Okinawan Diaspora

Okinawan Diaspora

Edited by Ronald Y. Nakasone

HAWAI

University of Hawai'i Press
Honolulu

© 2002 University of Hawai'i Press
All rights reserved
Printed in the United States of America

07   6 5 4 3

Library of Congress Cataloging-in-Publication Data

Okinawan diaspora / edited by Ronald Y. Nakasone.
   p. cm.
   Includes bibliographical references and index.
   ISBN 0–8248–2406–7 (cloth : alk. paper)—ISBN 0–8248–2530–6
(pbk. : alk. paper)
   1. Ryukyuans—Foreign countries. 2. Okinawa-ken (Japan)—
Emigration and immigration. I. Nakasone, Ronald Y.
DS832.5 . O55 2002
304.8'0952'29—dc21

2001045692

University of Hawai'i Press books are printed on acid-free
paper and meet the guidelines for permanence and durability
of the Council on Library Resources.

Designed by Kenneth Miyamoto
Digitally printed by Publishers' Graphics

To all ancestors
of the past, present, and future

Contents

Note on Transliteration and Conventions   ix
Preface   xi

PART I   Introduction

Chapter 1   "An Impossible Possibility"
                 RONALD Y. NAKASONE   3

Chapter 2   Theorizing on the Okinawan Diaspora
                 ROBERT K. ARAKAKI   26

Chapter 3   Okinawa in the Matrix of Pacific Ocean Culture
                 HOKAMA SHŪZEN   44

PART II   Journeys

Chapter 4   The "Japanese" of Micronesia: Okinawans
                 in the Nan'yō Islands
                 TOMIYAMA ICHIRŌ   57

Chapter 5   "The Other Japanese": Okinawan Immigrants
                 to the Philippines, 1903–1941
                 EDITH M. KANESHIRO   71

Chapter 6   Japanese Latin American Internment
               from an Okinawan Perspective
               WESLEY UEUNTEN   90

Chapter 7   Colonialism and Nationalism: The View
               from Okinawa
               NOMURA KŌYA   112

Chapter 8   *Eissa:* Identities and Dances of Okinawan
               Diasporic Experiences
               SHIROTA CHIKA   120

Chapter 9   Hawai'i *Uchinanchu* and Okinawa: *Uchinanchu*
               Spirit and the Formation of a Transnational
               Identity
               ARAKAKI MAKOTO   130

Chapter 10   Agari-umaai: An Okinawan Pilgrimage
               RONALD Y. NAKASONE   142

Appendix   157
Glossary   163
References   169
List of Contributors   191
Index   195

Note on
Transliteration and Conventions

While Okinawan and Japanese share a common linguistic origin, the two languages gradually split from each other about fifteen hundred years ago. The existence of only three vowels (*a, i,* and *u*) is one major phonetic difference that distinguishes the Okinawan language from Japanese, which has five vowels (*a, i, u, e,* and *o*). Okinawan retains traces of early Japanese; the most frequently cited example of this is the existence of *p* and *f* sounds, which have long disappeared from Japanese. The Okinawan *p* and *f* sounds are equivalent to the *h* sound in Japanese; thus, *hana* (flower) is pronounced *pana, fana,* and *hana* in different parts of Okinawa. Japanese linguistics refer to the dialects spoken on the four island groups of Amami, Okinawa, Miyako and Yaeyama as *Ryūkyūhōgen* (Ryūkyū dialects) in contrast to *hondo hōgen* (mainland dialects) spoken on the Japanese mainland. (For convenience Ryūkyū dialects will be referred to as Okinawan or Okinawan language.) For all practical purposes, Okinawan and Japanese are mutually unintelligible.

The 1879 dissolution of the Ryūkyū Kingdom and the establishment of Okinawa Prefecture had a profound impact on the Okinawan language. Standard Japanese became the medium of instruction in schools, and the use of Okinawan was discouraged. Okinawans became essentially bilingual; they spoke Okinawan at home and among themselves and conducted official business in Japanese. Although many families still speak Okinawan at home, the use of Japanese is increasing. As a result of speaking two languages, Okinawans often substitute Okinawan words for their Japanese equivalents or give Japanese an Okinawan pronunciation. In order to distinguish commonly used Okinawan expressions from their Japanese counterparts, the macron is not used with the former. Rather than use a macron to show long vowels, Okinawan doubles the letter in question, for example, *eisaa* and *agaari*. In general, the katakana rendering in the *Okinawa dai-hyakka jiten* (Okinawa encyclopedia 1983) is adopted, unless commonly accepted usage differs. Thus, the Japanese *kikoe-ogimi* is preferred over the Okinawan *chifigin*, but *arayachi* is used instead of the standard Japanese *arayaki*. In addition, as a rule, the romanization practices of the various publications cited are preserved—for example, *Ryukyu Shimpo*, the Okinawa daily, does not use macrons over *ū*s in *Ryukyu* or a macron over the *o* in *Shimpo*. Japanese words that appear in English-language dictionaries are rendered in roman type without macrons, as are common placenames, unless they appear with macrons in the titles of Japanese publications. *Art of Okinawa* (Okinawa Times 1989) has been relied upon for the translations of titles and the transliterations of ancient words and expressions.

Japanese, Chinese, and Korean names are given in the traditional order—family name first—except in citations of works published in Western languages, where they appear in the English order. Many Asian scholars publishing in English prefer to keep the traditional order.

Strictly speaking, *Okinawa* is the name of the main island of the Ryūkyūan Archipelago, but here *Okinawa* is used to refer to the entire archipelago. Similarly, *Okinawan*, as in *the Okinawan experience*, is used collectively to include those who live on the outer islands.

Preface

The first Okinawan immigrants left Okinawa on 5 December 1899 and arrived in Honolulu on 8 January 1900. Of the twenty-seven Okinawans aboard the *S.S. China,* one was refused permission to disembark—for health reasons—and sent home. The remaining twenty-six proceeded to Ewa Plantation on the island of O'ahu as contract laborers. The essays in this volume commemorate that event and the subsequent experiences of Okinawan immigrants and their descendants.

After that initial experiment, other Okinawans migrated to live and work in Hawai'i, the continental United States, Canada, Brazil, Peru, Argentina, Bolivia, Mexico, Cuba, Paraguay, New Caledonia, and the many islands of Micronesia. World War II transformed the political landscape, and many of these original immigrants and their children returned to Okinawa. For many of the contributors to this volume, the trials and triumphs of these immigrants are family lore. This project documents the experiences of their ancestors.

In retrospect, by agreeing to participate in this project, the contributors to this volume embarked on an adventure, one not unlike that their ancestors undertook on leaving their homeland for parts unknown. They become part of this project on trust. They did not know who I was, what form the project would take, or who would be publishing the final result. Work on the project proceeded in the cooperative spirit of *"yuimaaruu"* (mutual help) that emerged during the early stages of diasporic Okinawan society and helped sustain the first immigrant communities. I extend my appreciation to the contributors, not only for lending their expertise in crafting their essays, but also for enduring constant editorial critique.

Wesley Ueunten was especially helpful in identifying and introducing me to potential contributors. Raymond Aka's private archives of documents and other source material on the theft and recovery of the *Omoro-sōshi* and the still-missing royal crown revealed a fascinating adventure, one marked by international intrigue. Together with additional documents supplied by Kishaba Shizuo of the Ryukyu American Historical Research Society, I was able to reconstruct the disappearance and recovery of the *Omoro-sōshi*. After fifty-six years, however, the trail of the royal crown has grown cold; it has yet to be recovered—and may in fact never be. I must thank Irene, who selflessly read and reread each draft, critiquing and encouraging our efforts. Appreciation is also extended to Randy Shiroma, who rendered the cover illustration. But my greatest appreciation is extended to the many Okinawans whose stories inspired this book. Without their experiences, there would be no book.

This volume is an effort to introduce the Okinawan diasporic experience to the world. The essays in it cannot cover all facets of that experience. Much more work needs to be done, especially on the lesser-known Okinawan diasporic experience in South and Central America and the Ryūkyū trade missions to Southeast Asia. The growing scholarly interest in Okinawan studies ensures that more research will be forthcoming.

Part I Introduction

Chapter 1
"An Impossible Possibility"

RONALD Y. NAKASONE

On 26 May 1953, the hundredth anniversary of Matthew Perry's visit to Okinawa (see figs. 1 and 2), the Okinawan government gratefully received seven priceless treasures from Sergeant First Class William T. Davis. Representing the government of the United States, Sergeant Davis returned four ancient texts—the *Omoro-sōshi*, the *Chūzan seikan*, the *Chūzan seifu*, and the *Konkōken-shū*—as well as the *kugani ufu'n chanjasi*, three *tama kawara*, and sixty black-and-red lacquered tablets inscribed in gold with the names of Ryūkyūan kings.[1] These items had been seized only three weeks earlier, on 2 May 1953, by U.S. Customs agents from the home of Commander Carl W. Sternfelt in Scituate, Massachusetts. At the Naha City ceremony, neither Commander Sternfelt's name nor the manner in which these national heirlooms found their way to his home was revealed.

Unfortunately, the *tama'n chaabui* (Jp. *tama mi kabuiri;* also *hibinkan*), the royal crown (fig. 3), the symbol of Ryūkyū's political sovereignty, has yet to be recovered. The missing royal crown is made of twelve strips of black fabric sewn together and gathered at a wide headband to form a billowing headpiece. Running from front to back, narrow bands of gold-thread appliqués affixed with 266 multicolored pearls and other precious gems conceal the seams. A gold pin on which a dragon has been engraved is inserted crosswise near the top of the crown. Bands of gold cord circle the headband. The crown was granted to the Ryūkyūan king by the Ming emperor Xuande in 1427 as a symbol of investiture. It is similar to the crowns worn by the Ming emperors and is almost identical in color and shape to the crown discovered in the tomb of Emperor Wanli (1573–1620). Ryūkyū, a tributary state, maintained close ties to China until the Japanese annexation

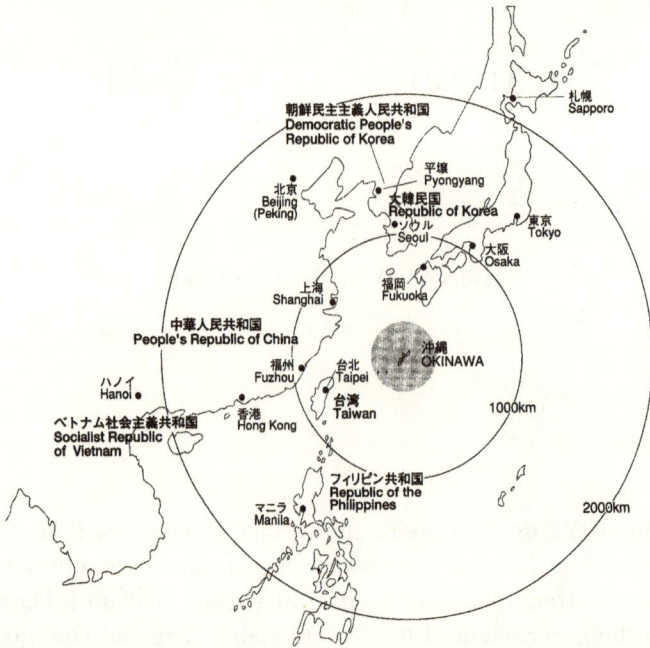

Figure 1. The location of Okinawa. Reproduced from *Okinawa Society and Economy* with permission from the Bank of the Ryukyus International Foundation, 2000.

in 1879. Even as late as 1895, the Okinawans expected a Chinese fleet to appear in Naha Harbor and vanquish the Japanese. China's decisive defeat in the Sino-Japanese War settled the question of Ryūkyūan sovereignty.

The loss of the crown can stand symbolically for the demise of the Ryūkyūan kingdom, and its possible recovery represents what Ōe Kenzaburō, the 1994 Nobel laureate, refers to as an "impossible possibility," the return to Okinawan sovereignty (Wilson 1986, 108). (The return of the *kugani ufu'n chanjasi* can likewise be understood symbolically as a partial restoration of their former sovereignty.) Even if the royal crown were recovered, however, Okinawans would be able to invoke only the memory of their former kingdom.

The Ryūkyūan kingdom was organized along a dual sibling sovereignty system, a feature of ancient Okinawan village and family life. Brother and sister had distinct yet complementary roles in ensuring the prosperity and well-being of the family. The brother attended to the secular affairs and the

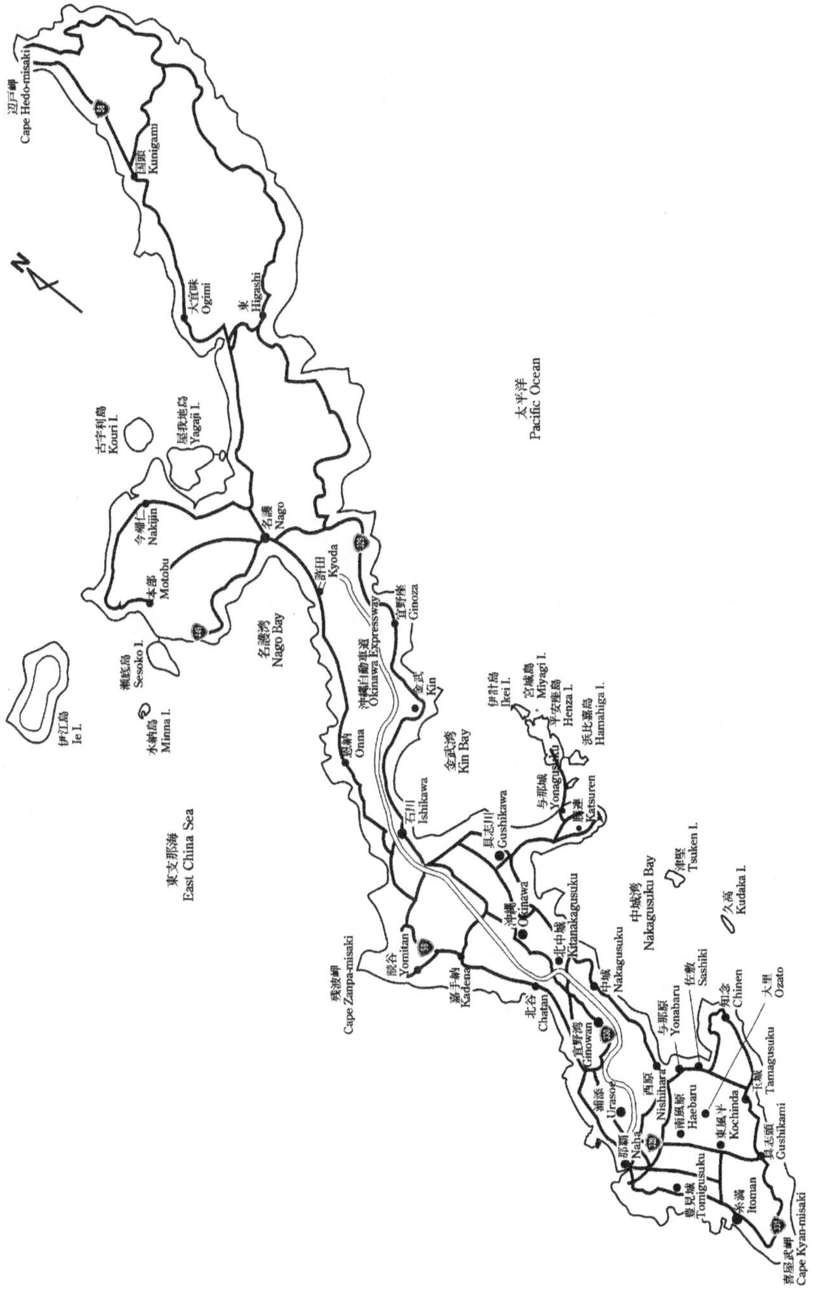

Figure 2. Okinawa main island. Reproduced from *Okinawa Society and Economy* with permission from the Bank of the Ryukyus International Foundation, 2000.

Figure 3. The royal crown, commonly known as *tama'n chaabui* (jeweled head-wear), was worn by the Ryūkyūan king at important state and religious functions. Okinawans believe that the crown was looted from its hiding place on the grounds of Shuri Palace during the waning days of the Battle of Okinawa. Reproduced from *Okinawa bunka no ihō* (1982) with permission from Iwanami shoten.

sister to the spiritual. In the same way, the king and the *kikoe-ōgimi,* the national high priestess, worked closely with each other to ensure the well-being of the country. Although the last chief priestess died in 1944 (Lebra 1966, 121), sacrifices of gratitude and memorials for the first ancestor, functions of her office, have continued through the family *Agari-umaai* (Eastern pilgrimage). Okinawans and those of Okinawan ancestry who continue to offer prayers to their ancestral spirits preserve these memories.

The recovery of the *Omoro-sōshi* was especially significant. The *Omoro-sōshi* preserves the earliest aspirations and memories of the Okinawan people. Scholars have suggested various meanings for *"omoro"*: "divine song," "songs sung in the sacred woods," "to think," "thoughts," and "reflections." These meanings are in keeping with the content of these ancient poems, which reflect the first Okinawan visions of the world, life, and the afterlife. The memories preserved by these archaic verses provided the foundations for the Ryūkyūan kingdom and articulate the earliest imaginings of Okinawan identity.

Memory and Imagination

Memory and imagination subvert ordinary notions of time and allow us to interweave past, present, and future. To divide time into past, present, and future and to understand that time moves unidirectionally from the past to the future or from the future into the past is to stand outside time and change. Thinking about time in the abstract permits the imagination to anticipate the past and to remember the future. Memories retrieve the past and transport it to the present. With such an exercise, we anticipate feelings of loneliness when we recall the loss of a parent or feelings of joy when we recall the birth of a child. Anticipating the past also raises fears that historical events will repeat themselves. When we anticipate the past, we construct the past with an eye to the present and thereby mold the present (Farriss 1995, 107).

To imagine the reality of the past and the future simply means that these time periods are linked to the present. We look back in time to understand the present; the present builds on the past and invites the future. We look into the future and imagine where we want to be and what we can achieve. When Takazato Shizuyo and other Okinawan feminists called for "recovering women's self reliance and to restore Okinawa as an island free from military forces and military bases" at the 1995 NGO forum in Beijing, they recalled the past and looked to the future (*Military Violence and Women in Okinawa* 1995, 13). On the one hand, their statement evokes the traditional role of women as equal partners with men in Okinawan life (see chap. 10 in this volume). On the other hand, they looked to the future and imagined the Okinawa they hoped for. Almost immediately after their return from the Beijing conference, they formed the organization Okinawan Women Act against Military Violence—in direct response to the abduction and rape of a schoolgirl by three U.S. military servicemen. By publicizing the incident, and by demanding justice, the women brought worldwide attention to the burden of the U.S. military bases on Okinawa. Their present actions evolved from past abuses and a future vision—their island home free from military control. The future holds limitless possibilities. Change and time thus originate in the future, appear in the present, and flow into the past.

But time is not simply an abstraction. Time is intimately related to being.

Dōgen Zenji (1200–1253), the Japanese cleric, writes, "Time, just as it is being. And being just as it is all time" (Dōgen 1967, 256). To claim that "being is time" is to articulate the understanding that we are irrevocably intertwined with the destinies of the world and all beings. To be intertwined is to be one with all things and to permeate all time. Being creates time and events. Conversely, events (time and change) have a direct bearing on our being and our lives. The experiences of each immigrant ancestor are such events. The diasporic experience affirms, in large part, who the Okinawans imagine they are. While the diaspora triggered the modern imagining of an Okinawan identity, the experience transformed how Okinawans remember their homeland and how they think of their new homes. Their memories and our reflective imaginings of those memories are part of the Okinawan experience.

Memory and imagination are the basis for reflecting on the experiences and on the imaginings of an Okinawan identity for present-day Okinawans, diasporic Okinawan communities, and those of Okinawan ancestry. Like the archaic voices from the *Omoro-sōshi,* the essays in this book reveal musings on an Okinawan identity; they also disclose each contributor's thoughts on such an identity. This book offers selected glimpses into the Okinawan diaspora during the past century (including the immigrant experience in the geopolitical context of East Asia and Japan), glimpses based on documentation, oral history, and personal experience. Thus, whatever their respective areas of interest, the contributors are all in a sense "informants." The insights that they offer are functions of their native talent, their professional training, and their personal histories. The issues that they discuss are self-selected, unique—and limited. The essays provide only a few clues to the nature of the Okinawan identity.

For successive generations of diasporic Okinawans and their communities, the memories of their immigrant ancestors link them to a past and a place. Ancestral memories—including the discrimination and hardship that immigrants almost inevitably face—become part of their present and future memories. For present-day Okinawans, the memories of World War II and the subsequent occupation and continued presence of the U.S. military also strongly color their imaginings of who they are. The "impossible possibility"—a return to political sovereignty, or the removal of the U.S. military bases, or the transformation of U.S.-Japanese military interests into more peaceful pursuits—is a memory of future imaginings.

In contrast to *Uchinanchu: A History of Okinawans in Hawai'i* (Ethnic Studies Oral History Project 1981) and *History of the Okinawans in North America,* which give a detailed accounting of the Okinawan experience in specific locales, the present volume introduces the Okinawan experience in a broader context—the Philippines, Micronesia, and Peru. More important, this volume attempts to understand Okinawan identity within the context of diaspora studies. In chapter 2, for example, Robert Arakaki offers a number of ways in which this experience can be approached and analyzed: How was Okinawan identity constructed across the various countries to which the Okinawans migrated? And how was the Okinawan diasporic experience shaped by the Japanese nation-building project and by globalization?

Toward an Okinawan Identity

The former commercial importance of the sixty-odd islands of the Ryūkyūan Archipelago stirs the imagination of modern Okinawans. For complex political reasons, the Chinese withdrew from the high seas during the late fifteenth century and the early sixteenth. Only two centuries earlier, the Middle Kingdom sent regular trading missions to India. Between 1405 and 1433, Zheng He (1371–1435)—who commanded a fleet of twenty-eight thousand sailors and three hundred ships—organized seven major expeditions, asserting China's preeminence in the world. His eight-masted, four-hundred-foot *bao chuan* (treasure ships) compare favorably with Columbus' eighty-two-foot caravel the *Santa Maria*, and traces of his explorations can be found as far away as Kenya. But, by the mid-fifteenth century, the Ming government had begun to limit the number and size of trading vessels constructed and to call for tough restrictions on foreign trade. By 1500, it was a capital offense to build ships with more than two masts. In 1525, the Ming government ordered the destruction of all oceangoing ships. Taking advantage of the Chinese absence, intrepid Okinawan sailors plied the trade routes and made direct contact with the major cultural centers of Asia. Between 1430 and 1512, the island kingdom became a crucial commercial link between Southeast and Northeast Asia (Tarling 1992, 120).

What was advantageous in one age, however, can be a liability in another. Since the late thirteenth century, Okinawa has been unwittingly caught up in the geopolitical ambitions of its larger neighbors. In 1272, Kublai Khan (1216–1294), emperor of China, ordered Okinawa's King Eiso (r. 1260–1299) to submit to Mongol authority and assist in the conquest of Japan. Eiso politely refused, and Kublai Khan's failed invasions relieved the Ryūkyūan entanglement in this early Sino-Japanese conflict. Three hundred years later, Toyotomi Hideyoshi (1536–1598), the Japanese shogun, pressured the Ryūkyūan kingdom to aid in his invasion of China. Hideyoshi's demands were ignored, and his death in 1598 temporarily eased the pressure being exerted by Japan. Nevertheless, eleven years later, in February

Figure 4. Reconstructed in 1994, Shuri Palace was the administrative center of the Shō dynasty. Ryūkyūan court culture was influenced by the cultural exchanges that resulted from the extensive international trade that took place under the dynasty. The vibrant colors of the *bingata* fabric favored in Ryūkyūan court costume and dance, for example, evolved from calico designs of the Majapahit court. Photograph courtesy Ronald Y. Nakasone.

1609, the Satsuma *han* (domain) dispatched three thousand warriors to subdue the insolent kingdom. After a spirited defense, the Okinawans succumbed, and on 5 April, Satsuma samurais entered and looted Shuri Palace (fig. 4). King Shō Nei was captured, taken to Japan, and paraded through the streets as war booty. The king remained in exile for three years, and the kingdom survived in name for another 268 years.

The fate of the kingdom was finally sealed on the evening of 30 March 1879 when King Shō Tai and his household left Shuri, the seat of authority and nationhood for five hundred years, and went into forced exile in Tokyo. Japanese troops immediately occupied the palace. Okinawa's destiny was now inexorably aligned with Japan's.

Matsuda Michiyuki (1839–1882), chief secretary of the Ministry of

Home Affairs, who accompanied the military contingent, announced the establishment of Okinawa Prefecture. The Chinese Ch'ing government protested the dissolution of Ryūkyū and suggested that the Miyako and Ishigaki island groups be placed under Chinese control. The fate of the island kingdom and the southern boundary of Japan was ultimately settled militarily at the conclusion of the Sino-Japanese War. The Japanese annexation of Ryūkyū exhibits the simultaneous rise of the modern Japanese state and the beginning of overseas imperial expansion. This development was significant for the Okinawans because they became Japanese citizens and imperial subjects (see Tomiyama 1997, 6).

In preparation for the defense of the homeland, the Japanese military excavated an extensive network of tunnels, now sealed, beneath Shuri Palace from which it directed the battle for Okinawa during the last few months of the Pacific War.[2]

America's battle for Okinawa began some sixty years later—on 10 October 1944—with sporadic bombardment by carrier-based warplanes. Over the next several months, 90 percent of Naha City was reduced to rubble. Finally, on 1 April 1945—Easter Sunday—American troops came ashore (and they have yet to leave).[3] A week after the American landing, the Japanese ordered the eight royal stewards to leave the palace grounds. The castle had been destroyed by the almost constant barrage from the U.S. warships, and the defenders wanted to take up defensive positions on the palace grounds. Maehira Bōkei, now eighty-two, assisted his fellow stewards to secure the royal crown and other priceless symbols of the Okinawan nation in three different locations on the palace grounds. In a 2 June 1953 memo to William T. Davis, Maehira recalled that the crown was placed in a black lacquered box bearing the Shō family crest and lowered into a drainage ditch next to the stone stairway of the third gate that led to the *Ue no udun* (upper palace). The ditch was not filled with dirt but covered with tatami and pine branches. The stewards took additional steps to secure the treasures before abandoning their posts. It was 8 April, Hanamatsuri, the day set aside to celebrate the Buddha's birth. Shuri Palace and its environs, once described by Yanagi Sōetsu (1889–1961) as the earthly embodiment of the Pure Land of Beauty, were nothing more than a memory (Yanagi 1972, 158–170; Coates 1996, 103).

Only two stewards survived the bloody onslaught. When Maehira, who was subsequently captured, returned at the end of August 1945 to retrieve the national heirlooms, he found nothing, although the site had escaped destruction. Not finding any splinters of the boxes in which the royal crown, the *Omoro-sōshi*, and the other treasures had been placed for safekeeping, he surmised that they had not been destroyed. He later learned from

Miyagi Saburo, an Okinawan who was recruited by the U.S. army, that American officers, with the aid of several Japanese American soldiers, looted the area. Kishaba Shizuo, chairman of the Ryukyu American Historical Research Society, and others believe that whoever took the treasures also took the royal crown. Maehira is the last living Okinawan to have seen the royal crown.

The horrific battle on Okinawa confirmed the worst fears of Ryūkyūan officials. After the unification of the kingdom in the fifteenth century, Shō Shin (1477–1520) ordered arms to be secured in the national armory. The kingdom pursued a foreign policy based on the premise that a military force would only attract the hostile attention of foreign powers. Thus, in 1894, officials protested the establishment of a Japanese military garrison. Okinawa was a small and impoverished nation, they argued, and had maintained centuries of peace with its neighbors through friendly negotiations (Kerr 1958, 369–370). Ryūkyūan reservations proved prophetic.

For the next twenty-seven years, U.S. interests and the relation between the United States and Japan determined the lives of the island people. Under American occupation, the armed forces requisitioned land, enlarging Kadena and Yomitan Airfields—which had been built by the Japanese— and establishing bases throughout the island. In 1953, under the provisions of the Land Expropriation Law, the military seized land in Naha City, Yomitan Village, and other locations to build new bases and enlarge existing ones. In one especially egregious incident, American soldiers with bayonets and bulldozers forcibly displaced thirty-two families from Isahama, now part of Ginowan City, the location of the present Futenma Marine Corps Air Station. Local residents protested unsuccessfully against the seizure of land on Ie, an island off the Motobu Peninsula in northern Okinawa. For a time immediately after the war, the U.S. government intended to control the former Japanese-mandate territories and Okinawa as strategic-trust territories. The military considered retaining the islands permanently and tried to foster Okinawan separatism. Okinawa was referred to as *Ryūkyū* (Aruga 1994, 10).

Okinawa Island provided an ideal base of operations for the U.S. military presence in the Asian Pacific. Ironically, Okinawa again became a vital link to other nations in the region, of strategic importance militarily this time instead of commercially. Okinawan bases continued to be vital to American military interests in the coming years—in the Chinese civil war, the conflict between Taiwan and mainland China, the Korean War, the Vietnam War, and the Gulf War. Okinawans fearfully imagine that their home, a military bastion, will be targeted in future conflicts in the region.

Table 1
U.S. Facilities

U.S. facilities on Okinawa Island:
Army Oil Storage Facility
Awase Communication Facility
Camp Courtney
Camp Hansen
Camp Kuwae
Camp Mctureous
Camp Shields
Camp Schwab
Camp Zukeran
Deputy Division Engineer Office
Futenma Air Station
Henoko Ordnance Ammunition Depot
Gesashi Communication Facility
Gimbaru Training Area
Ie Jima Auxiliary Airfield
Kadena Air Base
Kadena Ammunition Storage Area
Kin Blue Beach Training Area
Kin Red Beach Training Area
Makiminato Service Area

Naha Port
Northern Training Area
Okuma Rest Center
Senaha Communication Facility
Sobe Communication Facility
Tengan Pier
Torii Communication Station
Tsuken Jima Training Area
Ukibaru Jima Training Area
White Beach Area
Yaedake Communication Facility
Yomitan Auxiliary Airfield

U.S. facilities adjacent to Okinawa Island:
Idesuna Jima Range
Kobi Sho Range
Kume Jima Range
Oki Daito Jima Range
Sekibi Sho Range
Tori Shima Ran

Okinawa's reversion to Japan in 1972 did not lead to a reduction in the number of military bases, as the Okinawans had hoped. The Japanese-U.S. Security Treaty mandated that the Japanese government maintain the bases and guaranteed the United States free use of all of them. As of March 1998, the American military had thirty-eight facilities in Okinawa Prefecture (see table 1), covering a total area of 24,286 hectares.[4] While as of 31 March 1997 U.S. bases occupied almost 11 percent of prefectural land on the main island of Okinawa, they cover 20 percent of the total land area. Airfields, artillery ranges, ammunition depots, infantry training grounds, and other installations occupy 85 square miles of a 454-square-mile island (Okinawa is sixty-seven miles long and on average less than seven miles wide; see fig. 5). Military personnel and civilian employees on the bases numbered 50,893 as of December 1997 (Military Base Affairs Office 1998, 4).

The Okinawan prefectural government continually complains that military use of the land prohibits both the development of local industry and agriculture and urban development. In addition, the American military controls vast expanses of Okinawa's airspace. The military restricts landings and takeoffs from Naha Airport to a radius of less than five surface miles and an altitude of two thousand feet, adversely affecting domestic and international flights. The prefectural government has unsuccessfully lobbied for the return of the Port of Naha, where only one U.S. military transport

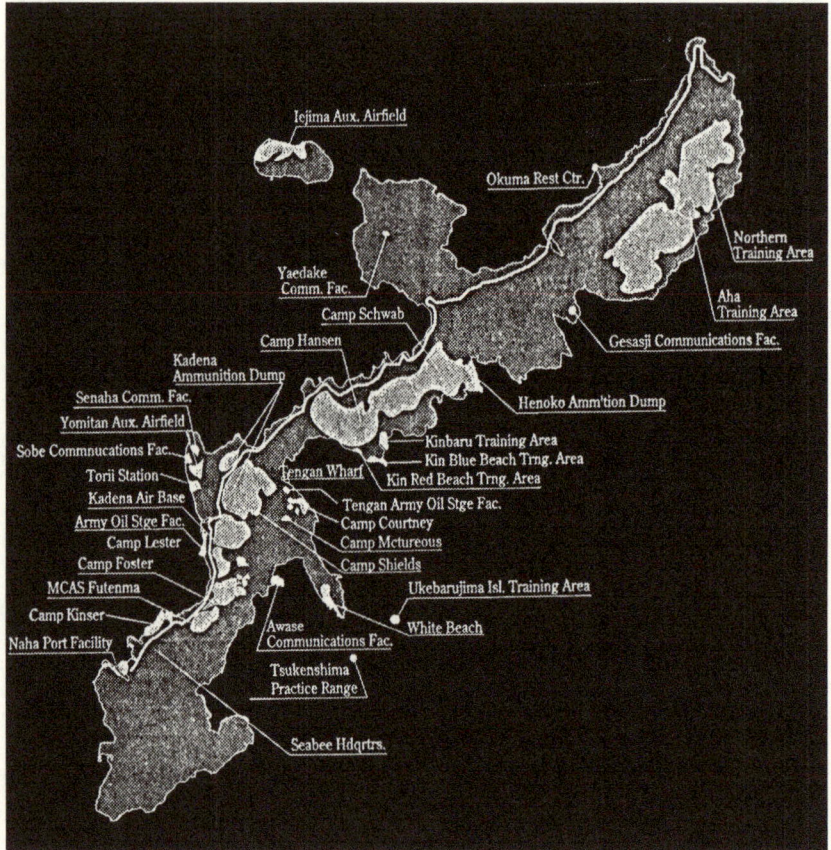

Figure 5. The U.S. military operates thirty-eight facilities in the region, thirty-two on the island of Okinawa and six adjacent to the island. The military facilities occupy approximately 20 percent of Okinawa Island. The Okinawan prefectural government has been lobbying for the closing of Futenma Air Station, which is located in the middle of Ginowan City, to permit the development of an academic and international hub.

calls in a month, and transfer of the wharves to local control and commercial use.

The Report on the Security Relationship between the United States and Japan submitted to the U.S. Congress on 1 March 1995 addressed the military-base issue. President Bill Clinton and Prime Minister Murayama Tomo'ichi promised mutual cooperation for the realignment of U.S. bases on Okinawa. In February 1996, the *Nikkei Weekly* reported that the U.S. government unofficially offered to reduce its military presence by 30 percent (Inose 1996). Although generous, this figure falls far short of the wishes of the Okinawan leadership. The U.S. withdrawal from the most important bases it currently occupies is contingent on their relocation in Okinawa Prefecture. The prefectural government, led by Governor Ōta Masahide, proposed to the Japanese government that the United States return Futenma Air Station (which is in the heart of Ginowan, a city of eighty thousand) and nine other facilities by 2001 and the remaining bases by 2015. An 8 September 1996 referendum indicated that more than 80 percent of Okinawan citizens support a reduction and realignment of the U.S. military bases (Military Base Affairs Office 1998, 11).

Prior to the May 1972 reversion to Japan, the U.S. military leased land directly from individual landowners. After the reversion, the Japanese government, acting as a trustee, leased the land from individual owners and in turn provided the rented land to the U.S. military. Many landowners resent the Japanese government's title for the compulsory use of their land. Governor Ōta, who was elected on a platform of reducing the U.S. military presence, refused to sign proxy documents that would forcibly permit the leasing of Okinawan land to the U.S. military. Ōta argued that forced land use by the U.S. military violated the Japanese Constitution's peace principle and a landowner's constitutional rights. The governor's yearlong defiance culminated in a high-profile five-hour confrontation with Prime Minister Murayama on 4 November 1995. Ōta's audacity stunned and bemused the whole of Japan. The Japanese government, specifically the prime minister, filed a court action to force the governor to sign the instrument. With unprecedented speed, on 28 August 1996 the Japanese Supreme Court unanimously rejected Ōta's contention that the expropriation of private land for use by the U.S. military is unconstitutional.

Two weeks later, Governor Ōta reluctantly signed the papers extending the current leases. His bold challenge called attention to the unreasonable burden that U.S. military bases have placed on Okinawa and its citizens and the Japanese government's discriminatory policies toward the prefecture. In the process of publicizing Okinawan aspirations, Ōta extracted from

Prime Minister Hashimoto Ryutarō, who succeeded Murayama, the promise that the bases would be reduced in number and that assistance in fostering economic self-reliance would be provided (Higa Kōbun 1997, 12–13). The Okinawan government's grand design for the twenty-first century is to take advantage of its strategic location and secure a chance at another "golden age" as a peaceful trading "nation" at the crossroads between Japan, China, Korea, and Southeast Asia (Kakazu 1992, 121; Okinawa Prefectural Government 1996b). Okinawans imagine themselves as the center of a vast trade network that would once again bridge the countries of the world. Okinawa would be Japan's bridge to South and East Asia, and its cultural and economic horizons would extend far beyond Japan. Such a vision invokes the glory days of the former kingdom.

To close the constitutional loophole that Governor Ōta exploited, in April 1997 the Japanese Diet enacted legislation to allow the continued compulsory leasing of private land for use by the U.S. military. Ōta lost his bid for reelection to a third term in 1998 to Inamine Kei'ichi. Okinawans, it seemed, wanted a less confrontational leader and elected a governor backed by the Liberal Democratic Party, the ruling coalition that Ōta challenged. The new governor, however, did not abandon Okinawa's call for a realignment of the all-pervasive U.S. military presence. On 1 March 1999, Inamine formed the Futenma Air Station and Naha Port Reversions Affairs Office. Pressing for a reduction of military bases, he proposed that Futenma Air Station be relocated to an area twenty-five miles to the north near Nago City and that the new facility revert to civilian control in fifteen years (Struck 1999). The U.S. government rejected the timetable. Although President Clinton wanted the issue resolved before the July 2000 Nago City G-8 summit, no agreement has yet to be reached.

Just as today, when the geopolitical interests of the U.S.-Japanese alliance have precedence, Okinawans had virtually no voice in their own affairs when they became part of Japan. Government officials and businesspeople from Kagoshima Prefecture (formally known as Satsuma) on Kyushu and from Osaka, the commercial hub of Japan, controlled the economic and political interests in Okinawa immediately after the 1879 annexation. Okinawans did not have a representative in the Japanese Diet until 1920, when the first full-fledged elections were held (Aniya 1974, 423–55). The Japanese heavily taxed their newest prefecture. In what amounted to taxation without representation, the Meiji Government collected ¥665,279 from Okinawa in 1882 but expended only ¥455,136 on the prefecture (ESOHP 1981, 14). Data from 1919 to 1928 show that Okinawa paid ¥68,000,000 in taxes, of which the Meiji government pocketed ¥45,000,000, money that could have been invested in the economic and social infrastructure of the struggling prefecture.

The Meiji government administered the prefecture as a virtual colony. Okinawa produced what it did not consume and consumed what it did not produce. The reliance on sugar as the primary cash crop exposed the Okinawa economy to worldwide economic fluctuations. While the Japanese were able to pay for food imports to feed a growing population from its industrial earnings, the benefits of the Meiji government policy of *sangyō rikkoku* (founding the nation on industry) did not extend to rural Japan. Industrialization had a negligible effect on Okinawa, which was far from industrial centers (Tigner 1954, 11–12). When the price of sugar on the world market collapsed in 1920, many Okinawans, deprived of their livelihood, were forced to consume *sotetsu* (poisonous sago palm), and many died from eating improperly prepared palm. Okinawans refer to this period of food shortage as "*sotetsu jikoku*" (hell).

Cycles of economic depression, population pressure, and lack of farmland forced many Okinawans to emigrate. In 1881, the population of the island of Okinawa was 150,000, or 114 persons per square kilometer. By 1914, the population had risen to 396,000. In 1940, while the population density of Japan proper was 204 persons per square kilometer, Okinawa, with a population of 475,766, had a density of 339 persons per square kilometer (Tigner 1954, 12). By 1935, approximately 15 percent of the population had emigrated to such Japanese cities as Osaka and Tokyo and overseas to Taiwan, Borneo, Sumatra, Java, Mexico, Cuba, Malaya, Micronesia, the Philippines, Hawai'i, and the Americas (Ishikawa 1980, 149).

More than 180,000 of an estimated 332,000 Okinawans and their descendants living abroad were forcibly repatriated after 1946. The war-torn Okinawa to which they returned could not support such a large influx of people, and the inevitable result was a second wave of emigration, not unlike the exodus that began at the turn of the century.[5] The first postwar emigrants left for Argentina in 1948. They were followed by others to Brazil, Peru, Mexico, and Paraguay. Officials of the U.S. Civil Administration of the Ryukyus (USCAR), which was set up to implement American policies and programs, also saw emigration as a solution to Okinawa's problems (which included overpopulation and a shrinking arable land base). *The Okinawans in Latin America*, a 1954 report by James L. Tigner of Stanford University's Hoover Institution, encouraged the shipping of repatriated Okinawans to Latin America. Emigration was also seen as a means to defuse the anti-U.S.-occupation sentiment that had resulted from the seizure of land by the U.S. military.

Between 1954 and 1964, approximately thirty-two hundred Okinawans immigrated to a settlement called Colonia Okinawa and other locations in Bolivia. Colonia Okinawa was not a happy place. The immigrants were essentially dumped onto a jungle floodplain. There were no adequate roads; settlers had to walk for miles to collect brackish water, and they were stricken with a mysterious disease. The colony ultimately failed. The original plan proposed to send twelve thousand emigrants over a period of ten years (Amemiya 1996, 2). Interest in emigration, however, waned after the late 1960s with the growing prosperity of Japan. Overseas immigrants began returning to Japan and Okinawa. Of the estimated two hundred thousand foreigners of Japanese descent living and working in Japan, about one-third, or sixty thousand, are of Okinawan ancestry. Of this number, about 70 percent are from Argentina, Peru, and Bolivia (Tamamori and James 1995, 74).

Imagining an Okinawan Identity

The current imagining of an Okinawan identity is both cultural and political. Okinawan identity is linked in part to nostalgia for the former kingdom. Ryūkyū fell victim to the early Meiji government's effort to solidify Japanese authority over nearby island territories, which had at one time or another been, however loosely, tied to Japan. The Japanese impulse to expand was motivated in part by the recognition of the country's vulnerability to Western imperialist designs and the need to create a modern nation-state (Peattie 1988, 2). Having incorporated these territories, the Japanese were confronted with the problem of how to integrate the indigenous inhabitants and at the same time maintain the purity and the hegemony of the Japanese race.

The process of crystallizing the modern Japanese identity required the creation of an "other" that would clearly underscore the uniqueness of the Japanese people. Thus, the growing empire's newly subjugated people became "*seiban*," or "aborigines." For the Okinawans, the implications of being labeled "*seiban*" were not simply theoretical. As "aborigines," they were to be civilized, and to become civilized meant to become "Japanese" (Tomiyama 1990, 1–19). The Japanese government initiated a series of measures intended to extinguish "uncivilized" Okinawan customs (including their language and their "irrational" shamanistic spiritual practices) and modernize the newly acquired territory.

The pressure to assimilate continued throughout the twentieth century, and resistance to assimilation remained strong as cultural differences between the Japanese and the Okinawans remained enormous and as Japanese discrimination against the Okinawans continued unabated.[6] After World War II, some Okinawans hoped that they might be able to secede from Japan.[7] But, for the next twenty-odd years, Okinawa was administered by the occupying American forces, and, in 1972, sovereignty reverted to Japan, a "reunification" that Okinawans accepted only unwillingly (Wilson 1986, 108).

Japanese imperialism resulted in pressure to assimilate of another sort, a pressure subtler and more insidious—the setting up of the diasporic Okinawans as the "other Japanese." In Micronesia, the racial hierarchy imposed by the Japanese colonizers—Japanese at the top, Okinawans and Koreans in the middle, and indigenous Chamorros and Yapese at the bottom—spurred Okinawans to become more "Japanese." The leaders of the Okinawan community in Micronesia, like the compatriots in Japan, even formed the Seikatsu kaizen undō, or Lifestyle Reform Movement, to abolish Okinawan customs and memories. (Ironically, when at the end of World War II both the Okinawans and the Japanese were forcibly repatriated, the Okinawans gained some measure of the equality they sought.) These issues are explored more fully by Tomiyama Ichirō (chap. 4) and Edith M. Kaneshiro (chap. 5). Wesley Ueunten (chap. 6) examines the plight of the Okinawans rounded up by the Peruvian government and sent to U.S. internment camps in the early years of the war, documenting yet another form of discrimination faced by the Okinawans as *otro Japones* (the other Japanese). The plight of these diasporic Okinawans highlights the tenuous existence of people with a hybrid identity in a world of nation-states that insist on an essentialized identity.

Nomura Kōya (chap. 7) reminds us that, both in Okinawa and in diasporic Okinawan communities, Okinawan identity cannot be understood apart from the effect of Japanese imperialism and colonialism. Early in the twentieth century, the Okinawan sense of identity was strongly affected by Japan's intellectual colonialism and became, as a result, ambivalent and uncertain: Are we really Japanese? If we aren't, what are we?[8] Reflecting on the Japanese attempt to re-create the Okinawans in their own image, Nomura notes how continued discrimination forced Okinawans to internalize a sense of inferiority. He goes on to discuss Okinawan complicity in the Japanese imperialist experiment, which left both colonizer and colonized deeply psychologically wounded. The recent protests against the continuing American presence in Okinawa indicate, Nomura claims, that Okinawans are finally beginning to reassess their collusion with imperialism (whether Japanese or American).

What are the solutions to the problem of Okinawan identity? Shirota Chika (chap. 8) argues for a transnational experience—specifically *eisaa,* a popular dance that is religious in origin and has been used recently to protest the U.S. military presence on the island. Drawing on postmodern theory, Shirota describes the human body as a canvas for artistic and political representation and posits the creation by *eisaa* of an inclusive space in which Okinawans and non-Okinawans can easily participate. Tens of thousands of American military personnel and their dependents live on the island at any one time, but their experience of Okinawa is limited to the cultural, social, and linguistic enclaves of the military bases, the cyclone fences meant to keep the Okinawans out also work to keep the Americans in. The internalizing effects of such isolation, Shirota argues, can and have been transcended by performing *eisaa*. She hints that the Okinawan *resistance identity* may be giving way to a *project identity* meant to transform modern society into something more humane and peaceful.

Arakaki Makoto (chap. 9) takes a slightly different approach, proposing a *pan-Okinawan identity* that links the diasporic communities. He appeals to the spirit of *yuimaaruu,* a giving and loving spirit of mutual help and cooperation. Such a spirit, perhaps the only common denominator in the multiethnic, hybrid, and global Okinawan community, embraces the Okinawan and the Okinawan at heart. It is fluid, decentered, nonexclusive, and transnational. This is the spirit of *bankoku shinryō no tami* (people bridging the world), which the former Ryūkyūan kingdom embraced and which the present Okinawan government hopes to revive. The success of the Worldwide Uchinanchu Festivals of 1990 and 1995 and the founding of Worldwide Uchinanchu Business Investment Inc. in 1995 represent evidence of such a possibility.

In reassessing their relationship with Japan and imagining their place in the world, many modern-day Okinawans wish to be released from political power entanglements and have more control over their lives. Their desire is like the plaintive longing of Queen Shō Nei:

> When the northerly wind blows,
> I wait only for the ship
> Of my king, the ruler of lords.
> When the tailwind, tailwind blows,
> [I long only for the ship
> Of my king, the ruler of lords.]
> (Sakihara 1987, 193)

Dating to 1610, a year after the Satsuma invasion, the queen's verse is the *Omoro-sōshi*'s last entry. The northerly winds now bring Japanese economic aid, culture, and tourists. The queen's yearning contrasts with the *omoro* (divine song) "Worship of the Sunrise," which reveals a deep reverence and gratitude for nature:

> Great Master of the East,
> Let us all be of one mind before you.
> And say, "How revered. How revered."
>
> Great Master of the Orient,
> [Let all be of one mind before you.
> And say, "How august. How august."]
> (Sakihara 1987, 61)

"Great Master of the East" refers to the sun. The east and the sun are highly symbolic. The east is the direction of *nirai-kanai*, a place of abundance, the home of the *kami* and other ancestral spirits who bring happiness and treasure when they visit this world. Although the legends associated with Seefa-utaki, the most sacred site of the Okinawan nation, place *nirai-kanai* to the east, popular myth also locates *nirai-kanai* beyond the horizon to the west or the north, indicating the directions from which the earliest settlers may have migrated.

The longing for *nirai-kanai* points to an earlier diaspora that brought the original settlers to the islands, an event recalled in the Agari-umaai pilgrimage. Weaving memory and imagination, I trace the mythic origins of the Okinawan people in chapter 10. Continuing the ritual responsibility of the former royal house, the pilgrimage preserves the memories of the earliest ancestors. Like the Japanese myth of Amaterasu Omikami, the myth of Amamikyu connects the Okinawan people to a divine origin and serves to justify the legitimacy of the Shō rulers. The validity of this creation myth has been compromised, however, by the incorporation of the Shō family into the Japanese aristocracy and by the destruction of the office of the *kikoe-ōgimi*. Still, the nostalgia for old Okinawa persists in the Agari-umaai pilgrimage.

Arakaki Makoto describes a similar pilgrimage—the grandchildren and great-grandchildren of Okinawan ancestry returning to the homes of their grandparents and great-grandparents, searching for origins and memories. Experiencing sights and sounds that they could only vaguely imagine from the stories they heard, the memories of their forebears became their memories.

The Search

Since the East holds an especially prominent place in ancient Okinawan mythology, it is ironic that the drama of the recovery of the *kugani ufu'n chanjasi* and the *Omoro-sōshi* unraveled on the U.S. East Coast. In December 1945, Commander Sternfelt, who had just returned from service in Okinawa, visited Langdon Warner at Harvard University's Fogg Museum, asking to have some Okinawan antiquities appraised. In a letter dated 26 December 1945, Warner, who had visited Okinawa in 1909 and collected artifacts for the Boston Museum of Art, thanked Sternfelt for showing him the treasures and mentioned Serge Elisseeff, the director of Harvard's Yenching Institute, as a potential buyer. Warner suggested that the commander have the articles appraised locally and then name a price. Apparently in an effort to learn about what he had in his possession, Sternfelt contacted Iwamuro Yoshiaki, a professor of Japanese at Harvard. In a letter dated 16 February 1946, Iwamuro notified Sternfelt that, together with a Mr. Yue, whom he described as a Chinese assistant at the Harvard-Yenching Library, the twenty-two volumes in his possession had been identified as the *Omoro-sōshi*.

The tempo of the search accelerated when Yoshizato Hiroshi (1883–1969), who was living in New York City at the time, learned of the theft of the *Omoro-sōshi*. Indignant, he contacted the New York State attorney general and lobbied the office of John Foster Dulles, the secretary of state, for its return. Yoshizato even wrote a letter (dated 23 February 1949) to Sternfelt inquiring whether the commander still possessed the *Omoro-sōshi* and other artifacts. Yoshizato, it seems, never got a response.

In the meantime, Sergeant Davis, who wished to locate a *sanshin* teacher, fortuitously contacted Yoshizato. During the course of their conversations, Yoshizato mentioned that the looted treasures appeared to be in the possession of a former navy officer. Yoshizato was instrumental in the recovery of the missing artifacts; from his conversations with Iwamuro, he was able to identify the missing items and link them to Sternfelt. Later, Davis, who had learned of the lost heirlooms while stationed in Okinawa, visited the Yenching Institute to verify Yoshizato's claims. Davis contacted the State Department, which in turn notified the Customs Service. The U.S. government viewed the seizure and return of the lost treasures as a way to improve Ryūkyūan-American relations. The Korean War was in full swing, and the U.S. military needed a friendly Okinawa.

Sternfelt—who passed away on 25 May 1976—had been in charge of the counterintelligence unit that had entered Shuri Palace and was later appointed chief of censor of the Tenth Army, a position equivalent to a customs agent, enabling him to confiscate artifacts that soldiers had looted and were trying to smuggle home. In 1988, Kishaba visited Sternfelt's widow in an attempt to pick up the trail of the missing crown. Kishaba is still trying to trace Sternfelt's steps in order to determine to whom or where Sternfelt may have unloaded items that he carried back with him. The Sternfelt family, who auctioned many artifacts after the commander's death, has been uncooperative. According to Kishaba, they are afraid that the Ryūkyū American Historical Research Society will sue the family to recover the money their father made from selling his wartime booty. It does not help the situation that antique dealers are reluctant to reveal details of their transactions.

The recovery of the royal crown would be an occasion of great joy among Okinawans. It would no doubt strengthen Ryūkyūan-American relations by defusing recurring anti-American sentiment. But what will the return of the royal crown, the symbol of past sovereignty, mean to the 1.3 million Okinawans and 400,000 people of Okinawan ancestry in North and South America, Asia, and elsewhere?[9] There will, no doubt, be renewed calls for independence and the removal of American military bases. Either scenario is an "impossible possibility."

Ōe Kenzaburō was impressed by the Okinawans' ability to retain their identity in spite of the homogenizing and centralist culture emanating from Tokyo. Ōe's interest in peripheral cultures emerged from his discovery of Okinawa, an island on the fringe of the Japanese cultural sphere. He perceived in Okinawa values that are embedded in other peripheral Japanese cultures: "No matter how Japanized (or 'Yamotonized') it may outwardly appear now, Okinawa still maintains its non-Yamato cultural identity; and, unlike the insular, unaccommodating and emperor focused culture of the rest of Japan, it is blessed with a richness and diversity peculiar to peripheral cultures. Its people possess openness to the world that comes from knowing the meaning of relative values" (Ōe 1995, 32). Ōe's assessment of "peripheral cultures" and their people is noteworthy. While we normally associate the periphery with backwardness and conservatism and the center with diversity and progressiveness, Ōe thinks otherwise.

It is important to note, however, that Okinawa is peripheral to cultures other than the Japanese. Ever since the Satsuma occupation in 1609, Okinawans have been caught between two masters—the Japanese and the Chinese.[10] Indeed, as Hokama Shūzen (chap. 3) points out, the network of relations can be traced far beyond China and Japan. For many years Okinawa was part of an extensive international commercial, political, social, and religious network, and the Okinawan cultural fabric is therefore richly woven with North, East, and Southeast Asian motifs. And the American military presence brings yet another culture into the mix.

In the end, however, it is 123 years of Japanese political and spiritual hegemony that is winning out, and it is becoming increasingly difficult to assert an Okinawan identity separate from a Japanese identity. Okinawans continue to hope, however, looking toward the future while searching the past. The past revisited in the light of the present can open new avenues for reflection. While to wish for *go-banken-sama* (honorable watchdog) to leave is to recall a future that in all probability will never come to pass, the precarious nature of the present and the uncertain nature of the future continue to give rise to creative imaginings of the Okinawan identity.

Notes

1. The *Omoro-sōshi* is a collection of ancient poems dating from the twelfth century. A second original version—the Aniya *Omoro-sōshi*—is still missing. The Aniya *Omoro-sōshi* had been held for generations by the Aniya family, whose responsibility it was to recite poems from the *Omoro-sōshi* to the royal family. The *Omoro-sōshi* had been hidden in an air-raid shelter in Ginowan City in central Okinawa, and, when Aniya Saneaki returned to retrieve the precious document, he found that it was missing. Because scholars did not have access to the *Omoro-sōshi* in the possession of the Shō family, they relied on the Aniya manuscript for their studies. The Aniya family has offered a $100,000 reward for its return.

The *Chūzan seikan,* the official history of the Ryūkyūan kingdom, was compiled by Haneji Chōshū (also known as Shō Jōken; 1617–1675). The six-volume history begins with a narrative of the mythical origins of the Ryūkyūs and states that Shun Ten was the first king.

The *Chūzan seifu* continues where the *Chūzan seikan* leaves off. There are two versions of the *Chūzan seifu.* In 1701, under government orders, Saitaku (1644–1724) revised and edited the original *Chūzan seikan.* Saitaku's son Saion (1682–1761) made corrections and additions in 1724. Of the nineteen volumes, one is devoted to correspondence between the Ryūkyūan kingdom and Satsuma.

The *Konkōken-shū* is the oldest Okinawan dictionary. With more than eleven hundred entries, it is an invaluable resource for understanding the ancient songs contained in the *Omoro-sōshi.*

The *kugani ufu'n chanjasi* (Jp. *kogane ryūhan ōkanzashi*) is a gold hair ornament, the symbol of supreme ecclesiastical authority in the former kingdom.

Tama kawara (Jp. *magatama*) are comma-shaped beads that were part of the regalia worn by the *kikoe-ogimi* (the high priestess) during important state rituals of the Ryūkyūan kingdom.

2. What is known as World War II in the West is known to the Japanese as the Pacific War. The Pacific War began, not with the attack on Pearl Harbor, but ten years earlier when, on 18 September 1931, a bomb exploded mysteriously on or near the Southern Manchurian Railway tracks near Mukden. On his own initiative, Colonel Itagaki Seishirō ordered his forces to attack Chinese troops stationed nearby. The Mukden Incident led to the Japanese occupation of Manchuria and eventually to war with the United States. Historians consider the Muken Incident the beginning of the Pacific War.

3. President Bill Clinton's remarks at the G-8 summit in Nago City, Okinawa, on 21 July 2000 gave no indication that the U.S. military would withdraw any time soon.

4. A hectare is 2.471 acres.

5. Most Okinawans emigrated overseas, but many were sent to settle remote off-shore islands.

6. For example, in 1969, Yamazato Eikichi, a former official of the Ryūkyūan government Cultural Property Protection Commission, penned a series of essays for the *China Post* under the title "Japan Is Not Our Fatherland" pleading for a restoration of Okinawan pride and identity (see Yamazato 1969). In 1997, Mie Kawashima noted that, "instead of trying to assimilate culturally and linguistically with the rest of Japan—an aim at one time pushed by school dicta—Okinawans are increasingly looking to the past for inspiration" (7).

7. According to Berry Saiki (personal communication, 22 May 1999; see also Saiki 1995b), in 1956 a third of Okinawans wanted to maintain ties with Japan, another third advocated independence, and the final third favored becoming part of the United States.

8. Japanese imperialism created a similar confusion in Korea and Taiwan, where people began to think of themselves as Japanese (see Masalski 1999, 25; and Minear 1999, 31).

9. These population figures are taken from Higa Kōbun (1997). Other sources estimate that, in 1986, there were 272,800 Okinawans and people of Okinawan ancestry overseas (Tamamori and James 1995, 78).

10. The Satsuma subjugation of the Ryūkyūan kingdom placed the Okinawans in a difficult position. In an attempt to circumvent the strict seclusion laws of the Tokugawa shogunate, Satsuma ordered the kingdom to conceal its relation with Japan from the Chinese. Prior to the Satsuma incursion, Ryūkyū had enjoyed close ties with China, whose influence was much more benign. Ryūkyūans thus served two masters, the Chinese and the Japanese, and lived under "dual subordination" (see Kerr 1958, 166–169).

Chapter 2

Theorizing on the Okinawan Diaspora

ROBERT K. ARAKAKI

Centennials are milestones marking progress on a journey. The year 2000 has been designated as the centennial of the arrival of the Okinawan immigrants in Hawai'i. This book marks some of the complex journeys undertaken by Okinawans who left their homeland to sojourn in other parts of the globe and by their descendants who seek to recover their Okinawan identity.

This process of large numbers of people emigrating and settling abroad is referred to as *diasporic flows. Diaspora* is derived from the Greek noun *diaspora,* "dispersion." The verb form is *diaspeiro,* "to scatter abroad, throw about." The original expression described a farmer sowing seeds. The word later acquired its present meaning when it was used to describe the history of the Jewish people in exile. More recently, *diaspora* has been used to describe the experiences of other peoples. In this essay, I will discuss the recent theoretical debate surrounding the concepts of diaspora, diasporic flows, and diasporic identity and the ways in which these concepts are used to frame our understanding of the Okinawan diaspora as presented in this book.

The discovery of the Okinawan diaspora was a surprise for this sansei Okinawan born and raised in Hawai'i. I knew that there were Okinawan communities in Hawai'i, the mainland United States, and Brazil. But I was surprised to learn that the Okinawan presence extended to the Philippines, Micronesia, and Fukien, China, and Manchuria. I was fascinated to learn of Okinawans living as far away as Singapore, Java, Cuba, and New Guinea. These discoveries raised a host of questions: What were the political and economic forces that gave rise to the Okinawan diaspora? How was Oki-

nawan identity constructed outside Okinawa? How was the diasporic Okinawan experience shaped by the social processes of modernity, nationalism, and globalization?

Centennials, occasions for celebrations, are also times for critical reflection. Both are needed. Celebrations without critical reflection can easily
degenerate into self-indulgent narcissism. Approached constructively, centennials serve as means for appreciating the past, understanding the present, and preparing for the future. This book is intended to be a critical and
reflective work of scholarship. It is intended to be read by the descendants
of Okinawan immigrants and by descendants of other immigrant groups.
It is hoped that this book will be of interest to the scholarly community, especially members of that community studying modernity, identity politics,
ethnicity, nationalism, and Asia-Pacific history.

A New Field of Study

Only recently have scholars turned their attention to diasporas and diasporic flows. Gabriel Sheffer's collection *Modern Diasporas in International
Politics* (1986), Elazar Barkan and Marie-Denise Shelton's collection *Borders, Exiles, Diasporas* (1998), Robin Cohen's *Global Diasporas* (1997), and
Gerard Chalian and Jean-Pierre Rageau's *Atlas of Diasporas* (1995) deal
broadly with diasporic flows. Other books focus on particular diasporic flows.
Paul Gilroy's *The Black Atlantic* (1993) demonstrates how racial slavery was
integral to Western civilization and how modernity framed the experience
of black people. Gung Wu Wang's *China and the Chinese Overseas* (1991)
traces the different kinds of Chinese diasporas. Another excellent overview
is Jennifer Cushman and Gung Wu Wang's collection *Changing Identities
of the Southeast Asian Chinese since World War II* (1989). Lynn Pan's *Sons
of the Yellow Emperor* (1990) offers a more popular treatment of the Chinese diaspora. S. D. Goitein's six-volume *A Mediterranean Society* (1967–
1983) covers the cosmopolitan Jewish communities from the eleventh to
the thirteenth centuries.

The subject of diaspora is also receiving serious attention in academic
journals. William Safran (1991, 83) notes that very little attention has been
given to diasporas. James Clifford's "Diaspora" (1994) surveys the field. And
Adam McKeown (1999) gives the subject a theoretically sophisticated
treatment. The emergence of this new field has also been marked by the
launching of the journals *Diaspora and Public Cultures* and *Diaspora* in
addition to such established journals as the *Journal of Transnational Studies*
and *Cultural Anthropology*. Another indication of the serious attention be-

ing given to the topic of diaspora is the University of Washington Press series on global diasporas under the editorial leadership of Robin Cohen.

Research on diasporic flows has been stimulated by the emergence of
postmodern theory and cultural studies, disciplines that cover a wide range
of diverse topics such as globalization, identity politics, nationalism, transna-
tionalism, orientalism, postcolonial theory, and subaltern studies. Some notable works are Benedict Anderson's *Imagined Communities* ([1983] 1991),
Arjun Appadurai's *Modernity at Large* (1996), Kwame Anthony Appiah and
Henry Louis Gates Jr.'s collection *Identities* (1995), Mike Featherstone,
Scott Lash, and Roland Robertson's collection *Global Modernities* (1995),
Rajagopalan Radhakrishnan's *Diasporic Mediations* (1996), and Edward
Said's *Orientalism* ([1978] 1994b). Although much of the discussion in these
works focuses on the postmodern context of the late twentieth century, the
questions that they raise, their employment of an alternative lexicon, and
their challenging of conventional categories make this book possible. Without this current of scholarly debate, our understanding of Okinawan identity could not be framed in such terms as the response to relations of power
or to the transnational forces of capitalism, nationalism, and modernity.

What Are Diasporic Flows?

Diasporic flows are ancient phenomena. The history of humanity is filled
with individuals and groups moving from one place to another. The Jewish
diaspora is well-known. The close association between the expression *diaspora* and the history of the Jewish people evokes strong moral overtones.
It is only recently that appropriations of *diaspora* have moved beyond the
constrictive connotations of loss, exile, and the tenacious preservation of
identity. The more recent appropriations have sought to highlight trans-
formations and dislocations of groups by transnational forces, as well as
the fluidity of identity, as a way of challenging bounded and static under-
standings of society.

With diasporic flows, we are speaking about movements of significant
numbers of people and the relocation of cultural systems. A lone merchant
or even a small guild doing business in a port far away has a negligible effect on the local culture and society. It is when large numbers of migrants
begin to settle and replicate the cultural system of the homeland in a new
context that we can begin to speak of a diasporic presence.

Diasporic analysis is still being contested by competing approaches.
These approaches range from the postmodern hermeneutics found in
Barkan and Shelton's *Borders, Exiles, Diasporas* (1998) to Robin Cohen's

more historical *Global Diasporas* (1997). Tensions exist between the cen-
tripetal "diaspora as exile," which is based on the understanding of concrete
entities whose identities are indissoluble over time and space, and the centrifugal "diaspora as diversity," which shifts the emphasis away from bounded
groups to dispersed connections, institutions, and discourses (McKeown
1999, 311). Before undertaking diasporic analysis, we must clarify whether
our interest lies in the social structures of the diaspora or in the subjective
orientations of individual emigrants.

For the purpose of this essay, I will be defining *diaspora* broadly, as the
dispersal of significant numbers of people that results in the formation of
a minority culture in a different social context. My understanding of diasporas ranges from a group's merging or assimilating into the host society,
to a large-scale return to the country of origin, to a group becoming the
dominant power, to a group assuming a creolized or hybrid identity. In this
essay, *diasporic flow* refers to the social and institutional factors that facil-
itate the movement of people, *diasporic experience* to the formation of social identity within the dialectics of the ancestral homeland and the current
host society. Where the former is more structural and political in focus, that
is, objective, the second is more subjective and reflective.

Diasporic Flows and the Making of the Modern World

Diasporic flows have powerfully shaped the modern world; they are the
chief source of the multicultural diversity of many contemporary societies.
Examples in Europe include the Algerians in France, the Turks in Germany, and the Pakistanis and Indians in England. The Cubans in Florida,
the Irish in the United States, and the French in Louisiana and Quebec,
respectively, are North American examples. Asia-Pacific examples include
the Indian diaspora in Fiji and the Indian and Chinese diasporas in Malaysia and Singapore.

The United States is the result of a multiplicity of diasporic flows. The
English Puritans emigrated in search of religious freedom; the Africans were
transported across the Atlantic against their will as slaves; the Irish fled the
Potato Famine; and the Chicanos crisscrossed the border between the
United States and Mexico in search of work. More recent diasporic flows
originated from Ethiopia, Cambodia, and Vietnam. The long-dominant ethnic group in the United States, the Anglo-Saxons, was the result of the English diaspora that began in the seventeenth century. The English diaspora
is one of the most significant diasporic flows with respect to volume, duration, and effect (Cohen 1997, 67). Between 1846 and 1932, about 18 million

people emigrated from Great Britain and Ireland. This diaspora resulted in the formation of the United States, Canada, Australia, New Zealand, and South Africa.

Diasporic flows can give rise to diverse and tolerant societies like Hawai'i's (see below). Unfortunately, they can also give rise to intolerance, xenophobic racism, and apartheid. The American Exclusion Act of 1924, the neofascist attacks against the Turks in Germany, the antagonisms between African Americans and Korean immigrants in the Los Angeles riots, all point to the darker side of diasporic flows. The problem of ethnic pluralism and having an open and tolerant civil society is one of the major challenges of our time. A number of books have been written on this topic, for example, Crawford Young's *The Politics of Cultural Pluralism* (1976), Donald Horowitz's *Ethnic Groups in Conflict* (1985), and Joseph V. Montville's collection *Conflict and Peacemaking in Multiethnic Societies* (1990).

The study of diasporic flows is important for constructing an understanding of global history. Diasporic analysis links national history to the study of transregional and global history. For example, although the African diaspora and the Indian diaspora are distinct, there is a significant relation between the two. Both are examples of a labor diaspora. The slave trade was crucial for the emergence of the modern world economy. When slavery was outlawed, the labor needs of capitalists simply shifted from coerced African labor to indentured labor from India (Cohen 1997, 59). In a similar way, the demise of the African slave diaspora gave rise to the Chinese labor diaspora. Thus, although the African, Indian, and Chinese diasporas were quite different from each other, they are linked by global capitalism's evolving need for cheap labor. Just as the globalization of capitalism created an international economy, it also resulted in the ever-widening circulation of capital and, with that, a corresponding expanding dispersal of human labor, giving rise to a multiplicity of diasporic flows.

Diasporic analysis can be useful for bringing to light a hidden side of modern history. Until recently, much of modern history has been presented with reference to "national narratives" (McKeown 1999, 307). Constricted by the trope of nationalism, scholars have largely understood recent history as events within a nation's borders, ignoring transnational phenomena. For example, at the turn of the twentieth century, 62,000 Chinese laborers were recruited to work in the South African gold mines. A few years later, 140,000 Chinese were enlisted to build roads and dig graves and trenches in France during World War I. Although the laborers established no permanent presence, surely their contributions should be included in our consideration of history.

Diasporic analysis can also prove helpful in understanding contemporary developments. In *Ungrounded Empires* (1997b), Aihwa Ong and Donald M. Nonini discuss how the Chinese diaspora is giving rise to a transnational Chinese identity. Barbara Metcalf's collection *Making Muslim Space in North America and Europe* (1996) shows that diasporic identity need not be based solely on ethnicity.

Types of Diasporic Flows

Diasporas can take a number of forms. There are labor diasporas, in which people emigrate looking for jobs that promise economic improvement. There are political or victim diasporas, in which groups of people are forcibly ejected by a hostile regime or are fleeing civil war. There are slavery diasporas, in which groups of people are seized and transported against their will to meet labor needs elsewhere. There are imperial diasporas, in which the immigrants become the majority, dominating the original inhabitants.

A number of different typologies have been constructed to describe and differentiate the various diasporas. Milton Esman (1994, 6ff.) has formulated a threefold typology: hegemonic diasporas; bourgeoisie diasporas; and labor diasporas. Gung Wu Wang (1991, 4ff.) has created a fourfold typology to describe the Chinese diaspora: *huashang* (trader); *huagong* (coolie); *huaqiao* (sojourner); and *huayi* (reemigration or tertiary migration). Robin Cohen (1997, x) differentiated five types of diasporas: victim diasporas (the African and Armenian), imperial diasporas (the British), labor diasporas (the South Asian Indian), trading diasporas (the Chinese and Lebanese), and cultural diasporas (the Caribbean).

Differences in diasporic flows shape the diasporic community's interaction with the host culture. In the case of hegemonic diasporas, the immigrant community arrives in such numbers and with such a technological advantage that it dominates the indigenous peoples and in time claims for itself the status of homeland people. In bourgeoisie diasporas, immigrant communities enter host societies with commercial or educational advantages over the indigenous peoples. This often gives rise to a middleman minority group, both feared and envied by the host community, which can in turn give rise to xenophobic violence. In labor diasporas, a large-scale migration of workers and their families seeking a better way of life occurs. These emigrants often seek economic advancement and assimilation into the host country. Often, they engage in political mobilization to gain access to economic and political centers of power in the host country. On the other hand, in victim diasporas, communities forced from their homelands will often seek to return home and thus impede assimilation into the host culture.

Effect of Nationalism

Diasporic flows have been significantly affected by the nationalisms of the twentieth century. Nationalism has imposed on the majority of the world population the modern category of citizenship in which one's political identity, not to mention one's social existence, is determined by membership in a recognized state. In many ways, nationalism constitutes the height of the modernity project. It fuses the modern state with a precisely defined geography and a uniform populace with a uniform national culture. The essentializing of identity, a process that has come under rigorous scrutiny and critique from postmodern theorists, is crucial to the formation of the national identity. Under nationalism, political identity becomes linked with a particular "essence": race, language, religion, or culture.

Because nationalism assumes a fixed and stable identity, it is uneasy with communities with multiple or ambiguous loyalties. Hybridity and creolized identity are viewed as having the potential to undermine the nationalist project. In its quest for a uniform populace, nationalism gives rise to either assimilation or exclusion and has little tolerance for a transnational identity.

The host society's attitude toward diasporic communities is heavily shaped by its political culture. In countries such as the United States that define citizenship in civic terms (*jus soli*), the government will usually seek to assimilate the diasporic community into the national culture. In countries such as Japan that define citizenship in ethnic or racial terms (*jus sanguinis*), full citizenship is often denied to members of diasporic communities, even though they may be three or four generations removed from the original immigrants and may have no memory of their families' country of origin. In countries such as Malaysia that define citizenship in terms of consociation (i.e., democracy structured along the lines of institutionalized pluralism), ethnic diasporas are recognized as distinct communities and are guaranteed proportional representation; however, assimilation into the dominant culture is not encouraged.

Identity Politics

The construction of social identity is critical for understanding the diasporic experience. The question of identity, long taken for granted, has recently become the subject of vigorous academic debate. Primordialism—the understanding of identity as something stable and fixed—has long exercised a powerful influence on the way people understood social identity.[1] However, in recent years, social scientists have come to understand identity as something that is flexible and context dependent. Fredrik Barth's collection *Ethnic Groups and Boundaries* (1969) represents an early attempt critically to understand the nature of ethnic identity. In his introduction to the collection, Barth contends that it is the group boundary, not the cultural context, that plays a critical role in the construction of ethnic identity. Dru Gladney (1996) argues that identity is constructed through a series of binaries (us/them) that are dependent on the context in which the question of ethnic identity is raised. Norman Buchignani (1980) makes an argument for the interactionist model of ethnic identity.

Diasporic identity is not necessarily unidirectional. Robin Cohen (1997, 24) points out that the mere arrival of immigrants does not automatically signify the formation of a diasporic community. The migrants may seek to merge, shedding their prior cultural identity. Furthermore, assimilation can involve the forgetting or suppressing of one's ethnic identity, which the immigrant then later attempts to recover. My "Politics of Okinawan Identity" represents an attempt to describe this process (see Arakaki 1996). Ethnic identity can also result from outside pressure on a self-defined group. John Sorensen (1991) describes the attempts of the Eritreans, Oromos, and Tigrayans in Canada to resist being identified as "Ethiopians" by the Amhara elites from Ethiopia and the general Canadian population. Thus, identity is not static but dynamic. I suggest that we think, not only in terms of *identity* (a noun that implies something stable and static), but also in terms of *identification* (a process that implies historicity and change).

Although largely discredited in academic circles, primordialism is far from dead. It is still very much alive in the 1990s. The horrific ethnic cleansing in Kosovo by the Serbs represents an attempt to create an ethnically pure state through systematic violence. The white supremacist groups in the United States represent an attempt to preserve white identity in the face of population pressures that threaten to transform the white majority into a white minority. Primordialism is also very much alive in Japan, where the notion of *nihonjinron* (theorizing on the Japanese)—which assumes an unidentifiable "essence" that defines Japanese uniqueness—is still widely accepted (see van Wolferen 1990, 263ff.; and Reischauer 1977, 401ff.).

The ability to negotiate identity depends on the accessibility of the identity marker that a group uses to differentiate itself. An attribute or a practice that no longer distinguishes a group from its rivals or that has fallen

into widespread disuse cannot easily be used to assert a group's identity or
interests. One widely used identity marker has been religion. Catholicism
has been a powerful unifying marker for the Irish and the Poles. An Islamic
identity has been used in a similar way by the Algerians in France, the Turks
in Germany, and the Palestinians in Israel. Another powerful identity
marker has been language. The defense of the French language in Quebec
is one example of boundary maintenance. Similar instances can be found
in the case of the resurgence of Alsatian, Breton, and Flemish in France.
In Great Britain, Gaelic and Welsh have enjoyed a comeback after years of
domination by English. An identity marker can also take the form of a decisive historical memory. For the Jews, the traumatic event is the deportation to Babylon; for the Irish, it is the Potato Famine of the 1800s; for the
Armenians, it is the Turkish pogrom; and, for the Africans, it is the trans-
atlantic slave trade.

The signifiers of ethnic identity are often dynamic and shifting. In the
construction of a diasporic identity, manipulation of identity markers usually reflects power structures. Identity markers can be highlighted in such
a way as to exclude others or to establish hegemonic relations over others.
Or identity markers can be suppressed in order to gain access to the centers of power and obtain material and social benefits. This latter phenomenon is known as *passing*.

One of the fundamental assumptions of this book is that there is such a
thing as an Okinawan identity. But this leads to such questions as: What are
the signifiers of an Okinawan identity? What are the practices, values, rituals, and institutions that are uniquely Okinawan? Do these signifiers hold
across the various diasporic Okinawan communities? To what extent are the
signifiers of modern Okinawan identity shaped by the Japanese nationalist
project? Which theoretical approach best describes the way the diasporic
Okinawan identity has been constructed?

Creole Identities

The nature of diasporic identity can shift significantly over time. Where a
sojourner community regards the country of origin as its homeland, two or
three generations later the diasporic community will have evolved into a settled community loyal to the adopted country. This is manifested by the creolization of diasporic identity. Creolization retains some cultural practices
of the original ethnic community while fully participating in the social, political, and economic institutions of the host society, especially through in-
termarriage with the native population.

Hawai'i's diverse and tolerant multicultural society is the product of the creolization that resulted from the various labor diasporas that converged onto Hawai'i's plantations (see Okamura 1998). In the late 1800s and early 1900s, laborers were brought in large numbers from south China, Japan, Okinawa, Korea, the Philippines, Puerto Rico, and the Azores to meet the need for cheap labor to work on Hawai'i's plantations. The haole (i.e., European American) hegemonic diaspora from the mainland United States also had an effect. It was under the haole oligarchy that the various labor diasporic communities learned to live, work, and play together, giving rise to Hawai'i's unique *local* culture and *pidgin English*.[2] Modern Hawai'i is the result of the complex dialectic of Americanization (assimilation) and resistance to haole cultural and political dominance. The roots of this dialectic stem from tensions between various nonwhite labor diasporas and the white haole hegemonic diaspora.

Hawai'i's open society has made it possible for the Okinawans to make their own contribution to Hawai'i's unique blending of cultures. At first, the Okinawans were closely allied with the Japanese. Later, as they gradually became increasingly conscious and confident of their political ability, they began to field political candidates who won major political offices. In Hawaiian political circles, the Okinawan community has come to be widely respected for its ability to mobilize significant numbers of voters and resources.

However, creolization and assimilation are not necessarily inevitable. Several factors can impede creolization. If an immigrant community locates itself in a rural instead of an urban area—as Japanese communities in South America early in this century tended to do—it becomes isolated from the influence of the host culture. This isolation creates linguistic enclaves—for example, among South American Japanese communities, Japanese was used in public conversation and in signage, and libraries stocked only Japanese materials (Normano and Gerbi 1943, 52). Another impeding factor is loyalty to the home country. In Peru, for example, Japanese immigrants remained unflaggingly loyal to Japan and willing to follow the instructions of Japanese officials. That the native population resented the economic success of the immigrants further isolated the Japanese community, and tension grew to the point that anti-Japanese riots broke out in 1940 (see Gardiner 1975, 156, 61–65).

Diasporas and the Homeland

One of the variables shaping diasporic identity is how *home* is identified. Is home where one hopes one day to return, or is it where one's family has resided for the past two or three generations? I would argue that the return is not an essential part of diasporic identity. At the same time, the nostalgia of literally returning home can exercise a powerful influence on an individual's and a community's construction of a diasporic identity. Many settled diasporic communities regard the host country as home and have no desire to return to the country of origin. They are already home. However, it is possible that the desire to help out one's "homeland" can be used to mobilize the resources of diasporic communities.

Armenian immigrants to America who fled the 1915 massacres became withdrawn and sought to forget the past. In the 1970s, the American Armenian community made a journey to the past that resulted in a political identity that unleashed a burst of energy within the community. The end of the cold war resulted in the founding of the Republic of Armenia in 1990 and revived dreams of Greater Armenia. Armenia proceeded to lay claim to Nagorno-Karabakh, an Armenian enclave in Azerbaijan. The American Armenian community raised $1.5 million through telethons and fundraising drives to pay for food, clothing, and arms and ammunition. Other examples include the Irish American community's support of the Irish Republican Army and the American Jewish community's support of the nation of Israel.

In contrast, the diasporic Okinawan identity has, for the most part, been that of an apolitical labor diaspora. That, however, could change. Edith Kaneshiro (1999) describes how the Okinawan diaspora was rooted in the economic decline brought about by Japanese rule. Emigration emerged as an alternative when protests against Japanese rule were crushed by government authorities. Unable to improve their lot through political reform, and pressed by unemployment, Okinawans began emigrating in large numbers.

For me, the study of Okinawa's recent history has brought to light the forcible annexation by Japan and the attempts by the Japanese government to suppress Okinawan culture and stamp out the Okinawan language. For this diasporic Okinawan, these discoveries have given rise to a sense of moral outrage. As I became aware of Okinawa's past, I also became painfully aware of Okinawa's present status as a U.S. military outpost.

As one whose primary loyalty is to Hawai'i and the United States, my feelings about the oppressive presence of the U.S. military on Okinawa are ambivalent. My perception of Okinawan identity underwent another shift when I visited Shuri Palace, the site of Okinawan political sovereignty and of the theft of the Ryūkyūan royal crown in 1945 (see chap. 1). Previously, I understood Okinawan identity with reference to cultural practices: Okinawan dance; the *saataa-andagii* (a deep-fried ball-shaped sugar cake); and the *sanshin* (a three-stringed plucked lute). I now see Okinawan identity grounded in a historic tragedy and political sovereignty lost. My diasporic identity is now caught between the apolitical labor diaspora and the more political victim diaspora.

Double Minority within a Double Diaspora

One of the unique features of the Okinawan diaspora has been the Okinawans' position as a double minority. The Okinawans were often seen as "the other Japanese." They have been referred to as "the other Japanese" in Mindanao, "*otro Japones*" in Peru, "*Japan-pake*" in Hawai'i (by mainland Japanese), and "*Japonese-kanaka*" in Micronesia. In many instances, the diasporic Okinawans were forced to construct their identity against three axes of identity: the host culture, the Japanese diaspora, and the Okinawan diaspora. They were often *both* Japanese and non-Japanese.

The Okinawan diaspora is also significant because there were two Okinawan diasporas: one within the Japanese colonial empire and one beyond. Okinawans who moved within the Japanese Greater East Asia Co-Prosperity Sphere were forced to negotiate their identity against the Japanese imperial center and Japan's other colonial subjects. Okinawans who moved beyond Japan's colonial empire were forced to negotiate their identity against the host culture and in relation to mainland Japanese immigrants.

The contradictions embedded in modern Okinawan identity reflect the fact that, although officially a prefecture of Japan (which presupposes equality with mainland Japan), Okinawa was, in fact, an exploited colony (which presupposes a subordinate identity to mainland Japan; see chap. 7). With its annexation by Japan in 1879, Okinawa became subject to Japan's ambitions to become a modern nation-state. And with those ambitions came myriad Japanese normalizing practices: administrative laws, military conscription, language, education, and emperor worship. The nation-building project involved a series of measures to make the Okinawans into "good" Japanese. The attempts to emulate the Japanese reached ridiculous extremes, such as a newspaper editorial exhorting Okinawans to sneeze in a manner identical to that in which the inhabitants of other prefectures sneezed (Christy 1997, 155). However, because Okinawans remained different, they came to be regarded as inferior to the Japanese. This categorization of Japanese superiority/non-Japanese inferiority is an outgrowth of the Japanese construction of national identity.

Alan Christy (1997) notes that, unlike most other subject peoples, who by and large resisted the Japanese colonial project of cultural assimilation, many Okinawans accepted it. Within the context of the Japanese Empire, the Japanese polity was understood as a "family state." The Okinawans were the eldest son, the Koreans the second, and the Taiwanese the youngest. It was in the interest of many Okinawan elites to suppress their Okinawan identity in order to access the benefits derived from the Japanese. Christy notes, "The examples from both Taiwan and Osaka remind us that Okinawan struggles to deal with discrimination from Japanese and improve their economic lot must be understood within the context of the Japanese Empire, in which being Japanese was the only way to access power" (152). Many Okinawans immigrated to Taiwan, a Japanese colony at the time, seeking economic opportunity. Systematic discrimination forced the Okinawans to occupy the bottom rung of the labor market. Many changed their names in an attempt to pass as someone from Kagoshima Prefecture in southern Japan (Christy 1997, 150).

Discrimination in Taiwan forced many Okinawans to immigrate to the Osaka-Kobe area in search of work, where they also abandoned their Okinawan identity. The Seikatsu kaizen undō, or Lifestyle Reform Movement, founded in the Osaka-Kobe area, encouraged Okinawans to reject their traditional dress, speech, and recreational activities (Christy 1997, 146). Tomiyama Ichirō (chap. 4) notes that a similar movement was also founded in Micronesia.

The Okinawan response to Japanese colonialism was not one of unmitigated complicity. Many resisted assimilation and discrimination. In the 1920s, the various mutual-support groups in Osaka-Kobe came under the leadership of the leftist Kansai Okinawa Prefectural Association, which attempted to instill class consciousness in Okinawan workers. (The association collapsed with the Japanese government's antileftist crackdown in the late 1920s.) Another sign of resistance was the founding of the discipline of Okinawa gaku, or Okinawan studies, in the early 1900s in reaction to the Japanese exclusion of Okinawa's history in favor of the imperial version of Japanese history.

Castell's *Power of Identity* (1997) is useful for differentiating the different responses that Okinawans have made to the Japanese colonial project and the construction of diasporic Okinawan identity abroad. Castell argues that there are three types of identity: *legitimating identity,* which rationalizes the structures of domination; *resistance identity,* which attempts to resist domination; and *project identity,* which seeks the transformation of society. To these categories, I would add another, *colluding identity,* the response of a subordinate group that accepts the hegemonic project and subordinates its identity to that of the oppressors, even to the point of actively colluding with them. Using Castell's categories, I would say that the Japanese administrators utilized a legitimating identity to justify Japanese rule in Okinawa. The Okinawans responded by taking on either a resistance identity or a colluding identity. One sought to become Japanese, the other to maintain the uniqueness of Okinawan culture. It seems that the project identity has been largely absent in the history of the Okinawan diaspora. It is possible that the recent Okinawan protests against the U.S. military bases and the attempt to reaffirm Okinawans' identity as a peaceful people could form the basis for project identity.

Engaging the Japanese Identity Project

Further research on Japanese nationalism and the Japanese diaspora may shed additional light on how Japanese identity was constructed within and outside Japan. Such research is needed because the Okinawan diaspora, it seems, cannot be adequately understood apart from the Japanese diaspora and the Japanese colonial project. Okinawan identity has been constructed in four contexts: in Okinawa under Japanese colonial rule; in mainland Japan under the Japanese majority population; in diaspora alongside the Japanese diaspora and the native population under Japanese colonial rule; and in diaspora alongside the Japanese diaspora and the native population outside the Japanese polity.

One of the distinctive features of the Japanese construction of identity is the unusual stress on Japanese uniqueness (Reischauer 1977, 401ff.) and the invention of "one Japan" (Hashimoto 1998, 140–143). More important, the official ideology of modern Japan prior to 1946 stated that the emperor is the living embodiment of the *kokutai* (national essence), a position that can be traced to the *Kojiki* (Records of ancient matters), which was completed in 712, and the *Nihongi* (Chronicles of Japan; also called the *Nihon shoki*), compiled a few years later, in 720. This national essence consisted in the alleged unbroken imperial succession from the first emperor, Jimmu (660–585 B.C.E.), to the present, and these ancient documents trace the origins of the imperial line and the Japanese people to the divine. The myth of Japanese uniqueness was further reinforced by the isolationist policies of the Tokugawa shogunate (1603–1867), which shielded the country from the outside—especially the Western world—for several centuries. (The Bakufu government did maintain diplomatic relations with China, Korea, and Ryūkyū.) The cultural stress on group conformity and the centuries-long harsh authoritarian rule also perpetuated the belief in the singularity of Japan. These historical and sociological features gave rise to *nihonjinron* (theorizing on the Japanese), which permeates Japan's popular and official culture (see van Wolferen 1990, 263ff.).

It is important to note that, beginning in the Meiji era (1868–1912), the Japanese identity was also constructed against the *gaijin* (outsider, i.e., foreigner) West, an attempt to survive the onslaught of modernizing practices that threatened to undermine the Japanese way of life (Wagatsuma 1975, 314ff.). What is of interest is how the Japanese constructed a Japanese identity when Japan incorporated non-Japanese peoples into the Japanese polity in the course of colonial expansion.[3] Also of interest is how the construction of a Japanese identity defined, protected, and supported Japan's military designs and economic interests throughout the twentieth century.

Weiner's (1995) bibliography lists a body of literature that critiques the Japanese construction of identity and the hegemonic relations so engendered. I am not aware of any major study of the Japanese diaspora. James Clifford's (1994) survey article "Diaspora" does not discuss it. Neither does Robin Cohen's *Global Diasporas* (1997). There are a few works on the Japanese diaspora in Latin America. Gardiner's *The Japanese and Peru* (1975) and Normano and Gerbi's *The Japanese in South America* (1943) were written before the recent emergence of diaspora studies and postmodern theory. John Schultz and Kimitada Miwa's collection *Canada and Japan in the Twentieth Century* (1991) represents a good start. Further research is needed.

To conclude, the study of the Okinawan diaspora is more than an academic exercise. It is an attempt to recover the Okinawan voice, resist the violence of Japanese nationalism and the more recent American global imperialism, and raise questions about modernity and the nation-building project.

Unfinished Agenda

It is hoped that this volume will inspire additional research on the Okinawan experience. Further research is needed on early Okinawan incursions into Southeast Asia, especially before the Satsuma invasion. Researchers proficient in Thai, Chinese, Japanese, Arabic, Latin, Portuguese, and Javanese should be able to tell us more of the early Okinawa diaspora. Between 1430 and 1432, Ryūkyū sent at least seventeen trade missions to Ayutthaya, eight to Palembang, and six to Java. In the sixteenth and seventeenth centuries, Ayutthayan fleets called on Ryūkyūan ports. We can also assume that Okinawans were in contact with Indian and Arab traders when they disembarked in Melaka, Champa, and other Southeast Asian ports. The modern

Okinawan diaspora in Cental and South America merits further study. Whatever happened to the more than three thousand Okinawans who went to Manchuria? There is a critical need for American Okinawans to enter into dialogue with Okinawans from other diaspora communities as well as with Okinawans who live in Okinawa.

Also needed is a better understanding of the political and economic forces that drove the Okinawan diaspora. To what extent was it shaped by the initiatives of the Japanese government, by the local Okinawan community, and by entrepreneurs? How did Japan's annexation of Okinawa restructure Okinawa's place in the regional and global economy? To what extent did Japanese colonial rule result in the deterioration of the Okinawan economy?

More specifically, research is needed on the social institutions that structured the Okinawan diaspora in a manner, perhaps, outlined by McKeown (1999), who notes the development of well-integrated transnational business networks among the Chinese that facilitated the movement of people on a vast scale. Research is also needed on the institution of the *imingaisha* (emigration company) and the role of such Okinawan entrepreneurs as Tōyama Kyūzō and Ōshiro Kōzō in the shaping of the Okinawan diaspora.

A further area for future research is the search for literary voices articulating the recent Okinawan experience. Short stories, novels, poetry, songs, plays, and dance pieces can give voice to the Okinawan diaspora and identity in ways that formal prose essays cannot. The writings of Ōshiro Tatsuhiro, Higashi Mineo, Shun Medoruma, and others need to be introduced to a wider audience. We need translations that make traditional Okinawan literature accessible to diasporic Okinawans. And we need to hear the voices of Okinawan cohorts in other diasporic communities.

Another area for future research is ethnographic accounts of the diasporic Okinawan experience across time, space, and national cultures. As I mentioned in an earlier article (see Arakaki, 1996), the remembering, forgetting, and recovery of identity is closely linked to relations of power. What is needed are interviews with first-, second-, third-, and fourth-generation Okinawans that ask them to describe how they grew up, how they understood their national and cultural identity and the significance of being Okinawan.

Finally, there is a need for comparative analyses, the benefits of which would be twofold. First, the situation of the Okinawans is unique in that they are a double minority within a double diaspora. A better understanding of the Okinawan diaspora therefore has the potential for enriching our understanding of other diasporic flows. Second, a comparative analysis of diasporic communities can be used to test theories of how diasporic identities are constructed, how diasporic communities are affected by power relations, and how diasporic flows are shaped by such social forces as capitalism, nationalism, and globalism.

Chapter Sequence

Ronald Y. Nakasone's "An Impossible Possibility" provides an overview of the modern diasporic Okinawan experience and its effect on the imaginings of an Okinawan identity within the context of the theft of and search for the royal crown. "Okinawa in the Matrix of Pacific Ocean Culture," by Hokama Shūzen, recalls the early history of Okinawa within the broad sweep of South and East Asia. Hokama highlights Okinawan ceramics, textiles, and liquor as evidence of the extensive contact that Okinawan traders had with other cultures. This international reach of the Ryūkyūan kingdom provides some of the current imaginings of an Okinawan identity. Hokama's essay also asks us to imagine Okinawa culture as part of the intriguing notion of "Japonesia," a cultural sphere that includes Hokkaido to the north and the Ryūkyūan Archipelago to the south.

The essays in part II review specific Okinawan experiences. The first two essays—"The 'Japanese' of Micronesia: Okinawans in the Nan'yō Islands," by Tomiyama Ichirō, and "'The Other Japanese': Okinawan Immigration in the Philippines, 1903–1941," by Edith M. Kaneshiro—describe the Okinawan experience with reference to Japanese imperialism. In both Micronesia and the Philippines, Okinawans were "the other Japanese." Next, Wesley Ueunten's "Japanese Latin American Internment from an Okinawan Perspective" documents and reflects on the experiences of Okinawans from Peru and other Latin American countries who were seized and held as hostages during World War II. Ueunten also observes that Okinawans were distinguished from the Japanese. He weaves the memories of the Okinawan internees with reflections on the diasporic experience and questions of identity and concludes with the Latin American Okinawans' efforts to secure redress from the U.S. government. Ueunten's essay bridges the prewar and postwar Okinawan experiences.

"Colonialism and Nationalism: The View from Okinawa," by Nomura Kōya, examines the effects of Japanese colonialism on the modern Okinawan identity and on the Japanese colonizers. Nomura also reflects on the effects of the U.S. military bases on the Okinawan psyche. Shirota Chika's "*Eisaa: Identities and Dances of Okinawan Diasporic Experiences*" speaks of breaching through dance the cyclone fences that cordon off the U.S. military personnel and their families from the Okinawan citizenry. Arakaki

Makoto reviews Japanese discrimination against Okinawans in Hawai'i, arguing for a transnational and pan-Okinawan identity based on an attitude of openness and mutual cooperation. His "Hawai'i *Uchinanchu* and Okinawa: *Uchinanchu* Spirit and the Formation of a Transnational Identity" recalls the experiences of the earliest immigrants and the spirit of *bankoku shiryō* (bridge to the world) that Okinawans imagined themselves to be during the Ryūkyūan kingdom. Finally, Ronald Y. Nakasone's "Agari-umaai: An Okinawan Pilgrimage" remembers and reflects on the myth of Amamikyu and the origins of the Okinawan people. The Agari-umaai pilgrimage bridges the present, the past, and, with the memories that the pilgrimage experience continues to recall, the possible but highly improbable future.

Notes

1. For an insightful discussion of this topic, see Geertz (1973).
2. Technically, this language is referred to as Hawaiian Creole English.
3. Weiner describes how race became the dominant element of Japanese imperial ideology.

Chapter 3

Okinawa in the Matrix
of Pacific Ocean Culture

Hokama Shūzen

The announcement in 1970 that the fossilized remains of five humans discovered at the Minatogawa site in Gushikami Village in the south of Okinawa Island were approximately eighteen thousand years old stirred great interest in academic circles. On the basis of this discovery, scholars proposed that the Minatogawa Pleistocene human remains were closely related to the Liŭjiang fossils unearthed in diluvial formations in Kwangsi Province of south China and the Pleistocene Jōmon people of the Japanese mainland.[1] Some have suggested that the Liŭjiang and Minatogawa peoples may be distant ancestors of the Jōmon people. Although it is premature to trace the migratory route of the Japanese from southern China through the Ryūkyūan Archipelago with these bits of information, it is certain that, during this period, south China, Okinawa, and mainland Japan were closely connected. The discovery of the Minatogawa fossils established Okinawa as a legitimate research site in the study of the migratory route of the Japanese people.

While scholars have advanced theories that identify the Ainu as part of the Caucasoid racial stock or related to the Australian aborigine, recent research has suggested that they belong to the Mongoloid racial lineage and occupy a position between the Jōmon and the Japanese peoples. It has even been suggested that, more than any other people, the Ainu shared the same migratory route with the Japanese. The circle of Japanese migration thus includes not only the Okinawans to the south but also the Ainu to the north. If this is correct, then the Jōmon, the Japanese, the Okinawans, and the Ainu may be racially related.

Archaeologists believe that the Minatogawa people are related to the Yamashita cave people, whose fossils were discovered in 1962 at a site just south of Ōnoyama near Naha Harbor. Carbon 14 analysis has determined that these fossils are thirty-two thousand years old. Scientists also link the Minatogawa fossilized remains with the remains of the Kadabaru cave people of Ie Island, the Ōyama cave person of Ginowan City, and the Pinsa-abu cave person of Miyako Island. These discoveries and archaeological research without doubt connect the Okinawans to the recently discovered stone-age people of the Jōmon and Yayoi periods, especially in northern Kyushu.[2]

Japonesia

These findings, along with others in other academic disciplines, situate Okinawa studies within the broader context of East and Southeast Asia. The novelist Shimao Toshio was the first to coin the term *Japonesia* in his *Japonesia no nekko* (Roots of Japonesia), which appeared in 1961; it has since entered the Japanese cultural vernacular. *Japonesia* refers to a long and narrow cultural sphere in the northwest Pacific that stretches from Hokkaido in the north and Yonaguni Island in the south. The Ryūkyūan Archipelago, with Okinawa Island at its center, constitutes the southern sector of this great geographic arch. The Japonesian cultural sphere is distinct from that of the four great archipelagoes of Indonesia, Melanesia, Micronesia, and Polynesia, which together constitute an area inhabited by a racial group that shares a common language and culture. And it is on the basis of this cultural distinction that Japonesia has been proposed. The notion of Japonesia freed the Japanese from the traditional belief that their historical links lay with continental Chinese culture and allowed them to imagine alternative origins for their culture and civilization.

Folkloric and linguistic analyses of the cultures of the Oceanic and Pacific archipelagoes has, for instance, traced the origins of Polynesian culture to Indonesia and even further into southern China. Similar studies have tracked the migration of peoples and their culture from Indonesia to the far-flung South Pacific island groups of Samoa, Tahiti, and the Marquesas and from there north to Hawai'i and south to New Zealand. The notion of Japonesia has not been fully systematized and is not accepted in the academic world. Nonetheless, by inquiring into facets of Japanese culture in this broad context, new possibilities for understanding its origins are opened.

Since my task is to consider Okinawa, I would like to highlight creation myths and music as examples that place Okinawa within the larger cultural matrix of Asia and the Pacific. The creation myth, centering on a brother-sister original ancestor and the deluge pattern found on Kouri Island, Miyako Island, Ishigaki Island, and other locales throughout the Ryūkyūan Archipelago, is common throughout East Asia, Southeast Asia, and Polynesia.[3]

Ifa Fuyū (1876–1947) was the first to report the example of brother-sister founders on Kouri, an island just off Okinawa Island, and on the outer islands of Miyako and Yaeyama. The following brother-sister original ancestor/deluge creation myth from Miyako Island is similar to many other Polynesian deluge myths:

> A long time ago, a long, long time ago, there were the Bunazee siblings. One fine day, the brother and sister went out to the fields to work. Suddenly, from far off in the ocean, they saw a mountain-like wave [coming toward them]. The brother, concerned for his sister, [carried her] with great difficulty up a high hill. [Later] surveying [the land below], they saw no one. The tsunami swept away all life from the land. Resigned, brother and sister built a grass hut and pledged to be husband and wife. The *ajikai* [*Tridacnidae*] mollusk was the first to be born from the two. Next a human child was born, and gradually the island became filled with people. The people honor the two as the *kami* who reestablished the island. (Ryūkyū daigaku Okinawa bunka kenkyū sho 1964, 179.)

The broad context of Okinawan culture can be seen in *ryūka* or (Ryūkyūan song). The *ritsu onkai ryūka,* or five-tone scale, a distinctive Okinawan genre, bears a great similarity to the Indonesian *pejogedan* scale, which is heard on the gamelan played in Java and Bali. According to Koizumi Fumio's research, a similar instrument is found in the hinterlands of India and in Sri Lanka, Burma, Nepal, Bhutan, Micronesia, and Polynesia. The wide distribution of *ryūka* suggests that it is especially old and that its presence in Okinawa is a revival (Koizumi 1979). While this thesis still requires further evidence, such findings place Okinawan music within a broad cultural context that embraces India, Southeast Asia, and the Pacific.

Okinawa in the Asian Context

From these broad geographic and historic contexts, we can surmise that cultural influences from East and Southeast Asia, and more broadly the Asian Pacific, of which Hawai'i is a part, swept onto Okinawa in many forms and at different times. When Okinawa appeared on the historical stage between the thirteenth and the fifteenth centuries with the emergence of the *aji,*

powerful provincial lords, the countries in East and Southeast Asia were experiencing political transformation. These events affected Okinawa and
quickened its development.

In Japan, the Kamakura shogunate fell in 1333 and was replaced five
years later by the Muromachi shogunate of Ashikaga Takauji. In China, the
Ming dynasty replaced the Yüan dynasty in 1338. In Korea, the Koryŏ dynasty, which had persisted for more than four centuries, fell in 1392 and
was replaced by the Yi dynasty. Of these developments, the establishment
of the Ming dynasty had the greatest affect on the subsequent history of
Okinawa and Asia. Meanwhile, the most significant developments in Southeast Asia were the establishment of the Majapahit kingdom of Java in 1293,
the Ayutthaya kingdom of Thailand in 1350, and the kingdom of Melaka
in 1402.

The Majapahit kingdom experienced its golden age in the middle of the
fourteenth century. The literature, dance, (gamelan) music, and (calico) fabric art that blossomed from its court culture in turn stimulated the culture
of the Ryūkyūan court. The Ayutthaya kingdom, which established the first
independent Thai nation, flourished for more than four hundred years as
a Southeast Asian commercial hub. Okinawa enjoyed its longest trading relations with the Thai nation. The establishment of the Melakan kingdom in
1402 accelerated trade activity in Southeast Asia. Meanwhile, peoples and
cultures from Indonesia to the vast expanse of the South Pacific settled on
the archipelagoes of Melanesia, Polynesia, and Micronesia and established
kingdoms on Hawai'i and on Tonga. Kingdoms in Java and Vietnam also
appeared.

During this interval, the influence of Indianized Islam arrived in regions
such as Malay, Sumatra, and Java via port cities. From the fourteenth century to the fifteenth, trade grew rapidly, and Islam spread with it. Ming
China's lack of interest in maritime trade and the appearance of the *wako*,
Japanese pirates, proved opportune for the three Okinawan principalities
of Hokuzan, Chūzan, and Nanzan that were subsequently united into the
Ryūkyūan kingdom. Okinawan traders reestablished the flourishing trade
routes that linked the countries of Southeast and East Asia. While Ming
China held other countries at arm's length with its antimaritime policies, it
extended special protection to the Ryūkyūan and Melakan kingdoms.

A survey of the history and culture of East and Southeast Asia reveals that
the Ryūkyūan kingdom was a unique experiment. During its four-hundred-
year existence, it evolved a culture and a government based on its far-flung
trade economy and extensive international contacts. The Ryūkyūan kingdom was not a regional cultural outpost of Japan. Okinawa's ceramics, tex-

tiles, lacquerware, performing arts, and music reveal its connections with cultures in East and Southeast Asia and the Pacific.

Toward an Understanding of Okinawan Culture

Scholars have only recently come to view Okinawa within the broad sweep of the Asian and Pacific cultural context. The results of scientific investigations have unexpectedly forced a keen awareness of this larger context. We do not know what kinds of connections further research will uncover or what other conclusions might emerge. But it will be useful to briefly review earlier thinking on Okinawa and Okinawa studies. For this, I turn to the ideas of Yanagita Kunio (1875–1962), Ifa Fuyū, and other pioneers of modern Okinawan scholarship.

Yanagita Kunio's last major study, *Kaijō no michi* (Ocean road), was published in 1961 (see Yanagita 1978). In it, he attempted to substantiate in great detail that the Japanese had migrated northward through the Ryūkyūan Archipelago. On the basis of the fact that, riding the Black Current, coconuts drift ashore on the many beaches and inlets of Japan, Yanagita traced the origins of the Yayoi rice culture to the southern regions of modern-day China, from which it island hopped to Japan. He first proposed this thesis in *Kainan shōki* (A short record of the South Seas), published in 1925 after his first visit to Okinawa. This work pioneered the thesis that the origins of the Japanese culture lay to the south.

Yanagita's research on Okinawa flowered after World War II. "Takaragai no koto" (The cowrie), published in 1950, was the first of many articles advocating the northward migration of the Japanese people to their present home. In it, Yanagita linked the abundance of the cowrie mollusk (*Cypaidae*) harvested from Yaebishi, the coral shelf that surrounds Miyako Island and its offshore island Ikema, with rice cultivation. During the warring states period (ca. 403–221 B.C.E.) and until the first Ch'in emperor unified China, the cowrie (*takaragai*), found in the southern oceans, was valued as currency. Even in the seventeenth century, the *Rekidai hoan* (Precious documents of successive generations) makes frequent mention of *kaiha* (an alternative name for *takaragai*) and notes its great demand. From the Ming dynasty (1368–1644) until the beginning of the Ching (1644–1912), traders procured cowrie shells from Okinawa and transported them to the interior of China. People living in the highlands of south China and Southeast Asia still use these prized shells for ornamentation. From his investigation of the cowrie shell, Yanagita surmised that people from south China, traveling to the islands of the Ryūkyūan Archipelago in search of these shells, brought with them the cultivation of rice to feed themselves during their long sojourn.

In contrast, Ifa Fuyū, "the father of Okinawan studies," believed that the Okinawan language and people migrated from southern Kyushu. He tried to systemize Okinawa studies on the basis of the southward-movement thesis. He notes that, about 36 C.E., the Amabe people, who lived on the southeastern shores of Kyushu, passed through Amami Oshima on their way to Okinawa. The name of Amamikyu, the creator deity of the Okinawan people, refers to this ancestry. Beginning with the Insei period (1086–1185), there were repeated incursions of Japanese culture, as evinced by linguistic and population traces. The idea that Japanese culture moved south to Okinawa was widely accepted during the kingdom period, beginning with the Ryūkyūan historian and political leader Haneji Chōshū (1617–1675).[4] This accounts for the dilemmas that arose with the Satsuma invasion and the call for an independent Okinawa. Ifa's research can be understood as an extension of this thinking. It is important to note, however, that his research was conducted in accordance with the tenets of modern scientific methodology.[5]

In addition to the theories advanced by Yanagita and Ifa, those of the folklorist Higa Shunchō (1883–1977), who asserted that Okinawan culture owes much to China, cannot be ignored.[6] Okinawa also shares many cultural features common to South Asia. This essay does not advocate any of these theories. It simply calls attention to the many cultural waves that washed over Okinawa's shores.

Many scholars favor Yanagita's thesis that rice cultivation was introduced to Japan from the south, and subsequent studies support the northward advance of what would become Japanese culture. Folklore, ethnography, comparative mythology, and archaeology provide evidence that prehistoric shell bracelets found throughout northern Kyushu were made from the gohōra (*Ticornis latissimus*), a mollusk found in waters throughout the Ryūkyūan Archipelago. Murayama Shichirō published a study linking the Ryūkyūan language, including Japanese, with the Austronesian linguistic lineage (Murayama 1988).

During the 1970s, research tended to focus on uncovering evidence to confirm the northern-migration theory. At the very least, it should be noted that, in contrast to the studies that presumed that continental influences (by way of Japan) formed the basis of Okinawan culture, this recent research introduced an alternative migration route. However, the origins of Okinawan culture still have not been definitively determined, and further research is necessary.

The Complexity of Okinawan Culture

Linguistics, archaeology, history, ethnography, and other disciplines indicate that the imprint of continental culture is especially strong in Okinawa from the Yayoi period until after Okinawa enters the historical age. Continental culture was first introduced to Okinawa by way of Kyushu. Subsequent cultural influence was unmediated, coming directly from Japan, China, and various other regions of Southeast Asia. The resulting culture was a complex blend that is most easily traced in the development of the material culture of Okinawa. I therefore briefly trace the history of *awamori* (distilled rice liquor), textiles, and ceramics to illustrate the complex fusion that is Okinawan culture.

Awamori

The history of alcoholic drink in Okinawa begins with the mention of *miki* (sacred wine) in the *Omoro-sōshi* and *amasake* in the *Konkōken-shū*. The early Okinawans, it seems, made this ancient type of sake, which was fermented with saliva. (Many highland peoples of Southeast Asia still produce and consume this type of brew.) After distilled liquor from China and Thailand entered Okinawa, brew masters learned to produce *awamori* from rice, millet, foxtail millet, and barley. Later brew masters used only rice.

With painstaking research, Higashionna Kanjun (1941) traced *awamori* to the Thai liquor *lao-lon*. Recent research has distinguished the different brewing techniques and yeasts used to produce *awamori* and *lao-lon*. Although both *mochikōji* (glutinous rice yeast), used in China and Thailand, and *barakōji* (boiled rice yeast), used in Japan, had been introduced to Okinawa, brew masters used *kurokōji* (black malt yeast) for *awamori*. It is not exactly clear when *kurokōji* came into use. Evidently, the use of *kurokōji* came from Japan, and the Okinawans incorporated brewing techniques from south, west, and north as they refined the taste of *awamori* to suit their subtropical environment. The use of *kurokōji* for brewing is unique to Okinawa.

Textiles

From the *Suishu* (Records of the Sui dynasty; ca. 643) section on Okinawa, "Liuqui guo-chuan" (Report on the country of Ryūkyū), we learn the following: "[The people] weave ramie, from which they make their clothes. They weave ramie to make their armor and helmets; [they] use white ramie to make-rope." Seven centuries later, Korean castaways reported in the *Yijo sillok* (Veritable records of the Yi dynasty) seeing clothes of ramie, the primary tributary payment to Satsuma and Ming China. Even today, Okinawans weave Miyako *jōfu* (high-quality ramie) and Yaeyama *jōfu*. Okinawans have woven ramie from fairly ancient times. The ramie that grows naturally throughout the Okinawa, Miyako, and Yaeyama Island groups is suitable for weaving cloth.

The overseas commerce that flourished under the Ryūkyūan kingdom introduced *bashō*, a nonfruiting banana plant from South Asia, to Okinawa. After the sixteenth century, the Okinawans used fibers from the plant to weave *bashōfu*. In hot and humid Okinawa, the thin and porous *bashōfu* weave was the garment of choice. *Bashōfu* production increased after the Satsuma invasion in 1609. Okinawa sent *bashōfu* as tributary payment to the Satsuma overlords. Silk arrived from China, cotton from Japan. The use of silk was reserved for the king and the nobility, while cotton was worn by the common people. The Kumejima pongee, *tsumugi* silk, woven on Kume Island, is highly prized. The common people wore *bashōfu* in summer and cotton in winter. *Bingata* and *kasuri* production techniques were introduced to Okinawa from the south sometime after the Keichō period (1596–1611). Okinawans created refined and elegant textiles that reflected their environment. *Bingata* exported to Japan influenced the development of *yūzen*. *Kasuri* made its way to Japan and became popular after the middle of the Edo period (ca. 1741).

Ceramics

Foreign cultures and trade economics likewise nurtured the development of a distinctive Okinawan ceramic art. Sometime during the fifteenth century, the Thai liquor *lao-lon* arrived in ceramic containers that inspired the production of *arayachi* (unglazed hard-biscuit stoneware also known as *nanbanyachi* and *Ryūkyū nanbanyachi*) and spawned the beginnings of the ceramic arts. During the reign of Shō Hō (1621–1640), three Korean potters, including a Chō Kenkō (?–1638; also known as Nakachi Reishin), brought with them distinctive decorative techniques. Until the Korean potters introduced glazed stoneware, Okinawan pottery had continued the Southeast Asian tradition of simple, unglazed earthenware. Chō Kenkō was the first to produce high-fired stoneware in Okinawa. Hirata Tentsū (1641–1722) and others later studied ceramics in China and returned with the knowledge of Chinese style *aka-e* (polychrome overglaze enamel painting with red as its primary color) that led to the development of Okinawan *aka-e* stoneware. Subsequently, Nakandakari Chiken (1696–1754) and others imported Satsuma-style stoneware from Japan. Okinawan potters went on to create ceramics rich with the Okinawan sensibility by "fusing" advanced ceramic techniques and South Asian, Chinese, Korean, and Japanese aesthetics. The Okinawans evolved a distinctive aesthetic in their ceramics, with a lightness, an openness, and a gentleness that reflected the land and its people.

Questions Arising from Cultural Appreciation

In the variety and complexity of form of Okinawan crafts can be found the evidence of the movement and development of cultures. But the interpretation of that evidence is complicated by the fact that the various cultural influences—those of Japan, China, and Southeast Asia—were not adopted unchanged. Thus, whereas at first glance Okinawan cultural artifacts appear to be incredibly eclectic, they are best appreciated when viewed from an international perspective.

Folklorists and cultural anthropologists propose the categories *great* (national) and *small* (village) *traditions* in an attempt to grasp the complexity and variety of languages, ethnicities, and nationalities that constitute European society. The small tradition of Okinawa and its culture transcends the categories of ethnicity and nationality to embody many cultural layers. I anticipate that this approach will lead to more effective methods of understanding Okinawa and its culture.

One final point. There is a tendency to compare Okinawan culture with Japanese culture. Should we not expand our consideration of Okinawa to take account of the vast expanse of East Asian, Southeast Asian, and Pacific cultural spheres and speak of similarities and differences within these larger contexts? If we do, we affirm that Okinawa with its long history, especially during the Ryūkyūan kingdom with its more than four hundred years of interaction with other cultures, is not an isolated and forlorn orphan island.

Notes

This essay has been adapted from Hokama Shūzen's *Okinawa no rekishi to bunka* (History and culture of Okinawa) (Tokyo: Chukoshinshō, 1997), 2–17, and translated by Ronald Y. Nakasone.

1. The Jōmon culture dates from as early as 4500–3700 B.C.E. to as late as 250–100 B.C.E.

2. The Yayoi period dates from 300 B.C.E. to 300 C.E.

3. James Frazer documents many deluge myths in his monumental *Golden Bough* ([1913] 1980).

4. Haneji Chōshū (also known as Shō Jōken) authored the *Chūzan seikan*. He advocated a policy centered on the need to reconcile with Okinawa's Satsuma overlords, accommodating their demands.

5. Working from the assumption that society is dynamic and ever evolving, Ifa Fuyū pursued the answers to two broad questions. Where did the Okinawan people come from, and what is their destiny? Ifa filled in the broad sweep of Okinawan history with details that he unearthed by applying methodologies borrowed from linguistics, folklore, and ethnography. Ifa (1907), e.g., used comparative linguistics to trace the origins of Ryūkyūan and Japanese dialects. Ifa (1927) used the methods of anthropology and folklore studies to explore the notion of sister-brother dual sovereignty on which Okinawan sovereignty is based.

6. Through careful reading of such texts as the *Ryūkyū-koku yuraiki* (Accounts of Ryūkyū), the *Ryūkyū-koku* (Old records of Ryūkyū), the *Chūzan seikan* (Mirror of the Chūzan dynasty), and the *Chūzan seifu* (Chronology of the Chūzan dynasty), Higa Shunchō traced the origins of Okinawan society within the broad context of continental Asia (see Higa Shunchō 1959).

Part II   Journeys

Chapter 4

The "Japanese" of Micronesia
Okinawans in the Nan'yō Islands

Tomiyama Ichirō

The Nan'yō Islands and Okinawa

In 1914, Japan entered into a war against Germany and, in October of that same year, occupied the German South Seas Island territories. Later, in accordance with the Versailles Treaty, Japan, under a League of Nations mandate, was given administrative control of these former German islands. Japan established, in 1922, the Nan'yō-chō (South Pacific government) on Palau in the Caroline Islands. Japan, which had earlier expanded its control over the Ainumoshiri, the Ryūkyū Islands, Taiwan, and Korea, thus came to occupy the Mariana Islands and Palau Island (excluding Gilbert and Guam), which are part of the Caroline and Marshall Islands of Micronesia.

The significance of the extension of Japanese imperialism into the Nan'yō Islands lay, not so much in the benefits of colonization, as in the fact that geographically Uchi Nan'yō (Inner South Seas) extends into Soto Nan'yō (Outer South Seas), a region that included the Philippines and Indonesia.[1] Shiga Shigetaka (1887) argues that, with the acquisition of the Nan'yō Islands, the southward expansion of Japan that began in the Meiji period with the takeover of Taiwan took on a military significance. After leading a marine brigade that secured the Nan'yō Islands, Lieutenant Commander Matsuoka Shizuo immediately set out to survey Dutch New Guinea, attempting to lease it. Matsue Haruji, president of the Nan'yō Kōhatsu (South Seas Development Company), the first enterprise to expand into the South Seas Islands, wrote, "Ever since Japan was given the mandate over the Nan'yō Islands, that is, Ura Nan'yō (Rear Nan'yō), Japan's relations with the Dai Nan'yō (Greater South Seas) have fundamentally changed, and our country is currently in a most favorable position with regard to our interests in the New Guinea region, which lies in those expansive reaches" (Matsue 1932, 3). With the support of the Nan'yō government, Matsue's vision led in 1936 to the formation of the Nan'yō Takushoku (South Seas Development Company), a joint capital investment enterprise established by Nan'yō Kōhatsu in partnership with Mitsubishi Bussan and Mitsui Shōji.

Okinawa provided the bulk of the labor necessary for the Japanese expansion into the Nan'yō Islands. The increase of laborers in the labor force during the 1930s—from 11,076 to 45,710—was especially noteworthy (Okinawa Ken 1974, 387–400). This essay seeks to highlight the Okinawan immigrants to the Nan'yō Islands. Chōdō Matsujirō, who in 1922 traveled to Saipan from Okinawa at age eighteen, provided the following testimony: "At the time, my family was poor. Since they could not [afford to] send me to upper school, I yearned to make a name for myself in some undeveloped land" (Okinawa Ken 1975, 1003). This testimony reveals the vision of many Okinawans who believed that their fortune lay in working abroad or emigrating. Those with little education saw immigration to the Nan'yō Islands as the road to success and prosperity.[2] Chōdō achieved success and was an important participant in the development of the Nan'yō Islands.

The Okinawan immigrants who sought success in the Nan'yō Islands were being mobilized to become a *gyokusai* (crushed jewel). In 1942, Nomura Kichisaburō, a former ambassador to the United States, addressed the Nan'yō Kōhatsu Club, issuing the following warning: "If we win, shall we Japanese remain in the Nan'yō Islands? After unifying all of Hawai'i and Southeast Asia, we will become administers and wear neckties in all these hot regions. If we lose, all Japanese will become 'crushed jewels'" (Matsue 1932, 13). Chōdō became a second lieutenant and, at the time of the American army landing on Saipan, said, "As a Japanese I will not be captured. I believe that to surrender is dishonorable." He did not surrender. In terms of success, Chōdō perceived the importance of his "Japanese consciousness" and was ultimately transformed into a "crushed jewel." The immigrant journey to the Nan'yō Islands is also etched on Saipan, which retains such placenames as Suicide Cliff and Banzai Cliff.

The Nan'yō Islands and Japanese Imperialism

Although the League of Nations declared the Nan'yō Islands a mandate territory, in actuality, contrary to the stipulations of its mandate responsibilities, Japan implemented assimilation and forced-labor policies directed at the native inhabitants. The islands became, in fact, colonies. Except for phosphate mining on Angaur Island, the Germans had refrained from colonial exploitation. From the outset, however, the Japanese engaged in imperialist exploitation and invested large sums of capital, especially in two ventures, Nan'yō Kōhatsu, formed in 1921 by Tōyō Takushoku (Oriental Development Company), and Nan'yō Bōeki (South Seas Trading Company), a firm that had engaged in trade since the Spanish occupation. Nan'yō Kōhatsu engaged principally in sugar production but was also involved in phosphate mining and the production of liquor, tapioca starch, and marine products (through Nan'yō Marine Products) and in ice manufacturing (through Nan'yō Ice Manufacturers). Nan'yō Bōeki conducted commerce, trade, maritime shipping, and coconut cultivation. In addition, the Nan'yō government controlled the phosphate industry, which it purchased from the German South Seas Phosphate Company. Okinawans provided most of the labor required to operate these colonial enterprises. This essay focuses on the composition of this labor force.

Believing that it would be unable effectively to utilize the native Chamorro and Kanaka workforce owing to its poor work habits, Nan'yō Kōhatsu recruited laborers from Okinawa.[3] To attract Okinawans, Nan'yō Kōhatsu offered loans for ship passage and a year's living expenses, which essentially amounted to an immigrant contract (Uehara 1940, 52). The Okinawans were recruited to cultivate sugarcane under two employment categories: agricultural laborer and tenant farmer. There was also a third category, part-time farmer (Uehara 1940, 52–53). Initially, the laborers were mostly single men who chose to work abroad, but, gradually, a more stable pattern emerged whereby whole households emigrated (Peattie 1988, 160).

In 1920, when Nan'yō Kōhatsu first began sugar production on the Nan'yō Islands, the price of sugar declined on the world markets, leading to a worldwide restructuring of the sugar industry. The situation prompted the Japanese government to consider whether its colonial enterprise should be provided with a minimum price support or whether it should be considered a domestic industry and be protected or perhaps even abandoned. The depressed market greatly affected Okinawan sugar production and led to *sotetsu jikoku* (*sotetsu* is a poisonous sago palm to which the Okinawans resorted for sustenance; *"jikoku"* means "hell"). The Taiwanese sugar industry, however, was maintained without concern for lower prices and even expanded (Tomiyama 1990, 78–82).

Nan'yō Kōhatsu initially determined that the sugar industry was stagnant and called for abandoning Nan'yō, but the industry gradually recovered, and the company expanded its operations from Saipan to Tinian, Rota, and Ponape.[4] The Nan'yō Islands challenged Taiwan's leading position in sugar production. Nan'yō Kōhatsu recruited the labor that supported the sugar industry from among the Okinawan immigrants fleeing from *sotetsu jikoku*.

Nan'yō Kōhatsu's management, concerned with overcoming "tropical laziness," stressed the importance of strictly observing the work schedule. Additionally, under the slogan *"harashōbu"* (victory or defeat), Nan'yō Kōhatsu organized teams of agricultural workers that competed in producing the most bountiful harvest. The company awarded the winners bonuses. The leader of the losing team was blamed for the team's poor performance and the reason for the poor performance analyzed. These competitions were designed so that the teams supervised each other (Matsue 1932, 102–141). For the company, the most important issue was maintaining labor discipline and encouraging diligence.

Okinawans also provided most of the labor for Nan'yō Kōhatsu's Saipan operations. However, after a 1927 labor dispute, when the company expanded into Tinian, it also recruited laborers from Kagoshima, Yamagata, Iwate, and other prefectures. As a result, in 1936, while approximately 74 percent of the 6,800 sugar employees on Saipan were Okinawan, only about 50 percent of the 9,231 employees on Tinian were Okinawan. Further, there was a shift from tenant farming to direct supervision of laborers on site (Uehara 1940, 62–63).

In 1927, and again in 1932, labor disputes over wage equality and other issues arose. As many as four thousand laborers participated in the first dispute and six thousand in the second. As noted earlier, after the first labor dispute, when Nan'yō Kōhatsu expanded into Tinian, Rota, and Ponape, the company hesitated to employ Okinawans, who had instigated the first dispute (Nan'yō kyōkai Nan'yō guntō shibu 1935, 1–5; Kagoshima daigaku 1985, 20; Matsue 1932, 62–63). Using statistics from the Home Affairs Ministry, Nan'yō Kōhatsu enlisted laborers from Kagoshima, Yamagata, and Iwate, regions with little history of tenant labor dispute. Outside Saipan, Nan'yō Kōhatsu engaged in direct management, created clear distinctions among the laborers, and employed persons who were not from Okinawa as labor supervisors (Urasoe Shi 1984, 421). On Ponape, the company paid wages on a descending scale: at the top of the scale were the Japanese, then the Okinawans, then Koreans, then the native islanders (Urasoe Shi 1984, 439–440). In this way, labor costs were kept low. The company engaged in discriminatory labor practices by recruiting from mainland Japan laborers whom it believed would not stir up labor unrest, as the Okinawans had done.

On Angaur Island, Chamorros and Kanakas provided approximately 80 percent of the labor force at the Nan'yō government's phosphate-mining

Table 2
Wage Scale

Japanese	3 yen and 45 sen
Okinawan	2 yen and 53 sen
Chinese	2 yen and 15 sen
Chamorro	1 yen and 40 sen
Kanaka	0 yen and 76 sen

operation. The Nan'yō government recruited native workers by letting the village chiefs know how many workers were needed. Whenever recruitment fell short, laborers were forcibly mobilized—a method reminiscent of "*karobos*," or forced labor under Spanish rule (Yanaihara 1935, 113)—to staff the public-works operations (Yanaihara 1935, 442). By assigning the village chiefs the responsibility of mobilizing the labor force, the Nan'yō government made the native leaders their partners in their imperialist designs.

In 1933, at the Nan'yō government's Angaur phosphate-mining operations, Okinawans were paid wages lower than the Japanese were but higher than the Chinese, Chamorros, and Kanakas were (Yanaihara 1935, 114–115). Table 2 illustrates the wage scale.

Colonial Society

Discriminatory wages paid to the Okinawans and the semiforced labor of some of the indigenous people supported the Nan'yō Islands colonial administration. The form of discriminatory labor practice utilized corresponded with the existing social structure. In the Nan'yō Islands, besides the native Chamorro, Kanaka, and Okinawan laborers, there were mainland Japanese, Taiwanese, and Koreans. Nishimura Shokusan (Nishimura Industries), the predecessor of Nan'yō Kōhatsu, recruited Taiwanese and Korean laborers. Each ethnic group occupied a specific place in the social hierarchy. Mark Peattie distinguished three social classes in the colonial society of the Nan'yō Islands. The Japanese occupied the highest stratum and enjoyed special privileges. The Okinawans and Koreans, the exploited laborers in the colonial economic system, filled the middle stratum. The Micronesians, the original inhabitants, occupied the lowest rung, with Chamorros enjoying a status above that of the Kanakas and Yapese (Peattie 1988,

111–112). The relation between the second-ranked Okinawans and Koreans and the third-ranked Micronesians exhibited many complexities. A
comic ditty (from Akamine 1990, 81) recited at the time reversed the positions of the native islanders and the Koreans:

Ittō kokumin Nihonjin	(First-class citizens, the Japanese;
Nitō kokumin Okinawajin	second-class citizens, the Okinawans;
Santō kokumin buta:	third-class citizens, the national pigs:
Kanakas, Chamorro	Kanakas and Chamorros;
Yontō kokumin Chōsenjin.	fourth-class citizens, the Koreans.)

Umesao Tadao, who was part of Imanishi Kinshi's 1941 Nan'yō Research
Team, noted the native islanders' perception of the social ranks:

> According to reports of the islanders concerning the social classes, the Japa-
> nese [ranked first], the islanders [second], and the Okinawans [last]. Re-
> cently, *mama* [a pejorative for Koreans] [have become part of the social]
> mix. From the Nan'yō government's occupation categories, it appears that
> the islanders, who were primarily engaged in agriculture, did not recognize
> an appreciable difference in status between the Korean laborers and the
> Okinawans.
>
> For a number of reasons, the native islanders harbored misgivings of
> their legal status. Under the League of Nations mandate provisions, the na-
> tives were Micronesians, not Japanese citizens. While the Koreans and the
> Okinawans received *awamori* [Okinawan liquor] distributions [from the
> colonial government], the islanders, bound by the League of Nations
> covenant, did not receive any. Further, young islanders who [having the
> benefit of Japanese education] were fluent in Japanese would direct their
> condescension toward Koreans, who were from isolated mountain villages
> and whom they thought to be culturally inferior, and would goad the Ko-
> reans, who did not know the Japanese language very well, by saying [to
> them], "If you are Japanese, speak Japanese." (Umesao 1944, 487–488)

The colonial society established by the Japanese in Micronesia was essentially three tiered. While the Japanese occupied the top tier, the social
boundaries between the second tier (the Okinawans and the Koreans) and
the third (the native islanders) were not clearly defined. The Okinawans
and the Koreans were manual laborers, an occupation that highborn Micronesians regarded with contempt. Upper-class and educated Micronesians who spoke Japanese reasonably well were shocked by the poor Japanese that the Koreans spoke. They were also aware that Okinawan speech
and behavior were incomprehensible to the Japanese, who perceived the
Okinawans as an underclass (Peattie 1988, 220–221).

The Umesao report revealed that Okinawans and Koreans felt it necessary to demonstrate that they were Japanese citizens in the colonial soci-

ety of the Nan'yō Islands. That they did was due in part to the Japanese imperial education that was instilled in the native people. However, let us carefully examine what Umesao observed: "Why can't the islanders become Japanese? Why must we urgently urge the islanders to become Japanese? Should not everyone who labors under the *hinomaru* [Japanese national flag]—the Japanese, the islanders, the Okinawans, and the Koreans—be considered Japanese?" (Umesao 1944, 487–488). More than the disdainful-mocking by the Islanders toward the Okinawans, to demonstrate that they were on par with the Japanese, Umesao portrays a society in which Okinawans competed through their work under the *hinomaru* to become Japanese. Let us now examine the meanings of *Japanese* and *Okinawan* as these terms were used in the Nan'yō Islands.

On Becoming Japanese

By focusing on the process of imperial expansion from Uchi (Inner) Nan'yō to Soto (Outer) Nan'yō, I mean to call attention to the enculturation of the notion of Nan'yō (Sugihara 1990, 487–488). For many Japanese and Okinawans the mention of "Nan'yō" quickened images of a new frontier and adventure. For Yoon Kun-cha, the expression *Nan'yō* gave rise to "imperial consciousness" (see Yoon 1989; Kang 1989; and "Nihonteki" 1987). For Kang Sang-joong, *Nan'yō* quickened in the "Japanese" consciousness "Japanese orientalism" (see Anderson [1983] 1991). At issue is the question of what *Nan'yō* invoked in "the collective imagination" of the Japanese?[5]

Note especially the difference between *nanshin ron* (the southward advance) or *nanshin netsu* (obsession for the southward advance), which originated in the Meiji period (1868–1912), and statements that emerged from the actual exploitation of the Nan'yō Islands. Asai Tatsurō, a member of Imanishi Kinshi's research team, wrote of the cultural perspective of "cultivating the superior tropical aptitude in the Japanese" and "developing tropical studies" (Asai 1944, 394). At issue is not simply the "Japanese" people in an imagined community but the particular qualities that gave rise to the notion of what a "Japanese" is. What desirable qualities did the "Japanese" have that enabled them to be colonialists, and why was it possible for the Japanese to be the overseers of the South Seas? These qualities of the Japanese ideal that were tested and developed in the Nan'yō Islands include "labor ability," "birthrate," "racial lineage," "cultural supremacy," and "number of sweat glands."[6] The notion "Japanese" that was inscribed in "Japanese orientalism" was concretely reexamined and restructured at a specific imperial location.

The Okinawans were the subject material for this imperialist experiment. At issue were the character of the Japanese as colonialists and the character of the Okinawans as immigrants to the Nan'yō Islands as subjects. How are we to understand the character of the Japanese in the South Seas? What kind of Japanese did the Okinawans become within the context of colonial exploitation of the Nan'yō Islands?

Yanaihara Tadao commented on the kind of laborers that migrated to the islands: "Frankly speaking, in comparison with the average *naichijin* [Japanese from mainland Japan], the Okinawans possess a lowly lifestyle, are culturally backward, and are heavy drinkers of strong liquor. Moreover, they remit monies home to build such nonproductive structures as family crypts. For that reason, while the very vigorous and most tenacious Okinawans are the most suitable laborers for developing the tropics, as an element of the new social establishment they leave much to be desired." Further, in as much as the Okinawans were called *"naichijin no kanaka"* and *"Japonese-kanaka,"*

> "the depraved Okinawan lifestyle was not approved by the native people. Thus, for the sake of upgrading Japanese colonial society in the southern regions, there was an urgent need to reform Okinawan education and lifestyle. I realized from my observations of the Nan'yō Islands that "the issue of Japanese foreign immigration is an Okinawan issue." . . . At present, with regard to the southern regions, I believe that it is important for intellectuals to carefully consider the question of colonialism and Okinawans when considering increasing the Japanese labor supply. Since the Okinawans constitute the bulk of this labor force, we must utilize their tenacious pioneering labor strength to have a most practical and effective labor policy. (Yanaihara 1942, 156–157)

Yanaihara assesses Okinawan "vigor" and "tenacity" positively but appraises the Okinawan "lifestyle" and "cultural development" negatively. He insisted that, unless Okinawans were "reformed" and "educated," it was only natural that they would be considered on par with the "Kanaka," a new subject (object) of "Japanese orientalism." Conversely, he intimates that, should the Okinawans reform their "lifestyle" and "cultural development," they would become "Japanese." We should note, however, that, for Yanaihara, *Japanese* meant "Japanese laborers for (colonial) development" and that *reform* referred to the Japanese colonial society, which was separate from the life of the island people. Yanaihara distinguished the Japanese, who were not only laborers but also colonists and overlords, from the island people, who were the objects of Japanese leadership.

Kiyono Kenji commented on the Japanese as overseers in Uchi (Inner)

Nan'yō with reference to the "Japanese ability to acclimatize to the tropics." He wrote, "As seen in the example of Uchi Nan'yō, the unsavory dis-
position of the Japanese in the tropics cannot, in the least, exhibit the overseer spirit, and [this trait,] which is similar to the psychological makeup of
the native islanders, becomes a source of ridicule toward the Japanese" (Kiyono 1942, 125). Kiyono's strong characterizations of the "unsavoriness" and
lack of "overseer spirit" of the Japanese corresponds to the "cultural inferiority" and the inability to speak Japanese fluently noted by Yanaihara and
Umesao, respectively. More critical than the dismissive *"Japonese-kanaka"*
voiced by the native islanders are the issues surrounding the idea of the Japanese articulated by Yanaihara, Umesao, and Kiyono. By highlighting the native islanders' reference to the Okinawans as *"Japonese-kanakas,"* these writ-
ers articulate an underlying message that leading and training the native
islanders were identified with becoming Japanese. Their writings gave birth
to the notion of the Japanese as overseer and the native islander as an object (of subjugation). Clearly at issue for the Okinawans was how to escape
from being called *"Japonese-kanaka."*

In 1935, interest swelled among the Okinawans in Saipan, and discussions ensued over the method of developing a concrete strategy to upgrade
the culture of persons from Okinawa Prefecture, whose "cultural level" was
"lower than the average educated person" (Nan'yō kyōkai Nan'yō guntō
shibu 1935, 1–8). This development was part of the Seikatsu kaizen undō,
or Lifestyle Reform Movement, which emerged in the 1930s, not only in
the Nan'yō Islands, but in Okinawa, Osaka, and other locations where Okinawans resided ("Chiji jimu hikitsugi shorui" 1978).

The Lifestyle Reform Movement became an important pillar in the Yokusan undō (Imperial [Rule] Assistance Movement). In fact, the Nan'yō Guntō
Taisei Yokusankai Bunkabu (Cultural Section of the South Seas Islands
Group Imperial Rule Assistance Association), which was established in 1941,
enacted the Hōjin kyōiku shinkō hōsaku (Japanese Education Promotion
Policy), which detailed qualities that would improve everyday life (Nan'yō
kyōkai Nan'yō guntō shibu 1941). The lack of civil morality, public health
and safety concerns, inferior dress and speech, and the *sanshin* cited by the
Okinawan Association on Palau indicate that the Okinawans perceived
themselves as possessing a lower culture and hence as deserving the epi-
thet *Japonese-kanaka*. The reformation of the *Japonese-kanaka* focused on
the "Japanese" ideal characteristics and, as one can imagine, therefore reinforced the position of the Japanese as overlords. This identification of the
Japanese as leaders in the southward advance grew only stronger with the
promulgation of the Greater East Asia Co-Prosperity Sphere.

Conversely, the movement promoting the Japanese as overlord gave rise to an effort to enhance traditional Okinawan character traits. The publication of Asato Nobu's *Okinawa kaiyō hattsu shi* (History of Okinawan seafaring development) in 1941 was such an example. Asato describes the Okinawans as a seafaring people who wandered throughout the South Seas from ancient times.[7] Further, in a July 1943 address at the Okinawan Teachers School, Tōjō Hideki reiterated this idea: "The citizens of Okinawa have inherited and are carrying on the 'enterprising spirit' of their forebears, who, in the past, explored Nan'yō and were warriors in the expansion into Nan'yō" (quoted in Ōta 1972, 102).

Clearly, the Lifestyle Reform Movement infused the imperial consciousness in the Okinawans, who were caught between the desire to erase their inferior cultural traits and the desire to demonstrate those "qualities" of an invented tradition intrinsic to the Japanese. In the effort to improve their lives, the Okinawans aimed for more than becoming "Japanese" (Hobsbawm and Ranger 1983).[8]

The Okinawan struggle to deal with social and economic discrimination must be understood within the context of the Japanese Empire, in which being Japanese was the only way to access political power and secure economic success. From their imperialist vantage point, the Japanese perceived Okinawans to be culturally backward, lazy, and unproductive, traits that Okinawans internalized. The Japanese disparagingly referred to Okinawans as *Japonese-kanaka*. Desiring to be rid of this label and to assimilate—to "become Japanese"—the Okinawan community throughout Micronesia engaged in discussions meant to develop a concrete strategy for upgrading Okinawan culture and Okinawans' lifestyle. Like their compatriots in the Osaka-Kobe region and in other expatriate communities, many Okinawans in Micronesia embraced the Seikatsu kaizen undō, a grassroots movement that urged the eradication of "Okinawanness." For example, the Okinawan *kenjinkai* (prefectural association) on the island of Palau sent the following memorandum to the governor of Okinawa asking for the prefectural government's assistance:

> The executive council of the Okinawan Kenjinkai convened a meeting on 3 November 1936 for the purpose of discussing ways of upgrading [the Okinawan character] and abolishing earlier Okinawan customs. Since it is difficult for Okinawan residents to accomplish this goal [by themselves], we are asking government assistance. . . . We propose that [potential] immigrants be educated with respect to other shipmates who are immigrating to foreign countries and to the Nan'yō Islands; we propose that [immigrants from Okinawa be educated] to develop civic morality and public health and safety [standards] and to equal the Japanese in dress and speech; we propose that

[immigrants from Okinawa] be prohibited from bringing aboard ship their *samisen* [*sanshin* in Okinawan]. (Hattori and Kakihara 1941, 31–32).

Similarly, the *kenjinkai* in Ponape "advised those who gambled to refrain and those with poor attendance records at work to be more responsible" (Urasoe Shi 1984, 439–440). The Okinawan *kenjinkai* took the lead in establishing the Kyōei kai (Mutual prosperity association) to counter the perception that Okinawans were lazy and unproductive employees. The new association coined such slogans as "rōshi kyōchō" (labor and capital harmonizing society) and "kyōson kyōei" (coexistence and coprosperity) "to uplift the character of company employees and promote the reform of the moral life" (Uehara 1940, 59). In the effort to improve their standard of living, the Okinawans strove to become Japanese, which degraded the Okinawan self-image while promoting an idealized image of the Japanese. The successful Okinawan was one who measured up to the Japanese ideal and was able to assimilate—that is, work and socialize—in Japanese society. To this end, many Okinawans changed their names and mastered the Japanese language and Japanese manners. While these reforms were part of the *kenjinkai* strategy to negotiate for higher wages, the reforms enmeshed the Okinawans in the Japanese imperial vision.

Most Okinawans, however, found economic success outside the imperialist economic system. Many of the successful persons listed in the *Gendai Okinawa kenjin meikan* (Modern directory of persons from Okinawa Prefecture)—compiled in 1937 by the Kaigai Kenkyusho (Foreign research institute)—were engaged in independent enterprises, such as fishing, general merchandising, and operating restaurants and brothels. These entrepreneurs initially immigrated to the Nan'yō Islands to work as tenant farmers and farm laborers, having been recruited by the Nan'yō Kōhatsu company as part of the imperialist economic effort.

Nan'yō Kōhatsu was not pleased with the Okinawans' penchant for leaving its employ before their contracts expired, whether to start their own businesses or to return home to Okinawa. The 1943 "Okinawa ken imin jigyō kihonhoshin" (Fundamental policy regarding immigrant enterprises)—prepared by the Naimubu ishokumin kei (Domestic affairs section, colonist group) and published in the *Chiji jimu hikitsugi shorui* (Governor's report, supplemental documents)—stressed the necessity "to discourage overseas workers from wanting to return home in embroidered finery" and "to train colonists to be steeped in the national mission." As the war effort strained the resources of the empire, the energy that fueled the personal dreams of enterprising Okinawans was diverted toward and eventually enlisted in "honorably" defending the empire.

Figure 6. The cliffs at Marpi Point (Suicide Cliff) on Saipan drop a hundred feet to the Pacific. On 7 July 1944, fleeing the American invasion, throngs of terrified non-combatants—mostly women and children—hurled themselves onto the jagged reefs below. This 1972 photograph of the artillery-scarred cliff is a reminder of a great tragedy. Photograph courtesy P. J. Hirabayashi.

Concluding Remarks

Although the goals of the Okinawans often differed from those of the Japanese colonists who labored for the imperial vision, the lives of the Okinawans and the Japanese were tightly entwined. Wanting to free themselves of the stigma of *Japonese-kanaka,* the Okinawans sought to "become Japanese." In re-creating themselves, they played a part in defining what it means to be Japanese and in creating the modern Japanese nation, but they also expunged a part of themselves.[9]

Early on the morning of 15 June 1944, an American mechanized army unit landed on the beaches of Saipan. During the ensuing battle, many Okinawans took their own lives, and many others were massacred by the Japanese military. But the struggle of the Okinawans mobilized on the Saipan battlefield had really begun much earlier. The battlefield memories of "crushed jewels" raise such questions as: How do Okinawans conceptualize being identified as "the other"? How do they counteract their desire to emulate the Japanese? How do they eliminate those traits that enabled them to be colonized? Attempts to answer these questions are opportunities to expunge colonialist perceptions of Okinawans—and other peoples—as Umesao (1944) and Yanaihara (1935) reported.

Human remains can still be found scattered on Saipan's beaches even today, although memories of that great battle are deeply submerged. From nearby Suicide Cliff (fig. 6)—a site popular with Japanese honeymooners— we can watch tourists enjoying themselves in the ocean surf.

Notes

This essay originally appeared as "Mikuroneshia no 'Nihonjin'—Okinawa kara no Nan'yō imin o megutte" (The Japanese of Micronesia—the view from Okinawa on immigration to the South Seas), *Rekishi gaku hyōron* (Historical studies review), no. 513 (1993): 54–65. It has been translated and adapted by Heather E. Nakasone.

1. *"Nan'yō,"* lit. "South Seas," is an extremely vague expression. At various times, it has included Micronesia, Melanesia, the South China Sea, and Southeast Asia from the Andaman Islands to Papua. Uchi (Inner) Nan'yō includes the Carolines, the Northern Marianas to the north, and the Marshall Islands to the east. The geographic reference of *Nan'yō* is to Japan.

2. For a discussion of the characteristics of immigrant social classes and their education level, see Mukai (1988, 115–116). The testimony that, "in Saipan, even if one is uneducated, one can become rich," is found in *Urasoe shi* (1984, 417).

3. *"Kanaka"* is a pejorative term applied to all Carolinians and Marshallese. The Japanese ranked the Yapese, who stubbornly resisted Japanese institutions, values, and administration, at the very bottom of their social scale.

4. If, in 1930, Taiwan's sugar production were rated 100 on a hundred-point scale, the Nan'yō Islands' would be rated 97 and Okinawa's 56 (Tomiyama 1990; Nihon satō kyōkai 1930).

5. I am indebted here to Murai (1992).

6. These kinds of statements should be understood within the context of the actual colonial administration. According to Asai, "The experiences gained from and the intent of the Japanese southern expansion are much greater and more substantive than imagined by those on mainland Japan. Today, in the aftermath of the Greater East Asian War, without question, they hold great significance" (1944, 352). The notion of "substantive experience" captures the "character" of the "Japanese" as it was manifested in colonial exploitation. This substantive experience expanded daily as the Great East Asian Co-prosperity Sphere developed and grew.

7. The same argument can be found in other places (e.g., "Nyuu-yangu-Okinawa" 1940; and "Shinario" 1941).

8. *Editor's note:* Eric Hobsbawm, Terrence Ranger, and other contributors to *The Invention of Tradition* (Hobsbawm and Ranger 1983) argue that the European colonials constructed a privileged and genealogically useful past to administer their numerous overseas territories. These ruling elites understood the importance of projecting their power backward in time, giving it a history and legitimacy that only tradition and longevity could give. Similarly, Japanese imperialism appealed to Confucianism and Shin-

toism as its justification. Both traditions linked Japan to a venerable past. Confucianism was used as the common heritage of universal principles linking Korea, China, and Japan. Japan associated its expansion with the defense of Confucian morality. The indigenous myth of Amaterasu Omikami, the sun goddess, relates the divine lineage of the imperial house and the Japanese nation. In Nan'yō, the Japanese propagated a state Shinto religion as a means to lead the Micronesians from savagery to civilization and as a means to strengthen the identification of the native islanders with the national ideals of Japan.

9. For a discussion of the "inner" other giving rise to self-discrimination and thus domination, see Tomiyama (1993).

Chapter 5

"The Other Japanese"
Okinawan Immigrants to the Philippines, 1903–1941

Edith M. Kaneshiro

Before the outbreak of World War II, immigrants from Okinawa established communities in regions as distant and diverse as the Americas, Southeast Asia, and the Pacific. Despite a history of struggle against economic hardship and racial prejudice, communities, most notably those in Hawai'i, Peru, and Brazil, have flourished. World War II fundamentally transformed all these communities, but those that survived now boast of a third and even a fourth generation of Americans, Peruvians, and Brazilians of Okinawan descent. Okinawan ethnicity and culture have been transformed in the process. The pre-World War II Okinawan immigrant community in Davao, Mindanao, in the southern Philippines, did not share this same historical experience. Established early in the twentieth century, by 1945 the Okinawan community in Davao ceased to exist. Numerous members died during the war, and survivors were repatriated to war-torn Japan. Like other Japanese immigrants in other areas of the Pacific and the Americas before the outbreak of war, Okinawan immigrants in Davao were suspected of being possible agents of the Japanese Empire. Residing in a region long troubled by a history of imperialism and colonialism, Okinawan immigrants in the Philippines could not escape the consequences of modern warfare as Japan began expanding into continental Asia and Southeast Asia during the 1930s and the 1940s.

Background to Okinawan Immigration to the Philippines

The history of Okinawan immigration to the Philippines is intimately linked to the history of American and Japanese expansion in the Pacific region.

After the end of the Spanish-American and Philippine-American Wars, the Philippines officially became a dependency of the United States. Former American military personnel became governors, administrators, and planters. Although local Filipino nationalists resisted the American occupation of the islands by forming small groups of resistance fighters known as *insurrectos,* the American military and civilian occupation of the islands was effectively secured by 1903 (Linn 1997, 23–49).

One of the first goals of the American administrators of the Philippines was to improve the economic infrastructure of the islands. According to the U.S. War Department, roads, bridges, and ports in the Philippines were in desperate need of repair, where they existed at all: "The conditions of all forms of public works, was such as to retard public service. Unimproved harbors, primitive roads, unbridged streams, and a crying need for schoolhouses was everywhere evident" (U.S. Bureau of Insular Affairs 1913, 39–40). One of the department's most famous public-works projects was the Benguet Road or the "Zig Zag Road" to Baguio, a city situated in the highlands of the northern Philippines. This road enabled American administrators and their families to travel to and enjoy the cooler climates of the tropical Philippines. Baguio became known as a mountain resort for the American and Filipino elite (Office of the Resident Commissioner of the Philippines 1942, 50–51).

Several thousand immigrant workers constructed the road, one of the most difficult civil-works projects in the Philippines. According to Hayase Shinzō, between 1903 and 1904, more than two hundred workers died, and more than nineteen thousand contracted illnesses and suffered injuries (Hayase 1984a, 116–132). Toward the end of the project, workers from Okinawa were brought to the Philippines to complete the road (Goodman 1965, 170; Quiason 1958, 217). Recalling the early contributions of Japanese construction workers in the Philippines, Willard Price wrote, "The Americans had recently taken over the Philippines and were building the famous Benguet Road up the mountainside to Baguio. They tried Filipino laborers, Chinese, Russian—all failed. Then they brought down two thousand Japanese from Okinawa. They were equal to the very difficult and dangerous work and the road was completed, but not without great loss of life due to accidents and epidemics" (Price 1936, 15).

Tōyama Kyūzō (1868–1910) and one of his most capable employees, Ōshiro Kōzō, arranged for the Okinawan immigrant workers (fig. 7). Both men were from the village of Kin. While Tōyama oversaw the immigration to Hawai'i, Ōshiro was charged with managing and coordinating the immigration to the Philippines. Dispatched to the Philippines in 1903 to oversee working conditions there, Ōshiro met the Japanese entrepreneur Ōta

Kyōsaburo. The two men realized that the Philippines provided numerous economic opportunities for underemployed agricultural laborers in Japan. Consequently, after the Benguet Road was completed in 1904, Ōta and Ōshiro led a group of construction workers to Davao, Mindanao, to work as laborers on American- and Filipino-owned abaca plantations (Hayase 1984b, 90–109; Ishikawa 1976; *Ryukyu Shimpo,* 5 November 1917).

Unlike the northern islands of the Philippines, Mindanao was not densely populated, nor was it Christian. Americans in the Philippines likened Mindanao to the American frontier, equating its local inhabitants with North American Indians and viewing its open lands as a vast resource. Soon after the end of the Philippine-American War, Americans separated Mindanao from the rest of the Philippines, called it the Moro Province, and instituted a military government (Hayase 1984b, 90–109; Hayase 1984a). The United States

Figure 7. Tōyama Kōzō recruited many Okinawans from his native Kin and other nearby villages to work in the Philippines and Hawai'i. The Nakasone family from neighboring Wakugawa Village sent sons and daughters to Davao, Hawai'i, Mexico, Peru, Brazil, and mainland Japan. Nakasone Shinyū, who immigrated to Hawai'i in 1906, visited his mother, Ushi (front center), and brothers who managed an abaca plantation in Davao. The caption inscribed on this photograph reads: "Commemorative photography occasioned by the visit of Nakasone Shinyū and Nakasone Zōji of Hawai'i to Davao. October 26, 1941." Photograph courtesy Ronald Y. Nakasone.

set out to pacify the indigenous peoples and to develop the agricultural and natural resources of the island. Abaca, one of the most important products of the island throughout the first half of the century, was used to produce heavy rope and cable for American industry. It was consistently one of the Philippines most important agricultural commodities (Hayase 1985a, 1984a).

Envisioning themselves as the principal producers and distributors of abaca, American soldiers turned planters formed the Davao Planters' Association in 1905 to promote the interests of American and Western planters in Mindanao (Hayase 1984b, 70–83). The shortage of labor was a pressing problem. On different occasions, the Davao planters entertained the possibility of using Italian, Chinese, Filipino, and even Russian laborers on their plantations (*Mindanao Herald,* 16 September 1905, 10 February, 14 April, 26 November 1906). While the planters were considering various options, Japanese laborers, particularly Okinawans, began arriving in Davao as a result of Ōshiro Kōzō's recruiting efforts.

Recognizing that they too could profit from producing abaca, Ōta and Ōshiro formed the Ōta Development Company in 1907. Ōshiro was named vice president. With Japanese investment and Japanese labor, the Ōta Development Company quickly became one of Davao's leading producers of abaca (Hayase 1984b, 155–162; Quiason 1958, 218–219). By 1917, the Ōta Development Company employed more than five hundred people and controlled between ten and twenty thousand acres of land in Davao (*Ryukyu Shimpo,* 5 November 1917). Filipino and American reports on the abaca industry often cited the productivity and efficiency of the Ōta Development Company. The company experimented with new varieties of abaca and new methods of cultivation, it constructed roads and piers, and it established stores for local people and immigrant families (Duckworth 1926; Quiason 1958, 218–219). Thanks to Ōshiro's influence, numerous Okinawans found employment as managers, shopkeepers, and laborers on plantations and farms owned by the company (Nakama Nabe, OH-KTHC).[1] At the beginning of the century, hopeful Okinawan immigrants looked, not only to Hawai'i, Brazil, and Peru, but also to the Philippines as a possible destination.

From 1904 up to the 1910s, Okinawan immigration to the Philippines was sporadic. Initially, a large organized group traveled to Manila to work on the Benguet project. Thereafter, Okinawan immigrants tended to immigrate as individuals or as sponsored relatives. Learning about the opportunities in Davao from friends and relatives who had settled there after working on the Benguet Road, single men migrated as *yobiyose* (summoned) or *dekasegi* (sojourn) laborers. These strategies for seeking employment were similar to those used by the early immigrants to Hawai'i.

World War I, however, marked a significant turning point in Okinawan attitudes toward the Philippines. No longer able to immigrate to Hawai'i as laborers after the enactment of the Gentlemen's Agreement in 1908, Okinawan laborers increasingly looked to the Philippines as a destination. Although the Philippines was a U.S. possession, Okinawans were attracted to Davao because of its proximity to Okinawa and high wages. As the price of abaca rose during the war, so did wages for workers and profits for farmers (Goodman 1965, 172; Hayase 1985a, 513; Kobashigawa Kō, OH-KTHC).

Tales about the Philippines and economic opportunities in Davao piqued the interest of young Okinawan men seeking adventure and wealth. Many young men applied for permits to travel to Davao during the later 1910s and the 1920s. Impatient with the time-consuming application and selection process, and unwilling to risk rejection, many young men illegally stowed away on ships bound for the Philippines and Southeast Asia (Afuso Seian, OH-KTHC; Yonashiro Shigeru, OH-KTHC). Alarmed that the number of illegal immigrants arriving in Davao would have a negative effect on the Japanese community, in 1918 Ōshiro corresponded with the prefectural governor of Okinawa, urging him to take a strong stand against illegal immigration (*Ryukyu Shimpo*, 10, 17 May 1918). Despite these warnings, young Okinawans continued to travel to the Philippines without proper documentation.

Once in Davao, and after working for a few years, documented and undocumented Okinawan immigrants had numerous opportunities to become small farmers. With the savings from his earnings, a young man could lease land from an American or a Filipino landowner and cultivate and harvest abaca on his own (Hayase 1984a, 85–188). Some men also formed *compa* (small companies) with friends and leased land (*Ryukyu Shimpo*, 28 April 1917; Igei Goze, OH-KTHC; Igei Yasutarō, OH-KTHC). As in California, many Okinawan immigrants in Davao gradually climbed out of the laboring class and began their own farms. By the 1920s, Okinawans in Davao were widely regarded as hardworking and successful farmers. In fact, many informants recalled that it was more desirable to marry Okinawan men in the Philippines than Okinawan men in Hawai'i (Nakama Goze, OH-KTHC; Higa Todo, OH-KTHC).

For many farm families, migrating to Davao became an attractive alternative to a life of underemployment in their homeland. After the 1924 passage of the U.S. Immigration Restriction Act, which prohibited further emigration from Europe and Asia, Okinawan farmers increasingly looked to the Philippines. Although American immigration laws, most notably the Chinese Exclusion Acts, were enforced in American Pacific dependencies, selective immigration of Japanese was permitted in the Philippines (Goodman

1965, 172). Noting this contradiction in American immigration policy, in 1937 the Japanese economist Ishii Ryoichi wrote, "In contrast to the situation that prevails in other Pacific possessions of the United States, there are no restrictions against Japanese emigration to the Philippines" (Ishii 1937, 201).

Despite restrictive immigration laws that were directed toward Asians in other parts of the American Pacific, Japanese immigrants were welcomed to work in the Philippines, where they were recognized as skilled agriculturalists. As early as 22 April 1905, the *Mindanao Herald* reported that "the Japanese make capable hemp strippers; the fiber cleaned by them being of finer quality than that cleaned by native laborers." Because the abaca industry was important to the United States, Japan, and the Philippines, selected immigrants from Japan were permitted to enter the Philippines to work. By the 1930s, in addition to Japanese laborers and farmers, Japanese businessmen who invested in and managed the cultivation and harvesting of abaca for the Japanese market immigrated to the Philippines (Goodman 1965, 172–193; Quiason 1958, 244–227; Yu-Jose 1996, 72). By 1928, Davao, which had once been referred to as "the most thoroughly American community in the Philippines," had become a predominantly Japanese colony (*Mindanao Herald*, 22 April, 5 May 1928). In addition to American and Filipino businesses, there were also Japanese stores, restaurants, and services in Davao (Quiason 1958, 224–225).

The Japanese presence in Davao was strong and influential. Contemporary observers praised the work ethic and business efficiency of the Japanese. "Davao would not have achieved its present state of progress had it not been for the pioneering spirit of the Japanese," wrote Pablo F. Sulit. "They were the ones who blazed the trail to the interior, defying the wilderness and the hostility of the natives." He added, "The Japanese . . . have converted virgin forests into seas of waving, green abaca fields from which is derived enormous wealth" (Sulit 1929, 3–4).

Daily Life on Okinawan Abaca Farms

By 1940, approximately ten thousand Okinawans were living in Davao; many were immigrant farmers (Taeuber 1958, 200). Acquiring land was essential to the economic strategies of these farmers. The earliest immigrants to the Philippines usually leased uncultivated land from American and Filipino landowners, and, after negotiating an agreement with a landowner, they cleared the land by cutting trees and burning the remaining stumps. Once the land was cleared, they dug holes and planted abaca plants in well-measured rows (Hayase 1984a, 185–188; Higa Todo, OH-KTHC). Writing for the *Philip-*

pine Journal of Commerce and Industry, David Alvarez described the neatness of these rows: "In hemp plantations of Davao abaca plants grow to a great height, in orderly groups arranged in straight rows, so that even in streches [*sic*] hundreds of meters long, workers at one end can easily be observed from the other." Having observed the methods of the Japanese abaca grower, Alvarez attributed the success of the Japanese to their meticulous attention to every aspect of the planting and harvesting of abaca: "Selection of the land for planting, the variety of hemp to be raised, the manner of planting in seedlings, and the cutting of the plants for stripping, all undergo careful scrutiny" (Alvarez 1934, 6).

When the abaca plant grew to a height of four or more meters and produced blossoms "like that of a banana plant," it was ready to be harvested. During the abaca harvest, the busiest time of the year, Okinawan farmers hired up to five additional workers to assist them with the cutting, stripping, drying, and bundling of hemp. Workers were required to clear the farm of leaves that had dropped from the abaca plant, and then they cut the stalks using machete-like instruments called *tonba* and *boro*. After the plant was cut, the fibers were separated—sometimes by hand, but more often by machine. This stripping process—to which Okinawan farmers referred as "peeling" or "sawing"—required the labor of at least five men. More often than not, the process of stripping hemp on Japanese farms was mechanized.

According to Hayase Shinzō, the *hagotan,* a portable stripping machine, revolutionized the way in which hemp was stripped on Japanese abaca farms. As early as 1908, planters in Davao had experimented with new hemp-stripping machines, but few proved to be successful. Heavy and expensive, many of these machines produced fibers of mediocre quality. Although the time that it took for abaca to be stripped was reduced, the product was poor in quality. Japanese immigrant farmers reportedly managed to produce high-quality fibers with the smaller and portable *hagotan* (Hayase 1984a, 189–190; *Mindanao Herald,* 1 February 1908, 30 October 1909). The Filipino writer David Alvarez described the *hagotan:* "For small plantation owners, the 'hagotan' or stripping unit is the most suitable, as it costs less and can be installed on a removable wooden base that can easily be transferred from one place to another, and may be rented or used by the other strippers" (Alvarez 1934, 6–7). The *hagotan* became the centerpiece of the stripping process in rural areas. Because of its portability, one machine was often shared by many Okinawan farmers. One Okinawan farmer who owned two such machines hired as many as seventeen workers to help him strip and prepare abaca for market (Ajifu Tatsu, OH-KTHC; Ginoza Masa, OH-KTHC). The machine gave the process of stripping hemp a factory-like appearance. As the farmer ran the machine, workers assisted him by gathering hemp, running it through the machine, and gathering it after it was stripped. In many cases, in addition to the farmer, four or five men were required for this process (*Mindanao Herald,* 30 October 1909). This mechanized process was equated with "men's work" because immigrant women and children rarely stripped hemp. Instead, women reported that they swept the floors of the work area and performed "traditional" women's tasks such as housekeeping and child rearing (Igei Goze, OH-KTHC; Nakama Nabe, OH-KTHC).

The mechanization of hemp stripping resulted in clear divisions of labor based on gender. Although women did not strip hemp, they played crucial roles as gardeners and animal keepers on abaca farms. While immigrant men cultivated and stripped hemp, Okinawan women reported that they kept vegetable gardens and raised chickens and pigs. Okinawan women also reported that they supplemented their food supply by searching the forests for "delicious mushrooms." And, in addition to preparing dishes that called for eggs, chicken, and pork, Okinawan women learned to prepare meals with corn, coconuts, and durian. As in Okinawa, immigrant families in Davao produced their own food and ate what grew around them naturally. Yet, unlike in Okinawa, in Davao they could purchase rice, bread, sweets, and canned goods at trading posts run by the Ōta Development Company. In addition to food products, immigrants could purchase manufactured goods such as sewing machines. The mechanization of agriculture and the availability of new technologies and store-bought goods in Davao led to new gender roles and new work responsibilities for Okinawan immigrant men and women (Ginoza Masa, OH-KTHC; Nakama Emi, OH-KTHC; Nakama Nabe, OH-KTHC).

The mechanization of agriculture also influenced the architecture and design of Okinawan abaca farms. Most Okinawan farms had three structures: a residence for the farmer and his family (which also functioned as a warehouse), a bunkhouse for workers, and a shed called a *makina goya* where the farmer kept his stripping machine. These three structures were usually made of wood and metal, and some roofs were made of thatched banana leaves. In two-story structures, the first floor was used as a warehouse, while the second floor served as a living space for the farmer and his family. Workers were housed separately, according to their ethnicity (Ajifu Nae, OH-KTHC; Ginoza Masa, OH-KTHC; Igei Goze, OH-KTHC; Kobashigawa Ko, OH-KTHC; Nakama Goze, OH-KTHC; Yonashiro Shigeru, OH-KTHC). And, in extreme cases, a separate shed was constructed for a worker with whom others would not share a room. For example, Yonashiro Shigeru's father had to build a separate shed for a Muslim worker because the other workers refused to live with him (Yonashiro Shigeru, OH-KTHC).

In addition to housing, work spaces were also very important. The stripping of hemp was conducted in an area called the *makina goya*. It was in this area that the most difficult and skilled work of hemp stripping was conducted (Ginoza Masa, OH-KTHC; Igei Goze, OH-KTHC; Nakama Goze, OH-KTHC). Many immigrants recalled that they were required to demonstrate at least a year's work in cutting and cleaning before they were entrusted with the responsibility of stripping hemp (Kobashigawa Kō, OH-KTHC; Yoshida Matsuzō, OH-KTHC; Igei Yasutarō, OH-KTHC). Although Japanese and indigenous workers were both hired to strip hemp, Japanese workers were paid a higher wage. Native workers were paid thirty cents for cutting abaca, while Japanese workers were paid fifty cents. And native workers were paid eighty cents for stripping abaca, while Japanese workers were paid one peso. One Okinawan worker said that such a differential resulted because there were some local workers who were "lazy" (*namasu*) and, as the boss, he could not trust them and had to check their work often (Nakama Masanori, OH-KTHC).

Once the hemp dried and was prepared in large bundles, Okinawan farmers turned to a vast network of brokers, primarily Japanese and Chinese, for assistance in selling their product. In order to get the best price, Okinawan farmers read the newspaper and checked the market price of hemp on a regular basis (Kobashigawa Kō, OH-KTHC). They also positioned their bundles so that the finest fibers were visible from the top, but, as one immigrant recalled, brokers were wise and flipped the product to one side to view the quality of fiber from beneath. Like the laborer who wished to receive a higher wage, the Okinawan farmer tried but failed to outwit the local merchant. Although worker, farmer, and merchant continually tried to outwit one another, in the end each benefited from the rapid growth of the abaca industry in Davao (Ginoza, OH-KTHC)

The Social Status of Okinawan Immigrants in Davao

Okinawan immigrants in Davao developed a reputation for being hardworking and shrewd. Although they were admired for their strong work ethic, they were continually reminded by Filipinos and Japanese immigrants from the mainland that they were not "truly" Japanese, as were the educated Japanese business elite of Davao. Filipino observers often referred to the Okinawans as "the other Japanese" (Hayase 1984b, 216). The historian Cecil Cody wrote, "One feature of the Japanese community stood out clearly to their Filipino neighbors: there were two kinds of Japanese in Davao—the non-Okinawans and the Okinawans. They dressed and spoke

differently and discrimination existed between them" (Cody 1959, 174). Because of perceived differences, Okinawan immigrants were especially self-
conscious of their social status.

Abaca growing was labor-intensive. Days spent under the hot tropical
sun darkened the skin of the immigrant farmers, and the work was dirty,
the sap from the abaca plant staining their hands and bodies. Nakama
Masanori explained that working with abaca often made his hands swell and
that sometimes they would become "completely black." The sap was "as
sticky as rice paste," he recalled, making it so difficult to clean stained work
clothes that he often had to prepare extra sets. Okinawan farmers tended
to be darker than their urban counterparts, and Okinawan farmers often
appeared dirty and unkempt to the business elite of Davao, who wore neckties and white suits, the formal attire of the Philippines (Nakama Masanori,
OH-KTHC; Murayama 1929, 16–17).

Okinawan immigrants were also criticized for keeping untidy homes. The
Okinawans' living spaces were closely situated to their work spaces; outside
observers often found it difficult to differentiate between the two. One observer stated that Okinawan homes resembled "pig styes." The sight of hemp
drying in front of homes, the difficulty distinguishing storage areas from living quarters, and the sight of immigrant farm families and workers clustered
in makeshift homes provoked condescension (Murayama 1929, 16–17).

Okinawan immigrant women were also criticized for being untidy and
unrefined (Murayama 1929, 16–17). Although relatively less demanding and
more comfortable than rural life in Okinawa, rural life in Davao still required
significant contributions from the women. Raising children, keeping house,
tending to the vegetable garden, and cooking meals for workers filled the
daily schedule. Although the availability of sewing machines enabled women
to produce more clothes, the demands of farm life ensured that the clothes
that they produced remained simple and functional (Ajifu Kayū, OH-KTHC)

Outside observers noted that Okinawan immigrants were clannish
and that they rarely participated in civic activities. Participation in urban-
centered activities was often difficult for farmers who lived between two
and three hours (measured in terms of travel on horseback) away from
urban centers such as Davao and Mintal. A few farmers had cars, and some
reportedly kept horses, but most had to walk to get anywhere (Murayama
1929, 16–17; Ajifu Nae, OH-KTHC; Ginoza Toshiko, OH-KTHC). The
lack of access to convenient forms of transportation prevented Okinawans
from traveling to urban centers. Rather than traveling to the city of Davao,
where the American and Japanese elite socialized in country clubs and on
golf courses, Okinawan immigrant farmers socialized among themselves

in their rural communities, conversing in their native dialects and reminiscing about Okinawa. They formed prefectural associations (*kenjinkai*), village associations (*sonjinkai*), and small clubs. Electing representatives and supporting a vast membership, these organizations printed newsletters that informed members of weddings, births, and deaths, and they coordinated various activities. One such activity was the annual sumo match between village associations, and another was the effort to raise funds to erect a statue in Okinawa to honor the memory of Ōshiro Kōzō. Okinawan immigrants led active and socially rich lives. For example, after the birth of a child, it was not uncommon for several families to gather and celebrate the occasion for three days, often in drunken exhilaration. Because of these activities and frequent social interaction, many Okinawans reported that they did not feel lonely or homesick for Okinawa. In many ways, Okinawan immigrants had successfully transplanted and adapted Okinawan village life to Davao (Nakama Chiyo, OH-KTHC; Ginoza Masa, OH-KTHC; Ajifu Tatsu, OH-KTHC; Nakama Kamado, OH-KTHC; Ajifu Kayū, OH-KTHC).

Change, however, was also evident. Interactions with non-Okinawans, particularly the native peoples of Davao, altered Okinawan views of themselves and of peoples of other racial and ethnic backgrounds. "It was the Okinawans who tended to live most intimately with their neighbors, especially in the areas of Bagobo settlement" (Cody 1959, 184). "The early Japanese and the Okinawans," wrote the historian Hayase Shinzō, "had far more opportunity to establish harmonious social relations with tribal people and they proceeded to befriend the Bagobo under the leadership of Ōta" (Hayase 1984b, 224).

According to Hayase Shinzō and Fay Cooper Cole, the peoples of Davao were organized into six tribal groups, distinguished by clothing, tools, and social organization. And, as in too many Southeast Asian countries, a large Muslim population existed in Davao. Islam had spread to Mindanao from Southeast Asia, primarily through Malay and Arabic texts, and found many devoted converts among the tribal peoples of Mindanao. Owing to the strength of Islam in Mindanao, Spanish and Catholic influences were not particularly strong among the peoples of Davao (Cole 1913; Hayase 1984b, 13–56; Saleeby 1905).

Like other newcomers to Davao, some Okinawans also believed and perpetuated stereotypes of their tribal and Muslim neighbors. Ironically, Okinawan descriptions of the native peoples were similar to Western and Japanese descriptions of Okinawan peasants. Many Okinawans believed that, had the "native peoples" been "a little more clever," the Philippines would have been a "great country." Some Okinawans assumed that the local people were poor because of their perceived "backward" cultures.

Describing the cultures of the various peoples of Davao, Okinawans stated that the "natives" with whom they had the most contact were the Bagobo and that, if possible, they avoided Muslims, to whom they referred as "the Moro." The Bagobo adorned themselves in elaborate red costumes and wore jewelry around their ankles that sounded when they walked. One Okinawan remarked that the Bagobo tended to gather in groups of twenty or more, and this made them appear threatening. In general, Okinawans perceived the Bagobo to be fierce and courageous, but they also stated that they were poor and hungry and that they lied and stole (Nakama Emi, OH-KTHC; Yonashiro Shigeru, OH-KTHC; Ginoza Toshiko, OH-KTHC).

Some Okinawans, able to see beyond the constructed and misleading stereotypes, referred to the native workers as *dekasegi* laborers and understood that cash was essential in Davao's rapidly growing economy. The native peoples, like the Okinawans, left their homes to work as wage laborers (Hayase 1984a). As recent immigrants, sympathetic Okinawans apparently understood that the tribal peoples' poverty was not a function of their culture but a result of their new and weakened status in a cash-based economy. Some Okinawan employers became friends with their workers. A former overseer recalled, "Because I learned the local dialects quickly, friendly relations between me and the natives developed, and I received invitations to the births of their children" (Tōyama Kamasei, OH-KTHC). Although cultural and linguistic barriers prevented most from becoming true friends, warm relations did develop between individual farmers and their workers. Realizing that their hired help were no different from them, one farmer's wife tried to help her workers and their families by feeding them and buying them clothes. Another Okinawan woman acknowledged that her family's success was directly related to the contributions of their workers and felt indebted to them. After the war, she returned to Davao for a visit and learned that a former employee died soon after the war had started and that another and his family lived in poverty in the Davao hills. She was saddened to see their condition (Kōhatsu Uto, OH-KTHC; Higa Todo, OH-KTHC).

Nonetheless, distrust ran high. Japanese farmers regularly armed themselves and cautioned their families of the dangers of living among "native peoples." One Okinawan woman remembered that a bell was rung to warn of possible attacks from the indigenous peoples (Yabiku Shuko, OH-KTHC). One Philippine-born Okinawan remembered that his mother had told him that there were "bad people" in the Philippines and that the family kept a Japanese sword for protection (Ajifu Kayū, OH-KTHC). Such fears were reinforced when Filipino workers threatened a newly hired Okinawan laborer with a knife. Another recalled that a native broke into an Okinawan home, bound the couple living there, and stole a jewelry box from Hong Kong (Ikehara Hiroshi, OH-KTHC). While it was not uncommon for an immigrant farmer and his family to be ambushed and killed, there were also outbursts of crimes committed by Japanese immigrants as well (Hayase 1984b, 257–262). These outbreaks of violence and crime led many Okinawans to believe that the indigenous peoples were uncivilized and lawless: "The Japanese were very frightened of the Moro" (Ginoza Masa, OH-KTHC).

Some Okinawans, however, attempted to find similarities between themselves and the peoples of Davao. For example, when Kobashigawa Sakukichi supervised indigenous laborers, he recalled that the peoples of the Philippines trusted Okinawans more than the Japanese from the mainland. "*Yamatunchu* [Japanese from the mainland] are proud," he said, "and because they treat natives and *Uchinanchu* [Okinawans] like fools, the natives trust *Uchinanchu.*" Kobashigawa believed that the Japanese treated Okinawan immigrants and indigenous workers alike and thus naively believed that his workers felt a sense of solidarity with him. However, his position as overseer, his superior earnings, and the sword that he carried while at work did not win him many admirers (Kobashigawa Sakukichi, OH-KTHC). Kurota Zenpachi also felt that he could develop friendships with his workers by sharing liquor with them. To Okinawans, drinking with friends is and was perhaps the most obvious sign of friendship. After one attempt, he never tried again. "When the natives drink, they become violent, so I never drank with them" (Kurota Zenpachi, OH-KTHC). Social relationships between Okinawans and non-Okinawans in the rural districts of Davao were, therefore, awkward and fragile. Language barriers, cultural differences, misunderstandings, and mistrust prevented Okinawan immigrants and their workers from developing strong and lasting relationships.

"Education Fever" and Japanese Nationalism

Life on the so-called frontier proved to be especially challenging for immigrant parents who valued education. Extremely sensitive about their perceived lower-class status, Okinawan immigrant parents were especially active in their children's education. As one Philippine-born Okinawan recalled, immigrant parents had "education fever" (Ikehara Hiroshi, OH-KTHC). This strong desire to see their children educated is not surprising. According to the demographer Irene Taeuber, of all the Japanese overseas, the immigrants in the Philippines had the least amount of formal education. Less than 6 percent of the male immigrants in the Philippines had attended middle school. In contrast, more than 14.7 percent of the male immigrants to Hawai'i and 25.9 percent of the male immigrants who settled in the continental United States graduated from middle school. Moreover, Japanese immigrant women in the Philippines received less education than their Japanese cohorts who migrated to Hawai'i and the continental United States; only 2.5 percent of the female immigrants to the Philippines had attended middle school, while 16 percent of the female immigrants to Hawai'i and 34.4 percent of the female immigrants who migrated to the continental United States graduated from middle school (Taeuber 1958, 2000). A contemporary observer of the Okinawan community in Davao noted that the level of literacy was "dreadfully low" (Murayama 1929, 16–17).

In Davao, there were two types of schools: Filipino and Japanese. In 1937, there were twenty-one schools in the city of Davao: seventeen were primary schools with a total enrollment of 3,165; three were intermediate schools with 800 students; and one was a high school with 437 students (Estuar 1937, 17). Although Japanese children were eligible to attend these schools, Japanese immigrant parents chose to send them to Japanese schools that were administered by the Japanese Ministry of Education. In 1940, there were approximately 2,000 Japanese schoolchildren and twelve Japanese schools in Davao, and the curriculum in these schools was similar to the curriculum in schools in Japan (Ayala 1940, 35; Ajifu Kayū, OH-KTHC). In an economy that depended highly on Japanese investment and trade, a Japanese education and Japanese credentials were required in order to advance beyond the status of farmer. The ability to conduct business in Japanese was essential. Thus, Okinawan farmers eagerly sent their children to Japanese schools if they could. Rather than experiencing a decline in status, many Okinawan immigrants viewed their immigration to Davao as an opportunity for economic and social mobility. Educating the second generation thus became an extremely important priority (Ajifu Kayū, OH-KTHC; Yonashiro Shigeru, OH-KTHC).

If they lived in the city, or if they could afford to board their children near the schools, Okinawan immigrants sent their children to Japanese schools in either Davao and Mintal. Whereas they themselves dressed in work clothes, parents dressed their children in formal attire. The boys wore white shirts, short pants, and shoes and some even neckties. These children were educated to become part of the Japanese middle class. Philippine-born Yonashiro Shigeru recalled that his teachers were "strict." He had lessons in Japanese ethics, Japanese calligraphy, and arithmetic. He also recalled that schoolchildren attended an English class "because the Philippines was an

American territory." In addition to these academic requirements, children also participated in sports festivals with other Japanese youths rather than with teams from Filipino schools (Ginoza Toshiko, OH-KTHC; Yonashiro Shigeru, OH-KTHC).

Many immigrant parents supported the activities of the Japanese schools, but, because so many families lived in remote areas, many found it difficult to send their children to these schools. The children within commuting distance came on horseback or bicycle or simply walked. Ajifu Nae stated that she rose before dawn in order to walk her children to school. Children who lived further away crossed rivers and passed through hilly terrain in order to reach the schools. Ajifu Kayu, a Philippine-born Okinawan, remembered that most of his Okinawan friends at school returned to their rural homes in the summer, leaving him with few companions in the city. Nakama Nabe recalled that some parents rented rooms for their children in homes near the schools. Boarding children in the city was costly; thus, many chose to send their children to Okinawa to live with their grandparents or close relatives in order to receive a Japanese education (Ajifu Nae, OH-KTHC; Ginoza Toshiko, OH-KTHC; Higa Todo, OH-KTHC; Kōhatsu Uto, OH-KTHC; Nakama Chiyo, OH-KTHC; Nakama Goze, OH-KTHC).

Children sent to Okinawa were accompanied by either a trusted adult or their mothers. This "education migration" was often filled with anxiety. Philippine-born children who were sent to Okinawa often excelled in school but regularly complained that life in Okinawa was "boring" and that the food was "miserable." Grandparents in Okinawa informed parents that their children often threatened to "run away" and return to the Philippines. Okinawan children born overseas, it seems, found it difficult adapting to life in rural Okinawa. Ikehara Hiroshi, a Philippine-born Okinawan, expressed his deepest sympathies for the immigrant women who chose to return to "miserable" Okinawa so that their children could receive an education. "The Philippines was like heaven," he recalled. "The warm climate, the fertile land, no typhoons. . . . Women's lives were not difficult. . . . How did the women who escorted their children back to Okinawa feel [about leaving Davao]?" (Ikehara Hiroshi, OH-KTHC). Although the sending of their children back to Okinawa evoked emotions of sadness, anxiety, and guilt, these immigrant parents, particularly immigrants from Kin Village, felt assured that their children would at least receive a Japanese education.

Outside observers viewed this return migration of women and children as an indication that Japan was preparing to invade Davao. Antonio Gabila wrote, "You must have read about it in the papers—the silent, 'unofficial evacuation' of Japanese from the South." A week before this was written, eighty-seven Japanese (mostly women and children) left Cebu and Davao for Japan. The evacuation, argued Gabila, was clear evidence that Japan was preparing to invade the Philippines. When he inquired about the "evacuations," he was told by Japanese representatives that "the women and children, they go home because the children they enter school in Japan." Unwilling to believe that this was indeed true, Gabila argued that the Japanese method of control and domination was "gradual and quiet." Warning Filipinos of an impending invasion, he wrote, "You many shove the little Japanese about in the beginning, but some day you'll wake up to find him grown so big and strong you can't budge him. And that's what happened in Davao" (Gabila 1941).

"The Japanese Menace," War, and Repatriation

The "education migration" of Philippine-born Japanese schoolchildren coincided with the rise of Japanese militarism in Asia. The Japanese presence in the Philippines had become both a national and an international problem. The Philippines would be a site where geopolitics and diplomacy had failed and war prevailed. The Philippines had sought independence from the United States by the 1940s. During the 1930s, and especially after the Philippines achieved commonwealth status in 1934, Philippine nationalists sought to restrict Japanese immigration and attempted to confiscate Japanese lands that were allegedly acquired through "extralegal" means. Japanese immigration and the "land problem" became two hotly debated issues among Philippine nationalists (Yu-Jose 1996, 74–78).

In the fall of 1935, Teodoro V. Nano warned readers of the *Commonwealth Advocate* that the Japanese community in Davao, Mindanao, would be a major obstacle to Philippine independence. "Japan's agricultural development of Davao," he wrote, "may be disguised penetration that will someday result in the annexation of the Philippines to the [Japanese] Island Empire" (Nano 1935, 44). Comparing the Japanese with the Chinese, the *Commonwealth Advocate* argued that Chinese immigrants were colonists, not colonizers. Unlike the Chinese, the Japanese have "ambition[s] of conquest and expansion" (*Commonwealth Advocate* 1, no. 1 [January 1935]: 15–16). Another Philippine nationalist wrote, "The continuous influx of a foreign population, strongly bound to their old country and unwilling to be absorbed by us, soon will usher in a social and racial problem that will rival that of California's" (Paguio 1930, 40). Like their cohorts in California, Japanese farmers in the Philippines were perceived to be unfair competitors and undesirable immigrants. However, by the late 1930s, the peoples and the government of the Philippines had cause for concern. Japanese militarism had increased, and Japan's invasion of China in 1937 provoked criticism from the international community. Although Japan's militaristic activities alarmed several Asian nations, the Philippines continued to welcome Japanese investment until the bombing of Pearl Harbor (Yu-Jose 1996, 74–78).

After Pearl Harbor, several Okinawan immigrants in Davao gathered at the Ōta Development Company offices and cheered after hearing of the successful attack. Other immigrants recalled that their neighbors regularly prayed for the emperor of Japan. With the outbreak of war, ethnic nationalism among Okinawan immigrants was pronounced. Within a few days, several Japanese immigrants were interned. In one camp, a Filipino soldier randomly fired a gun and killed five Okinawan immigrants. A few weeks later, the Japanese military landed in Davao and transformed it into a military outpost. Japanese civilians were drafted into the military; many Okinawans served as low-level soldiers, mainly cooks and attendants to Japanese officers. By 1942, the Philippines was under the control of the Japanese military (Ajifu Nae, OH-KTHC; Ajifu Tatsu, OH-KTHC; Ginoza Sengorō, OH-KTHC; Kurota Zenpachi, OH-KTHC).

During this time, the Filipinos formed several resistance groups. When American troops landed in Davao in 1945, they relied on these guerilla fighters to fight the poorly trained and ill-equipped Japanese army (Morton 1953, 586). Warfare in Davao was particularly ferocious. While Okinawan men served in the army, their wives and children fled to the mountains to avoid conflict and battle. Guerilla warfare, however, affected soldier and civilian alike. Attempting to flee from American and Filipino troops, civilians drowned crossing rivers. Without adequate food and supplies, many of the elderly and the young died of starvation. Nakama Kamado and Yabiku Shuko recalled seeing many abandoned children along riverbeds. In one instance, one survivor recalled seeing crying babies still strapped to the backs of mothers' whose heads had been cut off.

Despite numerous casualties, many Okinawan immigrants fled further and further into the interior of Davao. The American military enlisted the help of the local tribes to reach them. Igei Genichi recalled that members of the Bagobo tribe were sent to find and retrieve Japanese soldiers and civilians. They were rewarded with "canned goods" and "prizes" (Igei Genichi, OH-KTHC). But, rather than surrendering to the Americans, many Okinawans continued to retreat deeper into the mountains. At war's end, American aircraft scattered flyers indicating that the war had ended and that Japanese civilians should surrender to American troops. Ajifu Tatsu recalled that the local peoples attacked Okinawans with knives as American troops transported them to internment camps, where survivors—who considered themselves "prisoners"—were processed for repatriation to Japan. By war's end, approximately seventeen thousand Japanese—soldiers and civilians— were killed, about twelve thousand surrendered, and approximately eighty-two hundred were declared missing (Smith 1953, 647). Many Okinawans were among the missing.

Okinawan repatriates were sent to Kagoshima, Oita, and Fukuoka prefectures. Many suffered from poor health and malnutrition. Because of their poor physical condition, many, particularly children, died. Those old enough and strong enough to work pieced together odd jobs on a daily basis. Beginning in 1946, many were able to return to Okinawa, but, on their return, they discovered that the island had been transformed into an American military outpost (Ajifu Tatsu, OH-KTHC; Nakama Emi, OH-KTHC; Nakama, OH-KTHC; Ginoza Sengorō, OH-KTHC; Igei Yasutarō, OH-KTHC; Yabiku Shuko, OH-KTHC).

Conclusion

Unlike Japanese expansion to Manchuria, which began with a military invasion, Japanese expansion to the Philippines began with immigration, followed by investment, and then invasion. The Japanese colony in Davao, Mindanao, was, as numerous scholars have argued, a creation of American and Japanese economic interests in the Philippines. The migration of Okinawans occurred within this international context. Excluded from the continental United States and Hawai'i, Okinawan laborers and farmers contributed to the expansion and economic development of the American Pacific empire in the Philippines.

Although the Philippines was an unincorporated U.S. possession, America's colonial presence failed to win the allegiance of Okinawan immigrants in the Philippines. As Davao's economy and trade became more and more dependent on Japanese investment, Okinawan immigrants began to identify with an expanding Japanese Empire. Japanese schools in Davao were instrumental in fostering this ideological tie with Japan. After the Japanese invasion of the Philippines in 1942, Okinawan immigrants openly expressed their devotion to the Japanese emperor and assisted with the Japanese military occupation of Davao. Unwilling to surrender to American and Filipino troops during the American liberation of the Philippines in 1945, numerous Okinawan immigrants became casualties of guerilla warfare. Survivors were repatriated to war-torn Japan, where many died.

The story of Okinawan immigrants in the Philippines is one of immigration, imperialism, and war. It is a tragic story of selective immigration to a country that was struggling to assert its independence, first from the United States, then from Japan. As the historian Grant K. Goodman noted, "Only when Japanese expansion and nascent Philippine independence confronted each other did the problem of Japanese immigrants and immigration come under close scrutiny" (Goodman 1965, 174). Within this colonial context, it appeared impossible for immigrants from Okinawa to be incorporated into the national life of the Philippines. With the outbreak of the Pacific War, and with the defeat of Japan, it was decided that the Japanese in Davao should not remain in the Philippines (Cody 1959, 186; Yu-Jose 1996, 80). The Okinawan immigrant community therefore was short-lived. Careful planning and cautious behavior failed to shield this community from the consequences of failed diplomacy and modern warfare. War would ultimately restrict the areas in which Okinawan immigrants could make their homes.

Note

A Fulbright dissertation research grant (1994–1995) administered through the Japan–United States Education Commission in Tokyo enabled me to conduct research in Okinawa. I would like to thank the Department of Geography at the University of the Ryūkyūs, and especially Professor Ishikawa Tomonori, for sponsoring me while I conducted research in Kin, a town located in northern Okinawa. I would also like to thank the Kin Township History Committee for providing me with primary and secondary sources and for pointing out the significance of the Okinawan experience in the Philippines. Finally, I would like to thank Yamamoto Yoshiko for helping me translate the oral histories. Any errors are mine.

1. Much of my work is indebted to the oral histories (OH) conducted and collected by the Kin Township History Committee (KTHC), Okinawa. To indicate that information reported in the text has been obtained from one of these oral histories, I give in parentheses the informant's name followed by the acronym OH-KTHC. None of the oral histories that I used is dated.

Chapter 6

Japanese Latin American Internment from an Okinawan Perspective

Wesley Ueunten

I tell this painful story in remembrance of my family so others will know how devastating this event was for us. Although I was just a young girl at the time, I knew that what happened to us was a grave injustice, and it should never occur again in a civilized world. I hope with all my heart that no group will ever have to undergo such an experience.—Carmen Higa Mochizuki et al. v. United States of America

Japan had lost the war and so we decided to stay in the U.S. until we could go back to Peru. Peru did not readily let us go back there and when the camps closed and we had to go out and work, my husband and I were already in our 50s and could not speak a word of English. To make matters worse, we had with us a granddaughter who was still a small child. I felt that it would be regrettable to leave this earth without telling the real story of our experiences in struggling with a life that was just better than death. Although I am nearly uneducated and ashamed of my writing, I decided to write things down.—Kamisato Kami, Ijū uchi de ikinuita

People . . . really lucky people travel smoothly through life, but life is really full of rough waves. My life was really full of rough waves.—OH-1

As a sansei Okinawan growing up on Kauai, I had few places to turn when I became interested in my Okinawan heritage.[1] At home, we had George Kerr's *History of an Island People* (1958), which I read cover to cover. Of course, we had my *baban* (grandmother). When she was temporarily bedridden after a fall, we would play Okinawan music tapes, and she would move her hands in the unique Okinawan clicking motions. I would try to mimic her hand movements. Observing my clumsy attempts, my mother suggested that I learn Okinawan dance from the Yamasatos in Kapa'a.

I spent many weekends with Mr. Toshio Yamasato (fig. 8) learning the dances that he had learned as a young man in Okinawa. Although I did not speak Japanese at the time, I eventually learned that the Yamasatos had come to Hawai'i from Peru via U.S. internment camps. At the time, I thought that it was a strange tale and wondered how it could have happened. Only years later, after I entered the doctoral program in the Ethnic Studies Department at the University of California, Berkeley, did I begin to piece together Mr. Yamasato's bizarre story and become involved with the Japanese Peruvian Oral History Project.[2]

The U.S. government illegally uprooted more than 120,000 U.S. citizens

Figure 8. Yamasato Toshio (center) with his family, 1958; (back row) Maurice, Kimiko, Eiko, Toshio, Yase (Mrs. Yamasato), Florinda, and Rosa; (front row) Mary, Fumiko, and Margaret. Mr. and Mrs. Yamasato were born on Okinawa, but the birthplaces of their children reflect the family's movements. Maurice, Florinda, and Rosa were born in Peru; Fumiko was born in Crystal City, Texas, in a U.S. Justice Department internment camp; Kimiko and Eiko were born in Okinawa; and Mary and Margaret were born in Hawai'i. Photograph courtesy Yamasato Family.

and permanent residents of Japanese ancestry in the Pacific Coast states, moving them into internment camps for the duration of World War II, even though there was no military necessity to do so since they did not pose a threat to national security. Very few know, however, that the U.S. government also rounded up 2,264 men, women, and children of Japanese ancestry from Brazil, Peru, Argentina, Bolivia, Mexico, and other Latin American countries and placed them in Department of Justice internment camps. In contrast, the War Relocation Authority (WRA) was responsible for the Japanese American internees. Of the 2,264 interned, approximately 1,800 were from Peru, and an estimated half were Okinawans.

The U.S. government exchanged more than 500 Japanese Latin Americans (JLAs) for its citizens stranded in Japanese territories between 1942 and 1943. The ordeal of the remaining 1,400 JLA internees continued long after the war's end. At the end of the war, the JLAs were told that they were "illegal aliens" and thus had to leave the United States. Between November 1945 and June 1946, the United States deported more than 900 JLAs to war-devastated Japan and Okinawa. With very few exceptions, Peru refused to allow any Japanese back. Three hundred Japanese Peruvians remained in the United States and fought deportation through the courts. It was not until June 1952 that the U.S. government allowed the Japanese Peruvians to begin the process of becoming permanent residents. Many became American citizens.

In 1988, Congress passed the historic Civil Liberties Act (CLA), which acknowledged the wrongs that the United States had committed against the Japanese Americans and provided former internees with $20,000 in redress and an apology letter. However, every JLA who applied for redress under the CLA was turned down, except for those who remained in the United States and obtained retroactive citizenship and those who were born in the camps. The JLA internees were denied redress because they were not citizens or permanent residents at the time of their incarceration.

"*Akisamiyoo!*"[3] Was it not the United States that sponsored their forced relocation across international borders and incarcerated them in Department of Justice camps? The United States even forcibly transported JLAs to Panama to labor in the jungles—a gross violation of human rights.[4] Did the United States not call the JLAs "illegal aliens" and deport most of them to war-devastated Japan and Okinawa?

Deeply disappointed, the JLAs sued the U.S. government to be included in the CLA. Two years later, after a determined effort, a settlement was reached. The JLAs were eligible to receive $5,000 and an apology letter. However, the figure was far short of the $20,000 provided to Japanese

Americans, and the apology letter was just a curt memo written on half a sheet of paper and stamped with the president's signature. Although it expressed regret "to those who endured such grave injustice," the apology shifted the responsibility to the past, and therefore excusable irrational behavior, by saying: "We understand that our nation's actions were rooted in racial prejudice and war time hysteria, and we must learn from the past and dedicate ourselves to renewing and strengthening equality, justice and freedom." The letter failed to mention the calculated actions of the U.S. government in kidnapping JLAs from their countries to be used in a hostage exchange.

Japanese and Okinawans in Latin America? Hostage exchange? Illegal JLA aliens? This little-known episode in the American wartime experience is shocking and complex. It took place in Okinawa, Japan, Latin America, North America, and Hawai'i. While engaged in this oral history project, I traveled from Berkeley to Los Angeles, Hawai'i, Peru, Japan, and Okinawa and interviewed people who spoke Okinawan, Hawaiian pidgin English, Japanese, Spanish, and English. This essay is an attempt to make sense of this story. I have divided my account into two parts. This first section relates Okinawan immigration to Latin America and immigrant life. In the second, I chronicle the internment and later resettlement. I begin each section with the voices of former Okinawan Latin American internees who give testimony to this strange tale.

Sweet sugar, bitter experiences

The women would sing about how the life of a boshikumaa [hat weaver] who worked day and night was hard. . . . They only got twenty-five sen for a hat. [In the 1920s, fifty sen equaled one week's wages (ESOHP 1981, 23–24). What can you eat with only that much? Twenty-five sen! Sometimes there were "smart" hat inspectors who would not pay anything if there was even a small dirty spot. That was one week's work. We [children] used to go there to make hats instead of going somewhere to play. It would take us a month to do the same work. . . . Boshikumaa awarinamun, Yuru hiru hatarachi [The life of a hat weaver is one of suffering, working night and day]. . . . It's been eighty years, how can I remember?—OH-1

In the early 1900s Okinawa was very poor. At that time, my mother already had two children. It must have been at that time that they had a dream to go overseas. I guess it was because their lives weren't too easy. So they left the two children with my grandmother, they were around twenty at the time, and they went to a place called Cañete in Peru as kaitaku imin [Immigrants who open up new lands to farm or ranch.]—OH-2

Japan forcibly annexed Okinawa in 1879 and made it a prefecture. In actuality, Okinawa became a virtual colony of Japan. Top officials in the prefectural government were predominantly from Kagoshima Prefecture (formally known as Satsuma) in Kyushu, the southernmost of the four main islands of Japan. People from Kagoshima and Osaka controlled the economic interests in Okinawa. Further, the Japanese government heavily taxed the new prefecture. In 1882, for example, while the Meiji government collected ¥655,279 from Okinawa, it expended only ¥455,136 on the prefecture (ES-OHP 1981, 14). Data from 1919 to 1928 show that Okinawa paid ¥68,000,000 in taxes while the Meiji government appropriated only ¥23,000,000 for Okinawa. In other words, the Japanese government pocketed ¥45,000,000. Much of this taxation was done without representation. It was not until 1920, thirty years after the rest of Japan, that Okinawa held its first full-fledged election for representatives to the Japanese Diet (Aniya 1974, 423–455).

To make matters worse, sugar became the main cash crop. Okinawans raised sugarcane to obtain cash to buy food from the mainland. In other words, Okinawans produced what they did not consume and consumed what they did not produce. When sugar prices in Japan fell in the 1920s, Okinawans suffered greatly. As a last resort, Okinawans were forced to consume *sotetsu* (the poisonous sago palm), and many died of eating improperly prepared palm. Okinawans refer to this time of food shortages as *"sotetsu jikoku"* (*sotetsu* hell).

By 1897, Japan had become a food-importing nation. Earnings from industrial exports paid for food imports. Although the Japanese government adopted a policy of *sangyō rikkoku* (founding the nation on industry) as the population increased, it did not relieve overpopulation in rural areas of mainland Japan. Industrialization had a negligible effect on Okinawa, which was far from the economic center of Japan (Tigner 1954, 11–12).

In 1881, the population of the island of Okinawa was 150,000, or 114 persons per square kilometer. By 1914, the population rose to 396,000. In 1940, the population stood at 475,766, or 339 persons per square kilometer. In the same year, the population density of Japan proper was 204 persons per square kilometer (Tigner 1954, 12).

I often wondered about the irony of the link between sweet sugar and bitter immigrant experiences. Many of the friends with whom I grew up in Hawai'i were from countries that raised sugarcane or had parents or grandparents from such countries. It seems strange that the production of white sugar involves the labor of so many brown-skinned people in and from such far-flung places as Puerto Rico, Cuba, the Philippines, Hawai'i, Peru, Japan, Okinawa, China, Korea, and Portugal. The Cuban writer Fernando Ortiz wrote in 1947: "The sugar industry . . . because of its exotic origin, its European antecedents, and the foreign capital invested in it, is economically centrifugal. It came to the country from abroad; it is the trader in it for foreign consumption who attempts to establish himself in Cuba and encourages its cheap production here; but those in control are not Cubans and the profits are reaped far from here" (Ortiz [1947] 1995, 69).

The international sugar industry was just one aspect of the world economy that had already begun developing when Okinawan immigration began. Cheap sources of labor have always been a prerequisite for the expansion of this global economy, and the excess population in Japan and Okinawa was one such source. But, even before Japanese and Okinawan immigration commenced, large numbers of Chinese immigrated to Hawai'i, the mainland United States, and Latin America. James L. Tigner writes in *The Okinawans in Latin America*: "From the time of their independence, early in the nineteenth century, up to the 1920s the general policy of Latin American countries was to foster immigration. The demand for workers in agriculture was unceasing and special efforts were made to attract Asiatic immigrants. The abolition of the African slave trade gave rise to the Chinese coolie traffic and its attendant evils. . . . Between 1849 and 1874 some 87,343 coolies entered Peru to work on coastal sugar plantations, in the guano deposits, and on railroad construction projects" (Tigner 1954, 5).

Japanese immigration to Latin America started in 1899. By then, Chinese immigration to Latin America had declined steeply because of rising immigration restrictions. After the Sino-Japanese War ended in 1895, Latin Americans became aware of differences between Asians and began encouraging Japanese to immigrate, believing that they might be better workers than the Chinese (Tigner 1954, 5).

Okinawan immigration to Latin America began in 1903 with laborers entering Mexico. Okinawan immigrants first went to Peru in 1906 to work in the sugar industry. Between 1906 and 1941, approximately ten thousand Okinawans entered Peru, where they constituted at least one-third of the Japanese population (Tigner 1954, 5).

Racism and Immigration

Grandfather had an uncle in Hawai'i. He wanted to go to Hawai'i, but because of anti-immigration laws, he had to come to Peru with his uncle and someone from his hometown.—OH-3

Mother wasn't able to get into the United States because of the 1924 Exclusion Law, and that's why they lived in Mexico.—OH-5

I always wondered why there were so many Japanese in Latin America and why, among JLA communities, Okinawans were numerically prominent. Why are there so many more Okinawans in Latin America than in the United States? Why does it seem that many Okinawans in Hawaiʻi also seem to have many more relatives in Latin America?

Okinawan overseas immigration began in 1900, and anti-Japanese immigration restrictions in the United States were launched with the Gentlemen's Agreement in 1908. Actually, the Gentlemen's Agreement was part of a series of measures that restricted Japanese immigration to other white countries: the Immigration Limitation Law of 1901 in Australia, the Lemieux Agreement of 1907 in Canada, and prohibitions on the entry and permanent settlement of Japanese in South Africa from 1913. Complete exclusion of Asians from the United States took place in 1924 with the Exclusion Act.

Soon after Okinawan immigration started, it became more and more difficult for Japanese to enter the United States and other mostly English-speaking countries. Latin American countries still welcomed Japanese immigrants, however, and thus became a destination for Okinawans who left in great numbers to relieve the overpopulated prefecture (Tigner 1954). Between 1899 and 1940, approximately thirty-one thousand immigrants left Okinawa.

Latin American Dream

In the beginning they were at a sugarcane plantation in the country under contract, but even in Okinawa sugarcane work—no like eh? At night, they went along the coast and ran away to Lima, where they heard that there was someone from Haneji. They had instructions about where to go in Lima. They were greenhorn immigrants and only had one month's—or was it one year's—pay, and they ran away. About five or six of them. They went along the coast and slept where they could at night. I wonder if there weren't any habu *[poisonous snakes]! [Laughs.] In Okinawa, everyone asks about* habu *when you talk about sleeping outdoors. Once at night a seabird flapped its wings, and they all shook from fear that someone was coming. I heard all kinds of stories.—OH-1*

Father had never done farmwork in Okinawa. He first went to do farm labor but ran away since he wasn't used to it. He and some others crossed the

desert and escaped to Lima. In Lima he worked for others and later met
mother. He also eventually started his own coffee shop.—OH-6

When I visited Peru in March 1999, I attended a memorial service for
the Japanese immigrants who died in Cañete. With a few hundred other
people, I got aboard one of the four or five buses that left the Japanese Cultural Center in Lima. The bus passed through congested streets and hor-
rible slums and along the dry and dusty coastal region. The bus driver drove
at breakneck speed trying to catch up with the other buses, which had left
ahead of us. He drove up and down the countless rolling hills that towered
between Lima and Cañete. We reached Cañete, a small agricultural town
near the ocean, more than two hours later.

The long drive to Cañete exhausted me, but I could not even begin to
imagine what it would be to walk the distance or what the conditions were
that forced people to walk that distance. What would drive people even to
attempt such a trek? Less than ten months after the first group of 790 emigrants from Japan reached Callaò on 3 April 1900, 124 workers had perished from disease, principally beri-beri and malaria. They were also victims
of physical attacks from the native Peruvians and were not given the wages
that they had expected. As Tigner points out, "The root of the problem then
was that the Peruvian plantation owners sustained their enterprises by using natives as virtual slaves. Having had long experience with slave labor,
they were not prepared to deal with workers in a civilized manner" (Tigner
1954, 584). Within a few years of their arrival, many Japanese and Okinawans
had made their way to the urban centers of Lima and Callaó, where they
became small business owners. By 1910, there were about 800 Japanese in
Lima and 150 in Callaó. The Japanese consul-general reported that there
were 67 barbers, 77 small traders, 68 restaurant operators, 45 grocers, 74
carpenters, 19 coal and charcoal vendors, and 40 factory workers. Others
were employed as domestics, restaurant waiters, masons, road repairmen,
gardeners, fishermen, dairymen, and laundrymen (Tigner 1954, 591). By
1940, about 80 percent of the Japanese in Peru were living in the Lima-Callaó
area. In the same year, there were 17,598 Japanese in Peru, and they represented 28.08 percent of the foreign-born population (Gardiner 1981, 5).

A review of the membership of Japanese business associations in Lima
in 1938 shows that Okinawans operated a majority of the small businesses
(see table 3).

Lima was a subarashii [wonderful] place. I was happy to be there. My
brother, who was already there and called us over, was a regular wage

Table 3
Japanese and Okinawan Merchants

	Total	Naichijin	Okinawans
Japanese Merchants Assn.	245	33	212
Japanese Bazaar Owners Assn.	107	75	32
Japanese Barbers Assn.	121	21	100
Japanese Café Owners Assn.	173	23	150
Japanese Charcoal Dealers Assn.	65	15	50
Japanese Build. Contract. Assn.	20	10	10
Japanese Hotel Owners Assn.	25	13	12
Japanese Restaurant Owners Assn.	30	10	20
Japanese Importers Assn.	35	19	16
Japanese Bakery Owners Assn.	25	10	15
Japanese Jewelers Assn.	32	20	12
Japanese Chauffeurs Assn.	63	32	31
Japanese Peddlers Assn.	26	13	13

Source: Tigner (1954, 592).

*worker. He did a lot of jobs. He had three children and later returned to Oki-
nawa after the war.—OH-7*

*My father was one who liked to stand out. That's why he became the pres-
ident of the Okinawan kenjinkai [prefectural organization]. He also rode
horses—not to compete in horse races, but to be in shows. He once rode in
front of the president. He used to take his hat off and do all kinds of things.
That's why his name was well-known. He had a horse saddle and a pon-
cho with four corners. He rode the horses in a figure 8 and did all kinds of
performances before the president. So that's why he was well-known in the
community.—OH-2*

After initial years of considerable hardship, the Japanese and Okinawans
in Peru began to fill a niche in Peruvian society as small business owners.
They enjoyed a relatively high socioeconomic status and employed local Peruvians, many of whom were from the indigenous population. The lives of
many, if not most, were far better than those of their counterparts in Japan,

especially in Okinawa. Many had maids, attended good schools, enjoyed sports, and hobnobbed with influential Peruvians. It was a dream come true for many Okinawans.

Anti-Japanese Sentiment

Just at that time, in March of 1940, there suddenly was a riot. Three such incidents happened when I was in Peru. The first two were only domestic political incidents, and no foreigners suffered damages. The third riot was a riot directed only at Japanese, and almost all the Japanese shops were all destroyed. The victims stayed in the Japanese school, and many went back to Japan. When the riot was starting, the neighbors came out and said, "If you destroy this shop, where are you going to get your bread tomorrow?" Because of that our shop escaped damage, but our home was badly damaged.—Kamisato Kami, Ijū uchi de ikinuita

I remember that very well. We had the big store, and people were throwing stones. We had to shut the store. We ran away because they were breaking the door. We had to go up on the roof. My sister-in-law was pregnant, and we had to push her up. . . . They looted everything we had.—OH-8

Rioters were mainly students at the beginning and later everybody else— rioting lasted for more than one day. I had brought a futon from Okinawa. I was scolded for bringing the futon since I could have bought one there. . . . There was an incident when houses were destroyed. . . . The futon that I brought, and our radio, was taken away. We had a steel door. We thought we had locked it, but they took everything away.—OH-1

The dream would not continue undisturbed. In March 1940, an anti-Japanese riot in Lima and Callaó resulted in the destruction of almost all Japanese businesses and many homes. The riot forced many to seek refuge in the main Japanese school in Lima. After the experience, many returned to Okinawa and Japan. The riot started after a Peruvian woman who worked as a maid for the leader of the Japanese Barbers Union died after sustaining injuries during a scuffle between her employer and men from a rival faction in the Japanese community. Tabloid sensationalism fanned antiforeign and anti-Japanese sentiment that had developed as the Japanese became more and more successful as small businessmen and as Japan became a military threat in the Far East.

Mother sometimes talked about the 1940 riot. She said that they were saved by the local youths because her father, who liked sports, supported sports for the local youths. The youths protected the store from the rioters. The store was untouched.—OH-5

After the riot . . . the people in Peru have their own religious beliefs. In Okinawa we would call them "yuta" [shaman]. . . . Someone wearing white clothes said that it was wrong to attack the Japanese. If that person hadn't said that, things would have been worse. . . . That person was like a yuta.—OH-1

A few weeks after the riot, a strong earthquake rocked Peru. Many Peruvians believed that the earthquake was punishment from God for attacking the Japanese. It is interesting that the religious beliefs of the Peruvians came in conflict with their anti-Japanese sentiments and actions, whereas, in many other ethnic and racial conflicts, religion is often used to justify grievous thoughts and deeds against fellow human beings.

The fact that religious beliefs clashed with anti-Japanese sentiments likely reflects complex social relations in Peru. While there was a white elite that controlled the economy and politics, whites were greatly outnumbered by mestizos (people of mixed parentage: white and indigenous) and indigenous people. Peru was also home to many Europeans. Further, as mentioned earlier, there was a large population of Chinese who had immigrated before the Japanese as well as a sizable population of African descent. Each of these groups probably had different attitudes toward and relations with the Japanese, and anti-Japanese sentiment was by no means uniform.

Nonetheless, the riot did cause widespread physical damage and psychological stress within the Japanese community in Peru. At the same time, it raised many questions. Did it happen mainly because the Japanese were economically successful and Japan was becoming a military threat? Or was it also tied to racist ideologies such as white supremacy, anti-Semitism, and "Yellow Peril" fear that were prevalent in the United States at the time?

This last question is especially serious because it brings into focus the relationship between the United States and Latin America. The United States has long had a strong presence in Latin America. It has taken much natural wealth from Latin America, but did it also export its racial ideologies?

Describing how American anti-Japanese racism found inspiration in Peruvian anti-Japanese racism, Harvey Gardiner relates how J. Edgar Hoover, director of the FBI, readily believed Raul Haya de la Torre from the out-of-favor Alianza Popular Revolucionariá Americana. De la Torre asserted that all Japanese had served in the Japanese army, many as officers, and that there were few Japanese women in Peru. Hoover was gullible enough to believe de la Torre's claim that Peru's Japanese population was mainly male and could take up arms against Peru and the United States at a moment's notice (Gardiner 1981, 10).

James Tigner writes that the eminent Peruvian historian and sociologist Francisco Garcia Calderón viewed Japanese immigrants as an "emissary of imperialism," the advanced guard of Japanese military aggression. Calderón was responding to Marquis Okuma Shigenobu's remark that "South America was comprised in a sphere of influence to which the Japanese Empire might legitimately pretend, and that persevering emigrants there might build up a new Japan" (Tigner 1954, 23). Okuma founded Waseda University.

Calderón's view of Japanese immigrants as the vanguard of Japan's military seems to echo a 1921 FBI report about Japanese in Hawai'i following the 1920 sugar strike by Japanese and Filipino workers (in which many Okinawans were involved). The bureau surmised that "Japan's program for world supremacy" began with the "peaceful invasion" of Japanese migrants into California (Okihiro 1994, 136).

The 1920 sugar strike had great repercussions, not only in Hawai'i, but also in the rest of the United States. The strike spurred sugar plantation owners in Hawai'i to make a trip to Washington, D.C., to try to convince a congressional committee to revise the Chinese Exclusion Act to allow the importation of Chinese to Hawai'i. The Hawaiian planters believed that the influx of Chinese would curb the threat posed by the large Japanese presence in Hawai'i. At the congressional hearings, members of the Hawaiian delegation tried to play on American fears of the Japanese threat to make their case. In the end, their bid to revise the Chinese Exclusion Act failed. However, they did succeed in heightening white fears of a Japanese conspiracy. Senator James Phelan, a strongly anti-Japanese senator from California who was present at the hearings, came away with a new campaign slogan to replace "Keep California White"—"Keep California from Going the Way of Hawaii." The Hearst newspaper chain ran a six-part series in 1921 in the *Los Angeles Examiner* with the headlines "Jap Menace Lies Black on Pacific!" The article declared that "Hawaii is a menacing outpost of Japan ruled invisibly by a carefully organized government that functions noiselessly and whose mainspring is in Tokio" (Duus 1999, 238). In 1925, Genaro Arbaiza, a Peruvian journalist, declared in the *Current History Magazine* that "Japanese immigration in Peru has grown and prospered much faster. It is well organized, systematical and has the Tokio Government behind it" (Arbaiza 1925, 738). Arbaiza's words are uncannily similar to the *Examiner*'s.

The Other Japanese

When I went to Peru in 1937, Okinawan immigrants were still being ridiculed. There was the term "otro Japones." "Japones" means Japanese in Spanish, and "otro" meant "other." "Otro Japones" meant that Okinawans were not "pure Japanese." . . . The Japanese mainlanders were saying [to the Peruvians] that "those Okinawans are 'other Japanese.'" They meant that Okinawans were not real Japanese.—Nomura Kōya, "Uchinanchu no seikatsushi."

The notion of Okinawa as part of the Japanese "nation" is so natural that we rarely question it. However, to incorporate Okinawans into Japan, the Meiji leaders had to abolish symbols of Okinawa's past and replace them with Japanese symbols. George Kerr describes the events that took place on 30 March 1879 when Japan physically, officially, and forcibly deposed the last king of the Ryūkyūan kingdom: "This was a most poignant and dramatic moment. Great crowds waited, tense and silent, as Sho Tai and his household passed from the castle grounds through the *Kokugaku-mon* (Gate of National Learning) into exile. This was the symbolic break with the past. For the first time in five hundred years the palace ceased to be the seat of authority and the symbol of nationhood. It was immediately occupied by Japanese troops from the Kumamoto Garrison" (Kerr 1958, 382).

The Japanese emperor became the new symbol to which Okinawans were expected to give their allegiance. Japanese government efforts to incorporate Okinawa into the Japanese Empire was backed by brute force and by legions of government officials and merchants. Japan's efficient education system indoctrinated Okinawan schoolchildren in the ways of emperor worship. Although it was slow in implementing other reforms in Okinawa, the Japanese government put great effort into the education system. As a result, by the turn of the century, the vast majority of school-age children attended public schools. The Japanese government may have intended to improve the lot of Okinawans, but the education system was also a means by which to create loyal subjects. Okinawan children learned that their native tongue and culture were barbaric and backward, not fitting for subjects of the emperor. Thus began the stigmatization of the Okinawan identity.

The tragic consequences of this stigmatization would be realized over and over again in the lives of Okinawans both in Okinawa and in the Okinawan diaspora.

✿ ✿ ✿

The development of global capitalism led to the movement of large numbers of Japanese and Okinawans throughout the world. Racism against
Asians in the United States diverted the flow of Japanese and Okinawan
immigrants to Latin America. Racism with ties to U.S. capitalism also adversely affected the lives of Japanese and Okinawans, especially those in
Peru. In the background of the Okinawan immigrant experience was Japan's
annexation of Okinawa. Within the framework of imperialism and nationalism, the Japanese government carried out a policy of suppressing the Okinawan language, culture, and identity. Capitalism, racism, imperialism, and
nationalism affected not only the lives of the Okinawan Latin American internees, but also how the Okinawan Latin American internees negotiated
with and resisted these "isms."

Hostages: *Lista Negra*

*Grandfather wondered why he was on the lista negra [black list]. He thought
maybe because he had traveled back to Okinawa. . . . Grandfather did not
know he was on the lista negra. He had gone fishing with his friends, and when
he came back, he was caught by police who were waiting for him at the en-
trance of the home. They took him to the police station. . . . After they took
grandfather, no one sold flour to us. We had to close the bakery.—OH-3*

*Father was detained in 1943. He did not know he was on the black list. I
was asked by detectives if my father was the president of the Japanese Association. I remember answering yes. They were men with guns. It was
around lunch, and there were many customers. My father was in the
kitchen. Without saying a word they put him in a car. My oldest sister prepared my father's clothes and some food, but he said later that he never
received anything. He probably thought his family was cold.—OH-9*

*It must have been from 1943 that detectives were trying to arrest him. He
was on the run for one year. [He fled] because he felt he hadn't done anything wrong. We went to Crystal City in 1944, so that means he was on the
run for a year. But during that time he was told by the government that if
he didn't come out [of hiding], he would be put in jail for the rest of his life
and wouldn't be allowed to meet his family. That's why he came out of hiding. He was forcibly deported as soon as he came out.—OH-2*

The United States needed hostages to trade for Americans trapped in Japanese territories. Michi Weglyn wrote that the government perceived a need to create a hostage reserve to counter the Japanese threat of "rampaging hordes of yellow 'barbarians' overrunning and making 'free fire zones' of American villages and hamlets—looting, raping, murdering, slaughtering." The government later changed its policy toward building up a "barter reserve" that was "sizable enough to allow for the earliest possible repatriation of American detainees, even at the price of a disproportionate number of Japanese nationals in exchange" (Weglyn 1976, 54–56).

The U.S. plan fit well with the Peruvian government's desire to rid the country of the economically successful Japanese. Henry Norweb, the U.S. ambassador to Peru, informed the State Department of Peruvian president Manuel Prado's desire to cleanse his country of Japanese: "The second matter in which the President [Prado] is very much interested is the possibility of getting rid of the Japanese in Peru. We would like to settle this problem permanently, which means that he is thinking in terms of repatriating thousands of Japanese" (Weglyn 1976, 60). The forcible detention of men, women, and children of Japanese ancestry from Peru was a convenience for both governments. The United States saw the Japanese in Peru as hostages and bodies to be bartered, while Peru saw them as stains on its national fabric. Further, both governments had together spun a web of racial hatred toward Japanese to justify their actions.

Coming to America

[The immigration workers] came around and sprayed us, "Shu-shu, shu-shu." It was some kind of medicine. They thought we had lice or something. . . . We were completely naked, yo! Okinawan women never ever completely undress. We were so surprised. When you're a child, you may be completely naked even without thinking about it, but as you get older, you naturally try to hide yourself with a towel.—OH-1

The JLA internees traveled to the United States via different routes. The men who were arrested early were first sent to Panama and put to work in labor camps. Working conditions were especially terrible. Most of the men had been in business for many years and were not used to manual labor. There are even reports of men going insane. Most of the women and children who arrived later to join the men traveled through the Panama Canal and entered the United States through New Orleans.

The first welcome was shocking and humiliating. Women and children were herded into one large shower room, where they were made to shower and then sprayed with insecticide (which many say was DDT).

Camp Life

While the internment-camp experience was psychologically stressful for JLAs, many of the interviewees remember camp life as physically comfortable. The JLAs, along with German and Italian Latin Americans, stayed in Department of Justice camps, not the WRA camps in which most Japanese Americans internees were confined. Because the U.S. government considered the JLAs and German and Italian Latin Americans as potential hostages to be used in exchange for Americans in enemy territory, they were treated relatively well. The camp administrators provided private dwellings, adequate food, recreation, and entertainment. The residents of the Crystal City Camp in Texas prepared their own meals in their own living quarters and were able to set up a Japanese school for their children, a situation unheard of in the WRA camps. The camp also allowed residents to put on Japanese plays and musical performances.

Nakasone Katsujirō, a well-known *sanshin* master from Peru, gave instruction while in Crystal City. What is interesting is that there seemed to have been many *sanshins* in the camps. One interviewee said that they had a very "nice" *sanshin* and speculated that the instruments were brought over from Peru. But, given that the internees were allowed to bring only a limited amount of luggage, it is more likely that many of the instruments were made in the camps. One interviewee spoke of her husband carving a *sanshin* with a knife in the single men's camp before joining his family in Crystal City. He made the strings out of the heavy thread used for sewing on buttons. Men often fashioned a sound box from a discarded tin can, much like the *kankara sanshin* that was constructed from cast-off tin cans in Okinawa in the aftermath of the war. The existence of *sanshin* and the fact that Okinawan music was played is indicative of the Okinawans' love of their music. One interviewee recalls, "They got together. It was their *kinagusame* [recreation]. Some people would dance and the others would play." On the other hand, I learned from other interviewees that Okinawan music was not performed in public at the Crystal City Camp, that it was usually just done in private at home.

The private performance of Okinawan music relates to the ambiguous position of Okinawa and Okinawans within the Japanese nation. Okinawans carried the stigma of being different, where *different* meant "inferior." Officially, Okinawans were equal to other Japanese, but this official status did not protect them from discrimination. To escape discrimination, many Okinawans changed their names to make them sound more Japanese. For example, names such as Kanagusuku, Naagusuku, Nakandakari, and Jitchaku were changed to Kaneshiro (or Kinjo), Miyashiro (or Miyagi), Nakamura, and Serikaku, respectively. Okinawans also refrained from speaking to their children in their mother tongue. Some of the Okinawan Peruvian intervie- wees mentioned that their parents spoke Spanish at home. They could not speak Japanese well and did not want their children to learn Okinawan.

The sad truth, however, was that Okinawans were under pressure to es- cape discrimination and display their loyalty to Japan. During the Battle of Okinawa, countless Okinawans killed themselves or let themselves be killed in the name of the emperor rather than surrender to the Americans. After the war's end, *katta gumi* (we won faction) or *kachi gumi* (winning faction), factions of Japanese who refused to believe that Japan had lost, sprang up in overseas Japanese communities. In Peru, one such group, the Shindo Renmei, was predominantly Okinawan.

Coming home?

In the camp, there were many people who believed that Japan had won. There were some who knew Japan had lost. We didn't know which side to believe, so we decided to go back and find out.—OH-10

Most of the people believed that Japan was shinkoku *[the land of gods], and so they didn't believe Japan could lose. Until they got off the ship at Uraga, no one could understand why there were American MPs aboard since they didn't believe Japan had lost. The kachi gumi was the majority.—OH-11*

We were going to get off the ship in our Boy Scout uniforms. We were go- ing to march off the ship and walk through the city. But that was canceled when we found out Japan had lost.—OH-11

For the issei it was nostalgic. But for us who were born in Peru and never saw Mt. Fuji before—we had only seen it in pictures—it wasn't really nostalgic. —OH-11

At the end of the war, the Justice Department informed the JLA in- ternees that they had to leave the United States because they were illegal aliens. Aside from a very few exceptions, most of the Japanese Peruvians could not return to Peru. Peru refused them reentry. About three hundred

JLAs remained in the United States and fought deportation. The large majority, however, returned to Japan and Okinawa, refusing to believe that they were returning to a defeated nation. Probably many more would have stayed in the United States had they not so adamantly believed that Japan had won the war and realized that there was little to go back to.

Another group of JLAs, including many Okinawans, was repatriated to Japan in exchange for Americans in Japanese territories. These Okinawans suffered through the Battle of Okinawa, and many who were lucky enough to survive subsequently died from malaria or malnutrition during the months immediately after the war's end. Serei Kyoko, one of the many Okinawans who was exchanged during the war, expressed her losses in her 1995 autobiography *Watashi no ayunda hansei* (Reflections of my journey): "I lost my husband in the war and my child died of sickness. Why did I have to suffer such a fate? How much did the gods hate me?" (Serei 1995, 24).

Facing Deportation and Discrimination

[Seabrook, New Jersey,] was very cold. We had nothing. It was miserable. Everything was given to us in the camp. . . . It was a rude awakening actually. It was cold. We had a potbellied stove, and the housing was like bungalows, so they didn't keep the warmth, and we didn't have a bathroom inside. . . . And my parents worked in two shifts. My father worked the day shift and my mother the night shift. They alternated.—OH-3

When I was in high school [in Los Angeles], I had a Spanish accent. And being Okinawan [the discrimination] was double. So most of my friends were Latinos because they were much closer to us than the nisei. The nisei people never got close to us at all.—OH-3

I remember grandma talking about the garment industry. . . . The people who helped her were Hispanics. . . . Not the nihonjin *[Japanese] from here. They in fact didn't want to have anything to do with us.—OH-3*

Some may believe that camp life was physically more comfortable for the JLAs than for the Japanese American internees in the WRA camps and that the JLAs therefore had an easier time. I would refrain from such comparisons. Additionally, the internment experience did not end when the gates to the camps were opened and the internees were allowed to leave. It continued as internees tried to pick up the pieces of lives shattered by forcible incarceration and make a new start in a new country.

Many of the JLAs who remained in the United States found employment in New Jersey at the Seabrook Farms food-processing plant. The former internees worked long hours for low wages. Seabrook Farms probably
benefited from the JLAs' insecure status as illegal aliens. Eventually, most
of the Okinawans found their way to Los Angeles, where the Peruvian Okinawans ran hotels, apartment buildings, and grocery stores and worked as
farmers and gardeners: "Everything they turned their hand to has been successful" (Okinawa Club of America 1988, 299–334). Many of the interned
Okinawan Peruvians who settled in Los Angeles were also involved in Okinawan music. In 1964, Nakasone Katsujirō held the first postwar Okinawan
music recital in Los Angeles.

*In the beginning they felt very bitter. I remember once this Italian person
who got my father's bakery store [in Peru] came to the United States to also
get our [other] property. My father just wouldn't do it. . . . Here we were
on skid row in a one-room apartment, and this man was all dressed up and
trying to buy my father's property. That time, yes, I saw how bitter my father was.—OH-3*

The price of whatever success the JLAs were able to achieve came at
great cost. Parents in their forties and fifties had to start over, doing menial
jobs, and their children, who spoke only Spanish, had to learn English and
a new culture. Often, the internees left behind property, other assets, and
family. Some families were scattered across Okinawa, Japan, the United
States, and South America.

Back to Sotetsu Hell

*Even the rice gruel [at the camp in Uraga where the JLAs disembarked] was
only a little rice at the bottom, and the rest was just soup. . . . That's why
everybody suffered from malnutrition. We even had to eat crayfish. . . . It
was the worst. There was nothing. We ate anything.—OH-11*

Meanwhile, JLAs who returned to Okinawa had to start all over again in
a country that had been essentially reduced to ashes. Most of the returning JLAs from mainland Japan were able to return to their homes soon after arriving in Japan. For many, however, there was not much to go back to.
Many JLAs were from Hiroshima, which had been destroyed by the atomic
bomb. The Okinawan Latin Americans were not able to return immediately.
Okinawa was occupied by the U.S. military. Many were forced to live in

camps near Tokyo, and some remained on the mainland. The U.S. military eventually allowed others to return.

The Okinawans from Latin America who returned experienced the Battle of Okinawa, which raged from April to June 1945 and caused the death of about 170,000 Okinawans, or one-third of the population of Okinawa (Ōta 1987, 301). Nearly all Okinawa's cultural treasures, including Shuri Palace, the seat of the former kingdom, were destroyed. Thousands of displaced Okinawans languished in such places as Yaka Camp in central Okinawa. *Yaka bushi,* a song composed after the Battle of Okinawa, expresses the lament of the Okinawan people:

Nachikashi ya uchinaa	How sad my Okinawa
Ikusaba ni nayai	a battleground you became
Umanchu tu tumuni	The flowing tears of
Nagasu namida	the multitudes

Do you know what sotetsu is? We ate that. It's poisonous, so it has to be fermented before you eat it. It tastes terrible.—OH-11

All we had to eat were sweet potatoes . . . and the root of the sotetsu. . . . It tasted bad. We really had kuro [hardships] concerning food.—OH-2

Okinawa was destroyed by the war. There was nothing. There were only tents. That's how we started.—OH-12

We even cooked and ate rats in Okinawa. . . . Yes, [we would even use motor oil to fry food]. The motor oil would not be absorbed by the body and would just come out the way it went in.—OH-11

With dreams of a modern day *nirai-kanai,* the promised land over the horizon, Okinawans had left the *sotetsu* hell of Okinawa for Latin America. Okinawan Latin Americans, who were placed in U.S. internment camps and then sent back to Okinawa, found themselves back in *sotetsu* hell once again.

Okinawan Diaspora?

Question: You were taken from Peru by the United States and placed in U.S. internment camps. Then you were deported by the United States to U.S.-occupied Okinawa . . .

Reply: Akirame ga tsuyoidoo ni mo naranaiteikoo shite modoo ni mo naranai [A feeling of wanting to give up was so strong nothing could be done about it even if we resisted, nothing could be done]. In Okinawa after the

*war we couldn't relax. At night, American military personnel would come
to the villages and rape women. Shimashi was near Ojana, which was near
a U.S. base. They would come in the middle of the night. Now one could go
to court, but at that time the only thing possible was nakineiri [weeping into
silence]. There were many such incidents. Many women who are now in
their seventies and eighties suffered much.—OH-13*

The Okinawan Latin American story presents another irony. Most of the
Okinawan Latin American internees were either sent back to Okinawa on
exchange ships during the war or deported after the war. The U.S. government arranged for them to be seized from their homes and transported to
the United States, where they were placed in internment camps surrounded by barbed-wire fences. These internees returned to an Okinawa
that is to this day occupied by U.S. military bases that are surrounded by
barbed-wire fences now meant, not to keep them in, but to keep them from
their lands. The U.S. military authorities often expropriated the land for
the bases by forcing Okinawans off it at bayonet point. Some displaced
landowners were never compensated, and bulldozers leveled houses and
cultural treasures (Ōta 1987, 293).

This irony reflects the Okinawan diaspora. This diaspora is intertwined
with the projection of U.S. influence across the Pacific into Asia and across
the Rio Grande into Latin America. The diaspora reflects the determina-
tion of the Okinawans in the face of the immense power discrepancy between the United States and Okinawa. How can Okinawa, a tiny island in
a poor archipelago, and the Okinawan people possibly challenge the United
States? Perhaps Okinawans fit into the minority paradigm that Gary Y. Okihiro, an Asian American historian, writes of in *Margins and Mainstreams*:
"What I would like to suggest is that the deeper significance of Asians, and
indeed of all minorities in America rests in their opposition to the dominant paradigm, their fight against the power, their efforts to transform, and
not simply reform, American society and its structures" (Okihiro 1994, 155).
Okinawans have been part of this challenge to America's society and history. Okinawans have enlarged the range and deepened the meaning of
American democracy (Okihiro 1994, 156). A large number of Okinawans
participated in the labor struggles in Hawai'i during the first half of the twentieth century. In the homeland, Okinawans have held mass demonstrations,
rioted, and struck against the U.S. military bases and unjust U.S. policies
during the American occupation (1945–1972). They continue to challenge
the continued military presence. Okinawan Latin Americans interned during World War II have been part of this challenge. Carmen Higa Mochizuki,

a Latin American nisei, is the named plaintiff in *Carmen Mochizuki v. the United States of America*, a class-action lawsuit that sought redress and an apology for the internment of JLAs. Other lawsuits have been initiated by people who opted out of the settlement. Among those is George Shima, who is also an Okinawan Latin American nisei.

In a January 1999 declaration, Mochizuki accepted the terms of the settlement but expressed reservations: "Although my family and others suffered the loss of liberty, freedom and assets as a direct result of the action of the United States of America, we can never be adequately repaid. The United States Government has seen fit to compound the travesty by offering to settle this case for far less than was deemed necessary for others interned under the same conditions. Why would the people, although not citizens of the United States of America at the time, who were kidnapped from their own country, and interned in the United States, be entitled to any less?" (Mochizuki 1999). She questions America's claim to be a leading advocate of freedom, democracy, liberty, and equality in the world.

Notes

1. I have refrained from identifying Okinawan Latin American internees whose oral histories I quote throughout this essay, assigning instead a number to each oral history (e.g., OH-1). The oral-history tapes on which I base this essay are on file with the Japanese Peruvian Oral History Project. They will eventually be handed over to the National Japanese American Historical Society.

2. The Japanese Peruvian Oral History Project commenced in 1993 to document the oral histories of Japanese Peruvians who were interned by the U.S. government during World War II.

3. An Okinawan exclamation.

4. Natsu Taylor Saito points out that article 49 of the Geneva Convention Relative to the Protection of Civilian Persons in Time of War (12 August 1949) states: "Individual or mass forcible transfers, as well as deportations of protected persons from occupied territory to the territory of the Occupying power or to that of any other country occupied or not, are prohibited, regardless of their motive." Article 146 allowed for penal sanctions to be carried out in actions such as "unlawful deportation or transfer or unlawful confinement of a protected persona." Saito draws attention to the fact that, even though the articles were drafted a few years after the war, they were merely codifying existing laws and customs of war that prohibited the deportation of civilians. In other words, the international community so deeply abhorred the deportation of civilians that it saw no reason explicitly to state the need to prohibit it (Saito 1998, 305–306).

Chapter 7

Colonialism and Nationalism
The View from Okinawa

Nomura Kōya

Persisting Colonialism

With its defeat in World War II, Japan—for the most part involuntarily—lost its colonies.[1] The Japanese majority refused to take responsibility for its country's colonial despotism, and, with this refusal, Japan forgot its colonial past. The loss of its colonies and its memory lapse, however, do not necessarily mean that Japanese colonialism is dead. First and foremost, colonialism is a problem of the colonizer, not the colonized. Stripping away colonialism should be the first priority for citizens of countries that engaged in it. The Japanese majority finds it difficult to comprehend that colonialism is really *its* problem (Kang and Oka 1999, 84–85). However, notwithstanding the loss of the colonies, colonialism will persist in Japan unless the Japanese expunge colonialism from within themselves.

Resistance and criticism from the colonized represent opportunities for colonizers to free themselves of colonialism.[2] The Japanese are under the impression that Japan has ended its colonialism and that colonialism is no longer alive. When such issues as the military "comfort women" arise, they turn a blind eye to, remain silent about, or express disinterest in the protests of the victims of colonization. Such issues only affirm that colonialism has not yet ended for the colonized and that they are compelled to vigorously fight the common perception that colonialism is dead.

For the colonized, the adversary is not just the colonialism of the colonists but their own complicity with colonialism: "Colonialism cannot function without the collusion of the colonized. It is an arrangement that cannot be reduced to simple opposition and conflict. The colonial experience leaves especially deep scars in colonized societies" (Ukai 1997, 259). The experience of colonial rule leaves deep scars in the colonized, who will never be able to return to their precolonial self. Might this be a matter of the colonized assisting their own colonization? Even if independence were achieved, it would not be possible for the colonized to immediately extinguish their collusive relationship with colonialism. Eliminating the attitudinal vestiges of colonialism is the first important requisite of a former colonizer. In contrast, how to overcome the scars of colonialism is a searing question that the colonized have yet to ask. It is not possible to eliminate colonialism by simply critiquing it as an adversary, external to the self.

With these thoughts in mind, I wish to reflect on the Okinawan experience, how colonialists co-opt those whom they oppress, and how the colonized themselves are scarred. Although the Japanese government has never officially considered Okinawa to be a colony, this does not mean that the people of Okinawa have not experienced colonialism. Japanese nationalism demanded that Okinawans be assimilated and become Japanese; it also served as an instrument to ensure Okinawan complicity with the colonizers.

Colonialism and the Subject of Nationalism

It is not self-evident to Okinawans, whose homeland has only recently become part of Japan, that they are Japanese. Even today they continue to ask, "Are we really Japanese, or are we? . . . " The persistence of this question is deeply embedded in the annexation of the Ryūkyūan kingdom by Japan, which "simultaneously gave rise [among the Okinawans to the task of] becoming Japanese in a modern-nation state and being governed by colonialism engendered by imperialism" (Tomiyama 1997, 6).[3]

The military annexation of the Ryūkyūan kingdom was part of the territorial expansion of Japanese imperialism and the beginning of colonial violence toward the Okinawans. As have others who have been colonized, the Okinawans were labeled as "backward," "uncivilized," and "second-class citizens" by the Japanese from the very beginning of annexation. Since simply discriminating against the Okinawans would only heighten their dissatisfaction and thus make it difficult for Japan to govern the colony effectively, the one issue that surfaced for the colonialists was how to have the colonized identify with Japanese nationalism. "In the modern world, imperialism is nationalism. Modern imperialism is thus imperialistic nationalism and a means to unify the citizenry" (Ukai et al. 1996, 28). "Colonialism embodies

the narrative of nationalism. Thus, a critique of colonialism is necessarily a
critique of nationalism" (Hama 1998, 270). Although annexation is possible through military force, the colony must still be governed, and brute force
is never a satisfactory means of doing so.

Not content simply to discriminate against the Okinawans, the Japanese
sought to transform them into Japanese. In this instance, assimilation
meant the deliberate use of brute force to suppress and to destroy Okinawan
culture, thereby forcing the Okinawans to become Japanese. Further, since
this kind of assimilation meant constructing a Japan of one people and one
nation by rallying the populace, the exercise was one in Japanese nationalism (Nomura 1997b, 76–78; Nomura 1998, 105–107). Many Okinawans
were deeply wounded by such discriminative labels as "backward," "uncivilized," and "second-class citizen." These labels accelerated assimilation.
Finding it necessary to transform the Okinawans into Japanese, the Japanese discriminated against them in order to effectively control them. Might
there have been other means of assimilating the Okinawans without wounding them so deeply?

The assimilation of the Okinawans was carried out under the guise of
rescuing them. The implicit promise was that, once the Okinawans were
assimilated, discrimination would cease. And the operating assumption was
that, the more painful the discrimination, the sooner assimilation would be
achieved. "Wanting to become first-class citizens, and wanting to become
Japanese," the Okinawans rejected and suppressed their culture (Nomura
1998, 112–113). Assimilation, however, did not extinguish discrimination.
Despite the best efforts of the Okinawans to become Japanese, the fact that
75 percent of American bases in Japan are on Okinawan soil is evidence of
continued discrimination. The Japanese have succeeded in preserving a two-tiered society. And the Okinawans, through the experience of assimilation,
were co-opted by Japanese colonialism.

Assimilation and Intellectual Colonial Control

Assimilation does not end discrimination because assimilation itself is
closely linked with discrimination. For the most part, assimilation does not
make equals by fusing one people with another. Assimilation results from
an asymmetrical power relationship between those who are doing the assimilating and those who are being assimilated. Even though two cultures
become one, those who are being assimilated suffer greater losses and make
greater sacrifices when taking another culture as their own. In contrast, those
who are doing the assimilating naturally perceive themselves as occupying

a privileged position and force a one-sided sacrifice on those being assimi-lated. Assimilation is nothing less than discrimination (Nomura 1999).

Assimilation is not a simple process whereby the oppressed acquire the culture of the oppressor. "In actuality," Yoshino Sakuzō explains, "the as-similation policy did not just ask [the Okinawans] to achieve complete iden-tity with the Japanese; rather, it demanded that the [Okinawans] become the people the Japanese told them to become" (Oguma 1998, 660). The col-onizer demands that the colonized become what is asked of them. Edward Said uses the expression *intellectual colonialism* to articulate the process by which the colonized internalize the values and substantive perceptions of the colonizers. Describing the Palestinian experience vis-à-vis the Israelis, he writes, "It's the internalizing of the colonizer's perspective on you that you are incapable of doing anything without his tutelage and without his support and that validation doesn't come from your own society and from your own values, but from his. It's so pernicious, so deep now that I won-der whether it can be stopped or changed" (Said 1994b, 151).

In their aspiration to "become Japanese," and in order to actually expel and suppress their deeply etched culture, the Okinawans had to first inter-nalize the notion that they were "backward," "uncivilized," and "second-class citizens." In addition to enduring such discriminatory insults as "You are backward!" "You worm!" and "You second-class citizen!" the Okinawans had to become the insults hurled at them (Nomura 1997a). In this sense, assimilation is also self-discrimination.

For the Japanese majority, being Japanese was self-evident: for the Oki-nawans to become Japanese through assimilation was a matter of appro-priating Japanese nationalism. However, *to be Japanese* does not simply mean "to become Japanese." *Japanese nationalism* meant that the Oki-nawans had to construct within themselves the colonizer as the colonizing other. The Okinawans have been impressed with this "double vision," not available to "uncolonized Indigenes" (Ashcroft, Griffiths, and Tiffin 1989, 26). "Although they are Japanese, they are not" points to an ambivalent iden-tity. "While the expressions *hybrid* and *mixed blood* honor such ambiva-lence, the promise that *mixed-blood culture* holds conveys a completely dif-ferent meaning than does the *creole* that emerges from historical violence" (Hama 1998, 268).

Violence and Complicity

Assimilation, violence, and Japanese nationalism contributed to the increas-ing complicity of the Okinawans during the period from the 1879 annexation

of the Ryūkyūs to the Sino-Japanese War (1894–1895). The father of Okinawan studies, Ifa Fuyū, wrote, "Those who did not want to die had to com-
ply. One by one, they became Japanese. In the end, when the Sino-Japanese
War was about to be won, we could hear from those who spoke ill of the Meiji
government, 'Teikoku banzai' (May imperial Japan live ten thousand years)"
(Ifa 1911, 96). Ifa's remarks were framed by a plan by the military, the
police, and the vigilance committee of the Japanese residents on Okinawa to
massacre the Okinawans (Tomiyama 1997, 6–7). From the beginning of annexation, Okinawa existed in an atmosphere of forced assimilation.

    Forced assimilation became a deadly reality when Okinawans were mas-
sacred during the Battle of Okinawa. "It was usual for the Japanese to slaugh-
ter Okinawans for conversing in their native tongue" (Ōta 1994, 29–30).
These massacres illustrate the extremes to which the Japanese would go in
pursuing their assimilation policy. The decision whether to assimilate often
determined whether one lived or died, and one had to assimilate in order
to live and prosper. This kind of experience, according to Tomiyama Ichirō,
deeply ingrained in the Okinawa psyche "a premonition of violence"
(Tomiyama 1997). Sakai Naoki explains, "Okinawans may assimilate and become Japanese, but their citizenship is linked [to the premonition that] at
some point 'They may kill me.' This fear is two pronged when it is linked
with racial nationalism: the desire to side with the many who would kill
rather than the few who would be killed and with Japanese nationalism"
(Sakai et al. 1998, 87–88).

    Describing *intellectual colonialism,* Edward Said wrote, "It's so perni-
cious, so deep now that I wonder whether it can be stopped or changed."
It is difficult to say whether contemporary Okinawans have completely rid
themselves of the stigma of being labeled "backward," "uncivilized," and
"second-class citizens." For instance, after Okinawa reverted to Japan in
1972, the unemployment rate in Okinawa rose to approximately twice the
Japanese national average. This phenomenon may be thought to be an
example of Okinawa's economic backwardness. However, economic backwardness is not inherent in any people. Rather, could we construe this "backwardness" to be manufactured by the Japanese government, which represents the Japanese majority? Needless to say, one of the primary reasons
for the high rate of unemployment in Okinawa is the fact that, in Japan, 75
percent of Japanese and U.S. military bases, which are an impediment to
economic development,—are located on Okinawan soil.

    High unemployment affects not only the unemployed. The fear of un-
employment extends to many others. The Japanese government has re-
peatedly intimated that, if Okinawa cooperates and continues to welcome

the U.S. bases on its soil, economic aid will be extended. Cooperation and unemployment are intertwined. The Japanese government continues to exploit fear of unemployment and Okinawans' "premonition of violence" to guarantee the acceptance of U.S. bases. (Does this mean that government inertia to implement programs that would reduce the high level of unemployment is a way of pressuring the Okinawans?)

Ishida Takeshi believes that compelling Okinawans to acquiesce to the military bases is identical to the pattern of the earlier Japanese assimilation policy (Ishida 1998, 49). Like military force, law and democracy can intercede with violence: "In *Zur Kritik der Gewalt,* Walter Benjamin categorizes violence into the particular and the universal. Violence appears in the particular when it is posited as the law; violence appears in the universal when forced on others. For example, when an army occupies a country, a particular reality, and projects itself as the law or authority over the occupants, this is an act of violence" (Tasaki 1996, 23).

Japanese law that allows 75 percent of the U.S. military bases (see fig. 9) in Japan to be placed on Okinawan soil engages in violence. Violence in the

Figure 9. Futenma Marine Corps Air Base from Kakazu Heights, 1996. Photograph courtesy Ronald Y. Nakasone.

guise of law was established through democratic means. Recently, Okinawans raised the issue of democratic violence. The subject of this violence
is within each and every Japanese citizen. The Okinawans are asking, How
do we understand the violence that is embedded in the Japanese majority,
and how can we expel their complicity in this violence? There are no in-
nocent topos that select nonviolence (Kang and Oka 1999, 81).

Concluding Remarks—U.S. Military Bases and Colonialism

The issue of U.S. military bases on Okinawa does not need to be addressed
as urgently as do those of nuclear power plants or airports in Japan. Nevertheless, the questions about assimilation that have remained unanswered
since the annexation of the Ryūkyūs must be addressed. The question, "Are
we really Japanese, or are we? . . . " must be understood as a critique of Japanese colonialism.

And it is not simply the presence of the bases on their soil that Okinawans
resent but also the de facto colonial rule of the U.S. military. The Vietnam
War prompted Okinawans to ask particularly penetrating questions regarding the complicity with U.S. colonialism implied by their condoning of
the bases. And that questioning has only intensified with the Gulf War and
the subsequent bombing of Iraq. Seen in this light, rejection of the bases
becomes rejection of both colonialism and collusion with colonialism.

When Okinawans challenge the presence of U.S. bases on their soil and
the uses to which those bases are put, they are accused of selfish whining.
And what I hear in such accusations is the far-from-silenced voice of
colonialism.

Notes

This essay has been translated by Ronald Y. Nakasone.

1. Colonialism is not dead in postcolonial Okinawa. According to Ukai Satoshi, e.g.,
"The meaning of *post-* in such expressions as *poststructuralism* and *postmodernism* differs from the meaning of *post-* in *postcolonialism.*" (Ukai 1998, 42). *Post-* in *poststructuralism* and *postcolonialism* denotes the end of structuralism and modernism. In contrast, *post-* in *postmodernism* does not refer to the end of colonialism. *Postcolonialism*
means that colonialism is not dead, has not ended, and must be ended. While colonialism is thought to be a thing of the past, it is deeply ingrained in our society and our psyche. In addition, implied in the prefix *post-* is the question of the actions and directions
that we are to undertake with regard to this problem.

2. My statement is based in part on Edward Said's observation of colonized people:
"But I'm talking about organized movements, the liberal movement, the progressive

movement, or the working class movement or the feminist movement. They were all imperial by and large. There was no dissent from this. The only time that there began to be changes inside Europe and the United States was when the natives themselves in the colonies began to revolt and made it very difficult for these ideas to continue unchallenged. Then people like Sartre, in support of the Algerians, demonstrated on their behalf. But until then there was widespread complicity" (Said 1994b, 67).

3. "To say that the annexation process began in 1879, when Matsuda Michiyuki (1839–1882), chief secretary of the Ministry of Home Affairs and the official responsible for the dissolution of the Ryūkyūan kingdom, arrived in Naha with a military contingent and military police and announced the establishment of Okinawa Prefecture, is not the whole story. Subsequently, the Chinese Ch'ing government protested the dissolution of Ryūkyū and suggested that the Miyako and Ishigaki island groups be placed under Chinese control. The negotiation of national boundaries was ultimately settled militarily at the conclusion of the Sino-Japanese War. The annexation of Ryūkyū exhibits the simultaneous development of the modern state (by determining the boundaries of Japan) and the beginning of overseas imperial expansion "Significant for Okinawans because they became both Japanese citizens and imperial subjects at once" (Tomiyama 1997, 6).

Chapter 8

Eisaa
Identities and Dances
of Okinawan Diasporic Experiences

SHIROTA CHIKA

On 22 May 1998, attendees at the Festival for Asian-Pacific American Heritage, which was organized by the Joint Services Asian-Pacific Islander
Council and held at a military-owned gymnasium at Pearl Harbor Naval
Base, witnessed a slice of modern Okinawan experience. The program concluded with the Okinawan *kachaashi* (from the Okinawan *"kachaasun,"*
meaning "to mix up"), a dance in which the audience is invited to participate. The mix of dancers and participants from the audience included, in
addition to U.S. military personnel, their "war brides" and children, former
immigrant laborers and their descendants, and the daughter of a former
Okinawan American prisoner of war/internee and her grown children.

Music and dance provide a space in which the Okinawan people have
been able to affirm their identity, mourn their dead, and identify with their
overseas Okinawan cohorts while simultaneously negotiating their identities vis-à-vis the post–World War II occupation by and continuing presence
of the U.S. military. Even after the reversion of Okinawa to Japanese sovereignty in 1972, the U.S. military did not relinquish the land that it had
expropriated.

This essay explores the significance and evolution of *eisaa,* a popular Okinawan folk dance and music in the modern Okinawan experience.[1] From
its religious origins, *eisaa* has evolved into a popular folk art in Okinawa and
in overseas Okinawan communities. More recently, its spectacular stylized
choreography and haunting rhythm have attracted large audiences and an
international following. Today, *eisaa* is performed by Okinawans and non-
Okinawans. On Okinawa, *eisaa* has even breached the fences that surround
and protect the U.S. military installations.

Stuart Hall's definition of popular culture is useful for understanding the importance of *eisaa*: "Popular culture carries that affirmative ring because of the prominence of the word 'popular.' And, in one sense, popular culture always has its base in the experiences, the pleasures, the memories, the traditions of the people. It has connections with local hopes and local aspirations, local tragedies and local scenarios that are the everyday practices and everyday experiences of ordinary folks" (Hall 1996, 469). As a medium of protest and resistance, the dance and music of *eisaa* is an expression of the Okinawan experience with the U.S. military and the Okinawan aspiration to return to the ancestral lands. It is also a reminder of the frustrations and the tragedies of the local people. At the same time, *eisaa* has given Americans, Okinawans, and diasporic Okinawan communities a way of moving beyond barriers (and over fences) of nationality and ethnicity. This essay begins with a brief description of *eisaa*, notes its importance in traditional Okinawa, describes its evolution into a venue of protest, and concludes with some reflections on the nature of contemporary *eisaa* in Hawai'i.

The Postwar Development of *Eisaa*

Eisaa has traditionally been performed during the summer in conjunction with the annual Okinawan Buddhist Obon, a ceremony that honors the ancestral spirits. *Eisaa* incorporates influences of the *nembutsu odori* genre introduced from mainland Japan. The dance is dedicated to the ancestral spirits, whom the villagers petition for prosperity and good health for each member of the household. Performers gather in a circle at the *kami asagi* (*kami* dwelling), located at a central village location, and dance to the beat of their drums in a ritual that bids their ancestral spirits farewell.[2] Subsequently, the performers dance and sing along the village streets and in front of each home. The festivities continue throughout the night.

Eisaa is accompanied by the *sanshin*, the large barrel drum, and the hand-held *paranku* drum. Men usually dance the more energetic drum sequences, while the *timoi* (Jp. *teodori*) is normally performed by women, although men can also join in. Essentially, *eisaa* consists of a synchronous and dynamic display of group coordination. The current popularity of *eisaa* can be attributed, in part, to its rhythmic drumbeats, which create a special time and space for both the performers and the audience.

Music and dance are important parts of life in Okinawa. In the aftermath of the war, *eissa*, its dance and music, offered a creative space in which a depressed and dispossessed people could mourn their dead, remember their former homes, and sustain their spirits. From military discards and broken tree limbs, they fashioned, in addition to the necessities of life, the *sanshin*. Recalling his time as an internee in a prisoner-of-war camp in Hawai'i, Sakihara Mitsugu, an Okinawan historian, described the effect when a crude *kankara sanshin,* an instrument made from an empty tin can, was strummed: "The sounds of the *sanshin* brought the Okinawan people together. When we gathered, we began to sing and dance" (Sakihara 1979, 5). A survivor recalled that, when *eisaa* was performed as part of a Buddhist requiem at a refugee camp near present-day Okinawa City immediately after the war, people from the locale and those who were not yet able to return to their homes danced together. The experience did much to reaffirm their ties to their ancestral lands and their identities (Okinawa zentō 1998, 139).

In the years after the war, *eisaa* performances were one of the few public venues through which Okinawans could vent their frustration toward the U.S. military's requisition of their villages and farmland. While painting or sculpture stand independent of the artist, music and dance do not. The body, the instrument and means of expression and representation for the dance, became the canvas through which Okinawans expressed their frustrations and aspirations. As a political act, the performance of *eisaa* has enabled Okinawans to articulate their aspirations for the return of their land, for justice for wrongs committed against them, and for peace. Okinawans have continued to negotiate their identities vis-à-vis the U.S. military presence.

In 1952, seven years after the end of World War II, the Ryūkyūan-American Cultural Center, the City Council of Ishikawa, and the Chamber of Commerce and Industry of Ishikawa organized the first major *eisaa* festival. The event, American-Ryūkyūan Friendship *Bon* Dance Festival, was held at the Ryūkyūan-American Cultural Center in Ishikawa City. The high commissioner of the Ryūkyūan Islands reported that 50,000 Okinawans attended the weekend event.[3] At the time, Okinawa had a population of 880,000.

The U.S. civil administration tried to project a positive image by sponsoring this "happy-friendship" Obon *eisaa* event. It also used the event in an attempt to depoliticize military issues. The 1956 friendship event was held two months after one of the biggest mass rallies against the U.S. military bases. On 21 June 1956, the *Ryukyu Shimpo* estimated that 200,000 attended the various rallies and meetings that were organized in response to Representative M. Price's report to the U.S. House of Representatives

(Nakano 1969, 190). Price had traveled to Okinawa in October of the previous year on a fact-finding mission. He conducted public hearings on the brute expropriation of land without owners' consent, forced removal, and the use of bulldozers to destroy homes. Price ignored the rights of the Okinawans and emphasized the importance of the military bases on Okinawa. After the 21 June demonstrations, the civil administration declared the towns neighboring the military bases off-limits to all service personnel, a move that severely affected those businesses that catered to military personnel (Sakihara 1981, 19).

Twelve days after the restriction was lifted, approximately 30,000 persons attended the first *eisaa* contest sponsored by the City Council of Koza (renamed Okinawa City after the 1972 reversion), the Chamber of Commerce and Industry of Koza, and the Seinenkai (Young people's club). A major purpose of the contest was to lift the spirits of a despondent people (Okamoto 1998, 55). And at this at least the event succeeded: "It seemed now Koza City has recovered the energy which was lost under the 'off limits.' It was hard to believe [that people] were depressed, from the tremendous applause" (Okinawa zentō 1998, 51). It is important to note that the event transpired in a city in which a civilian branch of the government of the Ryūkyū Islands was located. The U.S. Civil Administration of the Ryūkyūs, the civilian arm of the U.S. military, oversaw the activities of the government of the Ryūkyūs. Most of the *eisaa* groups came from areas where the U.S. military had requisitioned land. The troupe from Koza represented a municipality where 70 percent of the land was controlled by the bases; 18,000 of its residents had joined the earlier antibase rally. The group from Kadena Village represented a town where 80 percent of the land was taken over by the U.S. Air Force; Kadena sent 3,000 to the antibase rally (Nakano 1969, 190–191).

Shiroma Kikō, president of the Cultural Association of Okinawa City, observed, "It is very interesting that the popularity of *eisaa* spread from the middle part of Okinawa, where most bases are located. *Eisaa* began in resistance to Americanization" (Okinawa zentō 1998, 319). Concurring, Makiya Akira, a reporter for the *Ryukyu Shimpo*, stated, "It had a very significant meaning that the *eisaa* contest started in the 'City with the Bases.'" Makiya also reflected that "the revival of *eisaa* as a contest indicates that *eisaa* is the spirit of *Uchinanchu* and the heart of the ethnic people" (Okinawa zentō 1998, 317, 319). In the aftermath of the war, *eisaa* was one of the few forms of entertainment available to the Okinawan people. Protest and and entertainment intertwined.

A photograph of dancers from the 1956 *eisaa* contest, however, presents a more complicated reality. The photograph captures twenty *eisaa* dancers, all men, beating Okinawan drums, some of them wearing long-sleeve white shirts, long white trousers, and black shoes, items that had been distributed by the U.S. military government (Okinawan zentō 1998, 53). While the absence of traditional Okinawan costumes is indicative of the poverty of the Okinawans, this kind of mismatch or hybrid between Okinawan music and dance, on the one hand, and American or Western dress, on the other, reflects Okinawa's situation: proud and defiant, yet dependent on the largesse of the United States

In the 1980s and 1990s, as part of the organizing strategy attracting the Okinawan people to a series of large rallies, *eisaa* became identified with the revitalized peace movement. Organizers of the 21 June 1987 rally, "Getting Together with Joy," which surrounded the entire 17.4-kilometer circumference of Kadena Airfield, the largest U.S. base in Asia, scheduled *eisaa* performances, live *sanshin* music, and children's games. The event attracted 25,000 people of all ages. The Okinawan sociologist Ishihara Masaie pointed out that this event was different from other political rallies and was highly successful in that it involved the entire family, from children to the elderly (Ishihara 1977, 271). Three years later, in 1990, organizers were able to rally 25,000 persons for the first "Peoples' Link around the United States Bases." The rally took place two days before Irei no hi (Day of remembrance), the annual 23 June event commemorating the end of the Battle of Okinawa and memorializing those who perished. That same year organizers rallied 26,000 for a 5 August protest. A third protest mobilized 17,000 people, who circled Futenma Air Station on 14 May 1995, one day prior to the anniversary date of the 1972 reversion to Japan. The event also marked the fiftieth anniversary of the end of World War II and was part of the "Great Okinawan Peace Movement" project. This new peace movement rallied approximately 90,000 Okinawans on 21 October 1995 near Kadena Airfield to protest the 4 September 1995 abduction, rape, and brutalization of a twelve-year-old Okinawan schoolgirl by three U.S. military personnel. The incident "crystallized Okinawan fears and fueled popular demands for the closure of all U.S. bases" (Taira 1997, 173).

Articulating popular aspirations, Okinawan musician and activist Kina Shōkichi and 170 *eisaa* dancers and singers dedicated their performances as a message of peace at the 1996 Atlanta Olympics. Two of the servicemen accused and eventually convicted of the 1995 crime were from Atlanta. Later, representing Asia, Kina and his *eisaa* dancers and singers performed for the "AT&T Global Olympic Village Concert." The troupe's theme,

"Transform All Weapons into Musical Instruments," crystallized Okinawan revulsion of the war experience and the Okinawan people's aspirations for peace (Kina 1997, 13).

Performing Identities:
Eisaa Inside/Outside the U.S. Military Bases

In addition to the Okinawan *kachaashi,* the Festival for Asia Pacific American Heritage also featured a performance by the Hawai'i chapter of the RMD, or the Ryūkyū-koku Matsuri Daiko (Festival drums of the Ryūkyū nation). The Hawai'i chapter was established by Akemi Martin, the wife of an American military physician who, while living in Okinawa, introduced *eisaa* to other military spouses. After seeing a performance by the RMD, Martin asked members of the troupe who worked on Kadena Airfield to teach *eisaa* to interested U.S. military wives. She reasoned that learning *eisaa* might just spark an interest in Okinawa, its people, and its culture. Many of the wives were unhappy with their stay on Okinawa, and some never ventured beyond the confines of the bases. Further, the effort to establish better relations with the Okinawan people might be improved if the members of the American Women's Welfare Association (AWWA) could perform the Okinawan *eisaa* in addition to Western and American dances.[4] Martin worked as an interpreter for the AWWA, trying to promote better communications between the local communities and the U.S. military.

With twelve others, Martin learned *Mirukumunari,* the most famous of the RMD dances, which they performed when they toured the outer islands in the spring of 1995. "The Okinawan people were very happy to see our dance and welcomed us," she recalled. The Okinawans were appreciative of their effort. Even after the 1995 brutalization of a twelve-year-old girl, the American RMD dancers were welcomed by the local Okinawans: "*Ojiichan* and *Obaachan* (elder men and women) looked happy and some even had tears in their eyes when they watched our performance by saying 'Oh, blue-eyed foreigners are performing our *eisaa'*" (Martin 1998). The American RMD dancers also performed at Kadena Air Base at the 1996 "American Fest" that celebrated American Independence Day, when U.S. bases were open to the local Okinawan people. A Japanese magazine, *Friday,* reported this event nationwide, carrying a picture in which Martin, two American men, three American women, and two Okinawan women performed an RMD dance in front of military aircraft (see fig. 10). The article noted the obvious pleasure of an Okinawan visitor, who separated the American festival from the base issue. The writer may have thought that Okinawans were more flexible in the face of the reality of U.S. military bases on their island home.

RMD was established in 1982. Today, it has approximately five hundred members on Okinawa and another five hundred scattered throughout Japan, the United States, Argentina, Brazil, and Peru. As was noted earlier, some are members of the U.S. military stationed on Okinawa. It is important to note that RMD began in Okinawa City, where more than half the land is occupied by U.S. bases. Its first president was Ōyama Chōjyō, one of the early organizers of the *eisaa* contests in the 1950s.

The music and dance of RMD draw from many sources: Okinawan and Japanese folk songs, Okinawan pop and rap, and even the music of Michael Jackson. The group's choreography incorporates the traditional *eisaa* dance and karate movements. RMD performed at New York's Carnegie Hall in 1995, at the 1996 Atlanta and the 1998 Nagano Olympics, in China and Singapore in 1994, in Europe in 1993, and in Hawai'i in 1985, 1997, and 1998. It also performed in Brazil and Argentina in 1998 and most recently in Peru in 1999. RMD functions as an ambassador of Okinawan culture and promotes worldwide friendships.

Martin moved to Hawai'i in 1996, where she established an RMD branch.

Figure 10. *Eisaa* performers at "American Fest" at Kadena Air Base, 4 July 1999. Photograph courtesy Shirota Chika.

Two American women who performed *eisaa* with her in Okinawa also moved to Hawai'i and joined the group. As of March 1999, the Hawai'i branch had forty active members who vary in age and ethnicity. Some are affiliated with the U.S. military, and others are from the community. I made a special note of the fourteen Okinawan and two Japanese women who emigrated to the United States after World War II. They practice and perform *eisaa* throughout the year with their American husbands and their children. There were also Okinawans born in Hawai'i. One woman whose father was one of the 1,444 Japanese Americans and Okinawan Americans from Hawai'i interned in the United States during World War II was ambivalent about the presence of U.S. military forces and bases in Okinawa.[5] Still, she danced with her sons and daughter at the Festival for Asian-Pacific American Heritage. An American marine and his two multiethnic children joined the practice. Although the children are now busy with scouting activities, their father remains a member of the club.

The diversity of those interested in and performing *eisaa* is remarkable. The mix of dancers in the Hawai'i RMD chapter included U.S. military personnel, their "war brides," and families, former immigrant laborers and their descendants, and former prisoners of war/internees and their descendants. This mixture of ethnicities and cultures in dance speaks of the modern Okinawan experience. From its links with the Buddhist Obon, *eisaa* has evolved to embrace the Okinawan encounter with war and the U.S. military presence. The military presence transformed *eisaa* from a performance that distinguishes one village from another into a medium that defines the Okinawan people's frustration at and resentment of the U.S. military presence. In the process, the *eisaa* performance affirmed the Okinawan identity and helped negotiate new social relationships. The transforming effects of *eisaa* confirm Helen Thomas's thesis that "dance does not simply reflect social relationships, but can also contribute to shaping social relations and thus can contribute to change" (Thomas 1995, 170). At least in its Hawaiian experience, *eisaa* reflects ethnic diversity and social interaction. No doubt, *eisaa* provided an opportunity and a space for new friendships.

Although *eisaa* has undergone many changes, its essential rhythm has not. Okinawan pop musician Teruya Rinken, who incorporates *eisaa* movements and songs into his performances, explains, "Even though *eisaa* outfits have changed over and over again, the basic rhythm of the beat has never changed and has been handed down. . . . The unchanged beauty that is able to preserve the value of the arts, this might be called tradition" (Teruya, Naka, and Murakami 1995, 86).

This unchanging *eisaa* rhythm has been an important thread that unites the diverse Okinawan community. In 1990, at the first Worldwide Uchinanchu Festival, commemorating the ninetieth anniversary of the beginning of Okinawan emigration, and again in 1995, at the second Worldwide Uchinanchu Festival, *eisaa* was performed a number of times as a symbol of the Okinawan, diasporic, and pan-Okinawan identity. More recently, the Peruvian-born Latin and Okinawan pop musician Alberto Shiroma created a Spanish song, *Eisa*, in 1997. The lyrics read: "Bailando desde el Asia Uchinámoya América, Eúropa y África!" (The dance from Asia Uchina to America, Europe and Africa) (Shiroma 1997). Shiroma's music accompanies *eisaa* performed in other widely separated Okinawan communities and on the U.S. military bases in Okinawa and the United States. Like Shiroma, Kina's music and dance have spread beyond Okinawa. His greatest hit song, *Hana* (Flowers), has been recorded by various artists from Japan, Taiwan, China, Indonesia, Thailand, and the United States. He reports, "I want to keep singing this song with a belief in the power of the music's spirit, which reaches many people's minds and hearts faster than economic systems and deeper than political agendas" (Kina 1997, 79–80). He has performed at peace-movement gatherings and memorial services in Hiroshima and Nagasaki and at Ainu and Native American events. Kina's music and *eisaa* have been performed as a badge of the peace movement and as an embodiment of the rights of indigenous peoples.

The Hawai'i RMD chapter is a symbol of the diasporic and transnational Okinawan experience. The once ethnic-specific folk performance embodies the reality and aspirations of minority peoples attempting to preserve their ethnic identities in the face of foreign incursions and worldwide dispersal. But perhaps, while crystallizing the experiences and memories of a people, the international popularity of modern *eisaa* lies in its ability to articulate the hopes, local aspirations, and everyday experiences of ordinary people.

My focus on the U.S. military role in the promotion of *eisaa* should not be mistaken for optimism about the military-base problem and support for militarism. Rather, I seek to note that, through dance, the Okinawan people created a space in which they could continually renegotiate their relationship with the overwhelming presence of the U.S. military bases on their island home. I continue to perform and write on *eisaa*, aware that the U.S. military bases are superimposed on my ancestral land.

Notes

Portions of this essay appeared in "Dancing beyond the U.S. Military: Okinawan *Eisaa* as Identity and Diaspora," *Theatre Insight* 10, no. 1 (spring 1999): 4–13.

1. Hokama Shūzen (1986, 172) divides Okinawan performing arts into three cate-

gories: *saishiki geinō* (ceremonial performing arts); *minzoku geinō* (folk performing arts); and *koten geinō* (classical performing arts). *Eisaa* belongs to folk performing arts.

2. *Kami asagi* are small temple-like structures in which the priestess performs rites of thanksgiving and welcome for the ancestral spirits.

3. According to the report, 56,360 persons attended the festivities between 1 April and 30 September 1957 at the Ryūkyūan-American Cultural Center on the occasions of "lectures, contests, square dancing, quiz shows, O-Bon dance contests, cooking class, baby clinics, chorus, stage performances, tours, tournaments, instruction courses, clubs, etc." The report does not specify how many actually attended the Obon dance contests, but it can be assumed that about 50,000 persons did because the centers in Naha, Nago, Miyako, and Yaeyama had attendances of 4,995, 1,967, 3,049, and 3,029, respectively, on those occasions (High Commissioner of the Ryukyu Islands 1957).

4. The roots of the AWWA date to 1952, when the charitable organization was called the Ryūkyūan American Welfare Council. The AWWA comprises six organizations: the Army Women's Group, the Kadena Enlisted Wives' Club, the Marine Enlisted Wives' Club, the Kadena Officers' Wives' Club, the Marine Officers' Wives' Club, and the Navy Officers' Wives' Club.

5. Internees included 979 issei Japanese and Okinawan "aliens" and 525 nisei Japanese and Okinawan American citizens.

Chapter 9

Hawai'i *Uchinanchu* and Okinawa *Uchinanchu* Spirit and the Formation of a Transnational Identity

Arakaki Makoto

After "reannexation" by Japan in 1972, Okinawa struggled to reintegrate into the national life of Japan. After ten difficult years, the dream of returning to the Japanese motherland ended in the harsh realization that Okinawa would not become an equal partner with the other Japanese prefectures. It would remain instead a military zone. In the unequal power relationship that resulted, a positive Okinawan identity was guaranteed only by assimilating, by becoming "Japanese." Only recently has this identity been questioned.

On 1 January 1984, journalists at *Ryukyu Shimpo*, a major Okinawan daily, began a series, "Sekai no Uchinanchu" (Okinawans worldwide), that proved to be extremely popular. Soon thereafter, Okinawa Television launched a series of features that highlighted the success of *Uchinanchu* (Okinawans) overseas. The adventurous frontier spirit, hard work, and achievements of their overseas cohorts brought to mind for Okinawans the Ryūkyūan kingdom and their former independence as a nation that existed in peace with other nations. Joining in, the Okinawan prefectural government began promoting the image of the *Uchinanchu* as an "oceanic frontier people," "peaceful traders," and "a people bridging the world." These images are inscribed on a bell (ordered cast by Shō Taikyu [1415–1460] in 1458), Bankoku shinryō no kane, that once hung in the Shuri Palace.[1] The inscription describes the ancient kingdom's role as a prosperous trading nation that bridged the countries of East Asia: "The Ryūkyūan kingdom, ideally situated in the southern seas, gathers wisdom from Korea, maintains close ties with China, and is the entryway to Japan. Abiding between [China and Japan, our kingdom] issues forth as the island of the immortals. Her trading ships, as the bridge to all nations [*bankoku shinryō*], gathered treasures from countries of the ten directions" (original inscription reprinted in Okinawa Ken kyōiku'inkai 1996, 33).

Articulating Okinawa's singular historical experience, the phrase "*bankoku shinryō*," or "the bridge to all nations," projects a very positive identity and at the same time identifies Okinawa's unique place in Japan's current global economic and political position. The presence of overseas *Uchinanchu* communities lends credence to Okinawa's claim to being a land possessed of the "oceanic frontier spirit" and one that acts as a bridge between nations. The presence of a worldwide *Uchinanchu* identity supports the very foundation of Okinawa's identity as "*bankoku shinryō no tami*" (a people bridging all nations) and makes the vision of a global *Uchinanchu* community possible. Today, under the slogans "*bankoku shinryō no seishin*" (spirit of bridging the world), "worldwide *Uchinanchu*," and "*Uchinanchu* spirit," Okinawans are reconnecting with fellow Okinawans and Okinawan communities scattered throughout the world.

This essay has two purposes. The first purpose is to explore the identities of successive generations of Okinawans in Hawai'i. During the years since the first immigrant Okinawans arrived in Hawai'i in 1900, the issei (first-generation) Okinawan immigrants, their nisei (second-generation) children, their sansei (third-generation) grandchildren, and their yonsei (fourth-generation) great-grandchildren have positioned themselves in different discourses on the basis of their respective sociohistorical contexts and their relation to their ancestral homeland. The second purpose is to move beyond the social space of Hawai'i and discuss narratives of a new relationship between Hawai'i *Uchinanchu* and their cohorts in Okinawa. As mentioned earlier, an Okinawan's identity is empowered by his or her relation to overseas *Uchinanchu* communities; at the same time, an aspect of the Hawai'i *Uchinanchu*'s identity is based on his or her relation to Okinawa. Recently, with the emergence of a worldwide *Uchinanchu* network, Okinawans have articulated the *Uchinanchu* spirit as the common bond with generations past and with other Okinawan communities scattered throughout the world. Through interaction and the production of a shared narrative of this spirit, Okinawans around the world have begun to form a discursive connection beyond their ethnicities and national identities.

The notion of the Okinawans as other (in relation to the Japanese) persisted in Hawai'i, where Okinawans and *Naichi* (lit. "the Japanese heartland," but often used to refer to immigrants from mainland Japan) were initially recruited to work as agricultural laborers. Unable to comprehend the language of the Okinawan immigrants, *Naichi* often pejoratively referred to Okinawans as "*Japan-pake*" (Japan-Chinese), an expression akin to "*Japonese-kanaka*," coined in Micronesia. Reporting on the incomprehensibility of the Okinawans, the 7 February 1907 *Nifu jiji,* a vernacular daily, published the following observation: "Okinawan immigrants seem to like music. In the plantation camps, after returning from work, they play their shabby *jamisen* and sing unintelligible songs."[2] The immigrants from mainland Japan had presumed that the Okinawans would be Japanese, but experience soon proved them wrong. The first generation of Okinawans in Hawai'i also experienced the ambivalence of being "Okinawan" and being "Japanese."

The Okinawan-Japanese ambivalence persisted in the second-generation Okinawan community, and Okinawan-*Naichi* animosity also continued. But the ambivalence and animosity were based on different experiences. The prejudices of the issei *Naichi* were strongly impressed on the nisei *Naichi.* A second-generation *Naichi* man, for example, found that his mother belittled his Okinawan girlfriend because the Okinawans were *heta* (lit. "unskilled"); in this context, the expression meant "not smart"), they did not know how to speak "properly" to elders (Toyama and Ikeda 1981, 133). The first-generation *Naichi* judged the Okinawan language to be "loud," "rough," "coarse," "uncultured," and "obnoxious." Aware of this, Okinawans, often ashamed of their "unrefined" Japanese, would speak to *Naichi* issei only in English (Toyama and Ikeda 1981, 133–134).

Naichi discrimination pressured Okinawan issei to reject their language and culture and to encourage their nisei children to assimilate into Japanese and American communities. As a result, the schism between the Okinawans and the *Naichi* community began to diminish. In addition, the language barrier disappeared because both second-generation Okinawan and second-generation *Naichi* spoke English as their first language and shared similar experiences growing up in Hawai'i. Moreover, mainstream America discriminated against all Asian communities equally, and, during World War II, Okinawans were lumped together with the "Japs," further eroding the gulf between the two communities. Both Okinawan and *Naichi* shared the same subject position as Americans. Finally, since *Naichi* were not in positions of power in the greater Hawai'i society, their attitudes toward Okinawans had little effect on the socioeconomic advancement the Okinawan nisei. The Okinawan nisei excelled in various professions, thrived in business, and became vital members of the Hawai'i community.

The third and fourth generations of Okinawans constructed their subjectivity in the social context of the 1960s and 1970s, when "identity politics" were played out in the name of multiculturalism. Knowing one's cultural roots became a positive value, and Okinawans in Hawaiʻi began to form a new relationship with their ancestral homeland. During the 1980s and 1990s, as communications and interaction between the Hawaiʻi Okinawan community and Okinawa became more frequent, Okinawan identity in Hawaiʻi moved beyond its Hawaiian social space. At the same time, Okinawa identified itself as an island of *kaiyō minzoku* (oceanic frontier people) and began more actively to embrace its overseas communities, with which it had always maintained close connections. Remembering help received when it was most needed, Okinawa, its institutions, and its people were in a position to reciprocate by sponsoring leadership tours and awarding scholarships to overseas Okinawan students.

The Emergence of a Pan-Okinawan Identity

The emergence of a pan-Okinawan identity can be traced to the formation of the United Okinawan Association (UOA) in 1951, which emerged from a need to organize relief efforts in the aftermath of World War II. The Battle of Okinawa completely devastated Okinawa Island, and the survivors were in desperate need of aid. The Hawaiʻi Okinawan community was hesitant to organize a relief effort because of the prevailing anti-Japanese sentiment. However, with the aid of the American Friends Service Committee, a group of concerned Okinawans organized the Okinawa Relief Clothing Drive Committee. This initial effort was replicated by other groups, whose efforts often overlapped as each group competed for recognition as the representative of Hawaiʻi Okinawans. Recognizing the need for a united effort, the leaders of the Okinawan community revived a movement to establish an all-Okinawan organization that had been pursued before the war. After much discussion, the UOA was restructured as a congress of clubs rather than an association of individual members.

Membership in the clubs around which the restructured UOA was organized was determined largely by where in Okinawa immigrants had been born. The early immigrants established *chōjinkai* (block associations), *son-jinkai* (village associations), *shijinkai* (city associations), even *azajinkai* (hamlet associations). Before the war, such "locality" clubs had been for the immigrants a source of fellowship and mutual support. Shared memories and experiences formed the basis for a collective identity, the locality club even functioning as an extended family. But it was only after the war, with the organization of the clubs under the UOA, that a larger—Okinawan—collective identity emerged.

Remembering Okinawa: The 1980 Leadership Tour

The UOA commemorated the eightieth anniversary of the Okinawan immigration to Hawai'i with a year-long celebration underwritten by the state legislature. And, as part of the celebration, the Sonjinkai (Town and Village Association) of Okinawa Prefecture and the Okinawa Prefecture City Mayors' Association invited thirty-five young nisei and sansei between the ages of eighteen and thirty-five to Okinawa. These thirty-five young *Uchinanchu*, all representatives of locality clubs, were selected from among more than two hundred applicants.[3]

Prior to their departure, the (mostly sansei) representatives underwent several orientation sessions, including classes in Okinawan history, geography, and culture, conversational Japanese, and Hawaiian hula. Then, on 1 October 1980, they left for Okinawa. On their arrival at the airport, they were blinded by the lights of television cameras and greeted by waving hands and welcome signs as they made their way to claim their baggage. In the VIP lounge of the airport, they were presented with leis and greeted by government officials, including the mayors of various cities. They felt like "celebrities" (Study Tour 1981, 220) and "dignitaries" (Study Tour 1981, 194). The twelve-day tour, however, was more than a sight-seeing trip. The participants attended lectures on the history, culture, art, economics, and politics of Okinawa delivered by college professors and visited their ancestral villages or towns as official government guests. The participants were overwhelmed by the Okinawans' hospitality, which was described as "first-class all the way" (Shiroma 1981, 178) and "fit for a king" (Study Tour 1981, 194). One participant remembered: "The anxiety quickly diminished when my aunt hurriedly came and gave me a *big* hug. She was so happy to see me [that] she started to do a *kachashi* [Okinawan improvisational dance]. . . . We met for the first time, but I felt a bond, a closeness between us" (Study Tour 1981, 220).

Many felt a sense of belonging and a connection to their ancestral roots. One sansei explained: "From the moment I arrived at the Naha Airport, I had the feeling of belonging, the feeling of returning home, the feeling that this is where my ancestors came from" (Study Tour 1981, 185). All found the three-day stay in their relatives' homes—including a visit to their grandparents' birthplace—especially significant. Okinawan traditions and customs that had once been obscure and unintelligible became immediately lucid and comprehensible (Study Tour 1981, 205). Another sansei wrote: "I realize and understand now, why my grandparents . . . always spoke [with] such love and warmth for Okinawa. I now share their feelings for their and now somehow my fatherland" (Study Tour 1981, 123).

This new understanding and appreciation of their cultural heritage connected the participants to their Okinawan identity and roots. Their grandparents' memories became their reality; they reconnected with their grandparents and formed new connections with Okinawa. Okinawa was not simply their ancestral homeland; now it was part of them. Very deep feelings were generated by the experience:

> Meeting up with my roots has given me a kind of secure, deep-rooted feeling that this is where my *ojiichan* [grandpa] and *obaachan* [grandma] came from, and these [my relatives] are the people who have the same basic kind of understanding and feeling that I have been brought up with. . . . I felt so close to these people, like there was a mutual openness and sharing with one another. (Study Tour 1981, 192)
> From seeing where my ancestors descended from, I knew I would have a better understanding of why things are as they are, and why I am as I am. . . . I have learned a lot about myself, thereby I feel a more complete person. (Study Tour 1981, 138–139)

The warmth and hospitality of their reception in Okinawa made an indelible impression on the young sansei. Treated like family, they felt that they belonged. It was a highly emotional experience. One participant wrote: "Okinawa . . . the memories still brings tears of joy to my eyes" (Study Tour 1981, 141). They returned to Hawaiʻi with a renewed pride in their heritage.

The overwhelming hospitality and extensive generosity of the people and the prefectural government of Okinawa reflected their deep appreciation for the invaluable relief aid that Okinawa received from Hawaiian Okinawans after World War II. The Okinawan people had not forgotten what the grandparents and parents of the young sansei had done to help them survive the aftermath of the Battle of Okinawa. The postwar relief effort was reminiscent of the generosity of the first Okinawan immigrants, who, even after working from dawn till dusk to feed their families, found enough money to assist family members back home, build schools, and contribute to other much-needed projects in their hometowns. Thirty-five years later, they showered their appreciation on the children and grandchildren of the early immigrants.

The tour experience awakened the sansei to their heritage and instilled a pride in being *Uchinanchu*. They returned with the resolve to preserve and perpetuate Okinawan culture and the *Uchinanchu* spirit. At a reunion, the participants expressed their appreciation for the trip and dedicated themselves to launch a new movement, the Young Okinawans of Hawai'i (YOH), an initiative that neither the UOA leaders nor the prefectural government officials foresaw. The emergence of the YOH encouraged more members of the younger generation to participate in civic affairs and revitalized the Okinawan community.

The 1980 tour to Okinawa was a turning point in the history of the Okinawan community in Hawai'i. On returning home, the participants assumed leadership roles in various Okinawan organizations, including locality clubs. Three consecutive UOA presidents after 1981, in fact, were among the participants. Interest in Okinawan culture was renewed. Ten years after the 1980 tour, the Okinawan community again saw a need to nurture new young leaders to assume leadership positions. This led to a second leadership tour in 1993.

The 1993 Leadership Tour

On 20 July 1993, thirteen sansei and yonsei left Hawai'i for Okinawa as representatives of locality clubs. The ten-day historical, cultural, and business awareness program was modeled after the successful 1980 tour. The 1993 UOA Leadership Development Study Tour proposed to revitalize the Okinawan community by involving younger *Uchinanchu*. Participants applied to and were selected by their locality clubs, which underwrote one-third of the tour's transportation cost. The UOA covered another one-third, while the participants paid the remaining one-third. The Okinawan prefectural government covered all expenses in Okinawa. Before embarking on the tour, the participants attended an intensive, month-long series of lectures on Okinawan culture and society and workshops on such aspects of social etiquette as exchanging business cards. In Okinawa, they visited important government officials, businesses, and factories. The major part of the tour was the home stay with their relatives.

The participants found their home-stay experience the most rewarding. "That's where the *Uchinanchu* spirit really came on," one sansei, Wesley Waniya, reported enthusiastically (conversation with author, 12 September 1994). Echoing a similar enthusiasm, others recalled the deep attachment they formed with their relatives, whom they had previously met only once or twice. Jay Ogawa recalled that he was treated "just like their own children" (conversation with author, 13 September 1994). Another sansei was highly apprehensive; he spoke little Japanese, and his relatives knew no English. Notwithstanding the language barrier, they "got along perfect." Waniya explained:

> The more *awamori* we drank, the better my Japanese got, [and] the better their English got. By the end of the night, we *shaberu* [talked] plenty, talking, talking, talking all kinds of stuff. . . . I went to visit my uncle, and my uncle hugged me. The basic stuff, I could understand. He was talking about my uncles [in Hawai'i] and asking me specific questions. That's when I was looking through my dictionary. But he didn't mind. He was very patient. I didn't feel uncomfortable at all. I felt I could always open up. And of course, when we go out for drinking, then my cousin goes, "Give me the dictionary!" and threw it away. [Laughs.]

Other participants shared similar experiences. Despite language difficulties, they were "laughing and crying [while] talking with each other," Waniya recollected. For Kevin Uyehara, visiting his relatives was a highly emotional experience, one that left an indelible imprint. He felt a connection with his relatives in Okinawa, and it gave him a new understanding of the *Uchinanchu* spirit. He was touched when his grandfather's sister told him that she wished she had been young enough to learn English so that she could have talked to him. After he left her house, she followed him despite her feeble condition. As she pressed an envelop in his hand, he protested, "I am not here to take the money." Recalling that moment, he said, "I just wanted to meet them and pay my respect." Arguing with an "old lady that was [a] hardheaded Okinawan," he finally realized that she wanted to express her appreciation for the aid his grandfather sent her after the war. He was moved that she wanted to reciprocate after almost fifty years:

> Not forgetting what happened in the past. Eh, it's what I call Okinawan heart. It's a giving heart. It doesn't know any boundaries. Through the ocean, and through all these miles. . . . You can walk to that house, knock on the door, and they are going to welcome you into their house and treat you like one of their family. You always feel welcome. . . . Jesus, we are just about complete strangers! They know we are related, but [they are] not like your mother or father. When they have that kind of love for you, this is as much as that. It's really unique. And you are finding it so many thousands of miles away. I wanted to cry. This lady, she made me cry. (Conversation with author, 13 September 1994)

As Uyehara indicated, the overwhelming hospitality shown the participants demonstrated the appreciation for the postwar relief projects organized by the Okinawans in Hawai'i. The young Okinawan tour participants also gained a sense of belonging through interacting with their relatives and visiting the birthplaces of their grandparents and great-grandparents. Once a sansei or yonsei established which village his or her family came from, the connection provided substantive family history that further reinforced a feeling of belonging.

Uchinanchu Spirit

The participants from both tours often mentioned "*Uchinanchu* spirit." "If there is anything that makes us the same *Uchinanchu* as issei, it must be this spirit. And what could be more precious to give to the generations to come?" Uyehara declared. All the participants affectionately speak of the "giving and loving spirit" of the early immigrants. This legacy is cherished and is still evident in the work of Hui O Laulima, a volunteer service club, and in the cultivating hands of the gardeners at the Hawai'i Okinawa Center. The 1980 participants defined this spirit as "mutual cooperation," "hard work," "good heart," and "emphasis on family." In a spring 1994 workshop, the 1993 tour participants agreed on five essential components of "*Uchinanchu* spirit": an open, giving, sharing, supportive, helping, and encouraging heart; fellowship and cooperation; hard work; Okinawan cultural awareness; and emphasis on family. Although it did not appear on the list, humility was often mentioned as an important quality.

These definitions articulate the feelings of many Okinawans in Hawai'i. Some refer to this *Uchinanchu* spirit as "the spirit of *yuimaaruu*" (mutual help). Or is it the "aloha spirit," Okinawan style? Young Okinawans see parallels between the *Uchinanchu* spirit and the aloha spirit. They believe that the issei brought the *Uchinanchu* spirit to Hawai'i; they found the same spirit in their relatives and other Okinawans they met. One participant marveled that, even though the Okinawans in Hawai'i and in Okinawa proper were brought up in different countries, their "cultural spirit is still the same." The majority of the personality traits and social values that characterize the *Uchinanchu* spirit are shared by the traditional Hawai'i society that is passed on even today. The guiding principle of Hawaiian social relationships is "to minimize personal gain or achievement in order to maximize interpersonal harmony and satisfaction" (Okamura 1980a, 121).

Through their "local identity" and the "aloha spirit," third- and fourth-generation Okinawans found their discursive position in the *Uchinanchu* spirit. This discourse served as a counterdiscourse to the negative narrative produced by the notion of Okinawans as the Japanese other. The discourse was a consequence of revitalized interaction between the Hawai'i Okinawan community and Okinawa as well as of the compatibility of the *Uchinanchu* spirit with the aloha spirit that characterizes local identity. Today, the perceived *Uchinanchu* spirit of the issei is no longer the same. Mutual cooperation and assistance—values that were necessary to survive in the harsh colonial plantation environment and the rationale for locality clubs—are now embraced by the larger community. For the sansei and yonsei, traditional values have converged with local values. Discourses on the *Uchinanchu* spirit and the aloha spirit are interwoven at their subject position: the Hawaiʻi *Uchinanchu*.

Toward the Okinawan Diaspora

In 1990, the notion of a worldwide *Uchinanchu* community became a reality when the Okinawan prefectural government hosted the first Worldwide Uchinanchu Festival. Okinawans living abroad gathered in Okinawa for the week-long event. The event quickened a worldwide sense of an Okinawan community, and the prefectural government pressed ahead with plans systematically to develop a network with and among overseas *Uchinanchu*. This Worldwide Uchinanchu Network Project included the establishment of the Worldwide Uchinanchu Goodwill Ambassador program. This movement echoed *bankoku shinryō no tami* of an earlier time. Thirty-five hundred participants attended the second Worldwide Uchinanchu Festival in 1995 (see fig. 11).

As a result of the Okinawan prefectural government's initiatives, the Hawaiʻi Uchinanchu Business Group sought ties with Okinawan businesses in other parts of the world. In 1997, the group cohosted the first Worldwide Uchinanchu Business Network Conference in Honolulu and established the nonprofit Worldwide Uchinanchu Business International (WUB) in 1998 and the Worldwide Uchinanchu Business Investment in 1999. WUB Investment was established for the mutual support of its members, who purchase stock in cooperative ventures, the proceeds of which are then reinvested in the businesses of the group's members. The structure and spirit of the organization are reminiscent of the mutual-help associations established by the earlier immigrants. A portion of the profits is donated to WUB International to promote, in addition to business networks, the exchange of information—and especially new technology—between other professional groups.

It is too soon to assess the effect of the WUB. However, it seems likely to allow Okinawan businesses to expand their markets and engage in exchanges that can create new opportunities in Okinawa and other parts of the world.

Uchinanchu Spirit and Uchinanchu at Heart

Yuimaaruu is commonly articulated both in Okinawa and in overseas Okinawan communities. The cooperative spirit of *yuimaaruu* emerged in farming communities at a very early point in the evolution of Okinawan society. Mutual help was essential if the community was to be sustained. The old spirit has found new life. Pamela Tamashiro, president of the UOA, adopted *yuimaaruu,* which she believed defines the essence of the *Uchi-*

Figure 11. Poster from the 2001 Worldwide Uchinanchu Festival. Courtesy Third Worldwide Uchinanchu Festival, 2001.

nanchu spirit in Hawai'i, as her administrative motto for 1998. She reported her decision in the November/December 1997 issue of *Uchinanchu,* the organization's newsletter. The spirit of *yuimaaruu* is evident in other places. The 17 August 1999 *Ryukyu Shimpo* quoted Yonamine Shinji, the 1999 president of Worldwide *Uchinanchu*—Brazil: "The *Uchinanchu* spirit of *yuimaaruu* is still alive in Brazil. Because of the spirit, many of us have succeeded. I want to share the spirit of *yuimaaruu* with *Uchinanchu* all over the world." The spirit of *yuimaaruu* is the cornerstone for the Third Okinawa Promotion and Development Plan, currently in effect. The plan envisions Okinawa as Japan's southern hub for international exchange and cooperation with neighboring Asian and Pacific countries (Okinawa Prefectural Government 1996b). Others envision the creation of an "Asian Community" with Okinawa as its hub (Omae 1993, 79).

The global *Uchinanchu* community is multiethnic and hybrid. Okinawans in Hawai'i have very little in common with other Okinawans in other parts of the world, except perhaps for a willingness to share the spirit of *yuimaaruu.* Nonetheless, it is through this affectionate and humane discourse that *Uchinanchu* and the *Uchinanchu* at heart touch one another. Okinawa's spirit of *bankoku shinryō* and the overseas communities' *Uchinanchu* spirit embrace each other to form vital new connections. This mutual embrace articulates discourses on what it means to be Okinawan. Unlike exclusive and fixed identities established through national agendas, diasporic Okinawan identities may be nonessential, decentered, nonexclusive, transnational, and fluid, even for those from the Okinawan homeland. These diasporic identities, I contend, can form a global, hybrid, and inclusive *Uchinanchu* community that is neither ethnic nor national. Those who demonstrate the spirit of *yuimaaruu* are *Uchinanchu* at heart. In this diasporic space, *Uchinanchu* at heart is—as James Clifford (1994) would assert—continually challenged and transformed.

Notes

1. The U.S. military seized the bell as war booty in the aftermath of the Battle of Okinawa. It was hung on the grounds of the U.S. Naval Academy at Annapolis, Maryland, until it was returned to Okinawa in 1973 to commemorate its reversion to Japan. While at the Naval Academy, the bell was rung whenever Navy scored a point in Army-Navy games (Kerr 1958, 100).

2. *"Jamisen"* is an expression coined by the Japanese to refer to the Okinawan *sanshin. "Ja"* means "snake." The sound box of the *sanshin* is covered with snakeskin.

3. The project was supported wholeheartedly by the UOA and the locality clubs because their membership was aging and their nisei leaders saw in the project an excellent opportunity to nurture cultural awareness among the sansei.

Chapter 10

Agari-umaai
An Okinawan Pilgrimage

RONALD Y. NAKASONE

On 21 September 1997, I accompanied family elders on the Agari-umaai (Eastern pilgrimage), a pilgrimage dedicated to Amamikyu, the creator deity of the Okinawan and Amami Oshima Islands and the original ancestor of those islands' people. It was a journey that evoked memory and imagination. The pilgrimage reaches deeply into Okinawan notions of creation, spirituality, ancestors, death and the afterlife, and identity. Retracing ancestral pathways brings to consciousness layered memories that commingle past and present. For this pilgrim, the journey also suspended time.

All journeys depend on where one has ventured. My participation in the Agari-umaai pilgrimage heightened my interest in Okinawan spirituality, an interest that had been sparked in 1995 by my presence at an *umatchi,* an annual observance that honors the family's founding ancestor. During the course of conversation with family elders, I learned of the seven-year ritual cycle observed by the Nakasone *munchu.*[1] Agari-umaai is the first event in the cycle. Nakijin-nubui is the other major pilgrimage.[2] Kin groups carry on this once-royal pilgrimage that ceased with the dissolution of the Ryūkyūan kingdom in 1879.[3] For more than four hundred years, the king, together with the *chifijin* (hereafter referred to as *kikoe-ōgimi,* as it is known in the Japanese), the national priestess, made annual visits on behalf of the nation to offer prayers of thanksgiving and to observe memorials for the first ancestor. The pilgrimage reinforced royal authority and was a powerful focus of national identity that persists even today. Our pilgrimage retraced the royal route, but reduced the number of sites visited.

The modern Agari-umaai pilgrimage is an extension of the annual *kami-ugan* (prayers to *kami;* Jp. *kami ogami*) performed by kin groups, which visit

sacred wells and springs, grave sites, and other reminders of their immediate ancestors. The observances at well sites honor the resident water *kami*
for their life-giving gift. At these sacred sites, pilgrims engage in *ubiinadii*
(Jp. *obenade*), a ritual in which water from these sacred springs is dabbed
on the forehead to ensure divine protection. Pilgrims return to their villages and homes with the sacred water and repeat the ritual with those who
remained behind. The sacred water is also offered at the ancestral altar.
Family rites at grave sites and other places honor the memory of ancestors,
who after thirty-three years become *kami,* take on a spiritual identity, and
protect their descendants (Namihira 1997, 69). Likewise, on the Agari-umaai
pilgrimage, kin groups pay homage at sites honoring the original ancestor,
Amamikyu, and other sites important to their earliest ancestors.

Joining my extended family on this pilgrimage offered a rare opportunity to observe a significant component of the Okinawan spiritual experience. I participated in the ritual observances as a representative of my
branch of the family. With my father's recent death, I am now the patriarch
of my paternal grandfather's lineage. The pilgrimage was a journey to places
in my mind and heart. It is my intention to participate in subsequent pilgrimages and other observances special to my family and to sketch the seven-
year religious cycle of an Okinawan family.

A participant-observer, I alternated between the roles of pilgrim and
scholar. I eagerly noted my observations and conversations. At each site,
elders retold the associated myth and shared memories of previous pilgrimages and our common ancestors. Humor and story revealed deep feelings for the myth, the land, and the family. The storytellers, I realized, had
incorporated into their identity the myth, the pilgrimage, and its landscape.
Each retelling—and each visit—nurtures the identity of future elders. The
spiritual torch is passed along by means of participation and observation.

This essay offers a contemporary perspective on the meaning and
significance of the Agari-umaai pilgrimage, its specific sites, and rituals associated with Amamikyu. My reflections commingle the memories of family
elders, who invoke memories of earlier ancestors, and the scribbling of scholars, who record and comment on the recollections of others. Kneeling in
thanksgiving before sacred sites, images of the moment of first discovery,
the joy of landfall, the hardships of a new beginning, nostalgia for the home
left behind, and aspirations for progeny came to mind. Landmarks invoke memory and imagination, allowing thoughts to move effortlessly between past and present. Weaving memory and imagination with scholarship and observation, I describe and reflect on my pilgrimage experience.
How, I wonder, has a tiny island nation in the shadow of powerful civiliza-

tions been able to maintain its spiritual and cultural integrity? The effect of Chinese religions, the homogenizing efforts of the Japanese, the continuing presence of the U.S. military and modernization, all these things cloud ancestral memories. Will they lapse into forgetfulness? I begin with an overview of the myth of Amamikyu, continue with a description of the twelve sites that we visited, and conclude with some observations on the intersection of foreign religions and the resilience of the Okinawan identity.

Creation Myth

In *Okinawa kō* (Okinawan reflections), Ifa Fuyū (1876–1947) speculates that Amamikyu (lit. "Amami person") refers to the Amabe, fisherfolk who serviced the Yamato clan of Japan during the third century. The Amabe gradually moved from their original home in the Japanese Inland Sea south to the Ryūkyūs. Over time, Amamikyu came to be identified with the creator deity who arrived from the sea. The original home of Amamikyu is *nirai-kanai,* a great island that lies somewhere in the eastern sea. It is the dwelling place of the ancestors and the source of such knowledge as the agricultural arts.

The four written versions of the myth of Amamikyu were compiled within a span of approximately fifty years.[4] During this half century, the myth grew in detail and complexity, revealing an evolving centralization of power and a hardening hierarchical structure in Okinawan society (Sakihara 1987, 30–31). In *Chūzan seikan* (Mirror of the ages of Chūzan) by Haneji Chōshū (1617–1675; also known as Shō Jōken), its last official retelling, the myth legitimizes the Shō dynasty's authority. Since scholarly debate on the details of the myth is of little concern for pilgrims, I turn to the *Ryūkyū shintōki* (Records of Shinto in Ryūkyū), which relates the following:

> Long ago, in the beginning, before there were people, a man and a woman descended from the heavens. The man was named Shinerikyu; the woman was called Amamikyu. The two resided in huts standing next to each other. At the time, the islands were small and floated on the waves. *Tashika* trees, thus, were brought forth and planted to form the mountains. Next, *shikyu* grass and *adan* trees were planted. Gradually the island took form. Yin and Yang were never consummated between the two, but since their residences stood side by side, the woman became pregnant with the coming and going of the wind. Three children were born. The first was the progenitor of the masters of various regions. The second was the predecessor of the *noro* [priestesses]. The third was the forebear of the commoners. (Yokoyama 1943, 108)

Like the Takaragahama in the Japanese classic *Kojiki* (Record of ancient matters), the *Ryūkyū shintōki* posits an idealized heavenly abode

where Teda, the sun and principal deity, resides. Teda summons Amamikyu to create the Okinawa Islands and asks her to bear children. The
Chūzan seikan embellishes the myth. Amamikyu and Shinerikyu, female
and male, are asked to descend to the world below, procreate, and prosper.[5] The firstborn is the progenitor of the king, the secondborn the progenitor of the *aji* or local lords, and the third the progenitor of the com-
moners. The first female is the *kikoe-ōgimi,* the second daughter the
progenitor of the local priestesses. Continuing, the *Chūzan seikan* describes
the creation of the seven major *utaki,* or sacred groves.[6] They are, in order
of creation, Ashimui of Kunigami, Kubō of Nakijin, Chinenmui, Seefadake,
and Sosatsuno-Urahara, Amatsuji in Tamagusuku, Fubuumui on Kudaka
Island, Suimui, and Madamamui. (Amamikyu is the creator of all other
sacred groves and woods on all the islands.) Subsequently, Amamikyu
ascends to heaven and asks for seeds of the five staple grains. The story
of Amamikyu and Shinerikyu—the creators of the islands, the progenitors of the nation, and the bearers of agriculture—is an important theme
in Agari-umaai.[7]

As was noted, the Ryūkyūan royal house embellished the ancient myth
of Amamikyu to legitimate its authority. However, in addition to this official
version, in the far-flung villages and on isolated islands a second oceanic
type of myth prevailed. First reported by Ifa Fuyū, a sister and brother pair
who escape a great flood are considered to be progenitors of the people.
Creation is not divine but much more humble. The survivors, after many
great struggles, carve out a life for themselves and repopulate the land. Sister and brother, the progenitors of the people, enjoy equal prestige and authority. The sister assumes the role of the spiritual patron of her brother,
who is in turn the sister's secular patron.[8] This dual sovereignty, spiritual
and secular, is a feature in Okinawan society.

The establishment of a hierarchical system of religious functionaries
presided over by a royal priestess was an attempt by the kingdom to ap-
propriate the folk religion (Mabuchi 1964, 86). Under the Ryūkyūan kingdom, this pattern of dual responsibility extended from the village level to
the national. The brother king held sway over political matters, and his sister attended to spiritual matters. The most important religious position,
kikoe-ōgimi, was reserved for a close female relative—a sister, a mother, or
an aunt. Sharing equal prestige and authority, the king and the priestess
consulted closely on matters of state. Similarly, the king accompanied the
priestess on the Agari-umaai pilgrimage. Since the sister held sway in religious matters, the king had to be ritualistically transformed into a woman
to enter Seefa-utaki and other sacred sites. While the Agari-umaai reinforces

the royal house and its relationship to Amamikyu, the supporting administrative structure is grounded in the brother-sister dual-sovereignty creation myth.

Pilgrimage

While there is no historical record marking the beginning of the Agari-umaai, the *Chūzan seikan* mentions that, in the mid-seventeenth century, the king, together with the *kikoe-ōgimi,* his spiritual counterpart, made annual visits to Kudaka Island in February for the *mugi no minkyoma* (first harvest) and in April, stopping at sacred sites in Chinen, Tamagusuku, Sashiki, and Ogata villages. On these visits, they prayed for national peace and a good harvest and conducted memorial services for the first ancestors. These pilgrimages drained the national treasury, and, in 1673, the regent Haneji Chōshū began sending a representative in place of the king. The ruling house continued the Agari-umaai pilgrimages until the Japanese destroyed the political and religious infrastructure of the kingdom. Soon thereafter, kin groups initiated the practice. The last *kikoe-ōgimi* completed her final pilgrimage during the Taishō period (1912–1926). She died in 1944.

Traditionally, the Agari-umaai and other pilgrimages observed by families occur on or about the twelfth day of the eighth lunar month. Since, according to the Okinawan calendar, the eleventh day of the eighth lunar month marks the first day of the year, the pilgrimage is essentially a New Year's ritual. This period also marks the lull between the summer harvest and the winter planting. Kinfolks escort the pilgrims to the outskirts of the village with music and festivities. As in the past, elders carry a *binsii,* a ritual tool and supply kit, and a *jubako,* a container filled with food offerings. Before the advent of the automobile, the pilgrimage took over a week. Ours was completed in a day.

Our pilgrimage began with rites honoring our immediate ancestors at the family altar. We left the Wakugawa section of Nakijin Village and traveled to Yonabaru Village on the Chinen Peninsula, continuing from there to Yonabaru-ieegaa, Teda-ugaa, and Seefa-utaki. After a break for lunch, we reassembled at Nakandakari-biijaa, continuing from there to Tamagusuku-nuru-dunchi and the shrine of the Tamagusuku shaman, Yabusaatsu-utaki, and Bin'nudaki. We skipped the rites at Sonohiyan-utaki for prosaic reasons—parking on a late Sunday afternoon in and around Shuri Palace is impossible. Our pilgrimage concluded at Saki-biijaa in Naha City. Our route, with a few notable exceptions, retraced that of the royal pilgrimage. The day ended with festivities.

At each site, elders from the various branches of the family withdrew *ukuu* (incense; Jp. *senko*), *uchikabi* (ritual paper money), *upanagumi* (pure rice; Jp. *ohanagome*), and *unsaki* (Jp. *osake;* rice wine) from the *binsii* and offered prayers of gratitude and remembrances on our behalf. The elders, the ritual leaders, occupied the front row, while other kinfolk settled in the back. When the elders signaled that preparations were completed, we knelt and drew our hands in prayer. The elders offered barely audible words of self-introduction to the *kami* and asked for health and prosperity for the family. Incense was not burned but laid on yellow sheets of paper that represent money. At the conclusion of the prayers, sake was sprinkled on the incense and around the *ibi,* the stone representation of the *kami* and the focus of veneration. Offerings of food were made at Seefa-utaki and Saki-biijaa. Except for the shrine at Tamagusuku, our rites were held outdoors. The sacred sites are always close to the earth.

We arrived at Udunyama a few minutes before the appointed 10:00 A.M. starting time. I was filled with excitement for this long-anticipated journey. Approximately seventy kinfolk, elders and children, from different branches of the family gathered. Relatives long separated greeted each other and exchanged news. A cousin formally introduced me, and we proceeded with our first ritual observance. The gentle sea breeze tempering the already warm midmorning sun reminded me of Hawai'i. I was struck by the simple, humble nature of the small cinder block and concrete shrine that sat on a concrete slab. No more than six feet high, about the size of a large refrigerator, the shrine was open on one side. A flat rock served as the altar. Located at the confluence of a river and the ocean, Udunyama marks the spot where Niruya-unusi, the principal deity of the Okinawan pantheon, revealed itself.[9] Also at this spot, Amakudi, a heavenly maiden, descended and *kikoe-ōgimi* rested on the occasion of her initiation.

Through subsequent research, I discovered the site's practical importance. Udunyama and Fubuu-utaki on Kudaka Island are sights that mark the inclination of the sun. The sunrise relative to these points determined the agricultural cycle and the departure of trading ships. From the Uteda-isi, a vantage point on Urasoe-gusuku, the sun rises exactly from the midpoint of Fubuu-utaki on the winter solstice. On this day, the sun marked the location of *nirai-kanai,* the abode of the *kami* and the land of the deceased ancestors.[10]

The Agari-umaai pilgrimage does not include a visit to Kudaka Island. However, this forlorn windswept strip of an island, *kami no shima* (island of the *kami*), is an integral part of the pilgrimage and the myth of Amamikyu. Fubuumui, one of the seven sacred groves that Amamikyu created, is lo-

cated on the island. It is here that Amamikyu chose to descend from the
heavens before making her way to the main island. Prayers are directed to
Kudaka from *utuusi* (Jp. *yōhaishō*), sites for prayers from afar located at
Seefa-utaki and Bin'nudaki and elsewhere on the main island.[11] On the
beach at Ishikihama is an *utuusi*, dedicated to *nirai-kanai*. Kudaka Island is
also associated with the initial cultivation of the five grains, which later
spread to the rest of the mainland.

Completing our rites, we cross a small stream to Yonabaru-ieegaa, where
Amakudi, a heavenly maiden, bathed her newly delivered infant. The artesian spring was enclosed by a small concrete structure resembling a Shinto
shrine. The king and *kikoe-ōgimi* made offerings there before proceeding
to Kudaka Island for other rites. Urban sprawl has encroached on both sites.
My cousins remarked on the many new buildings that had arisen since their
last visit, and we had difficulty locating Udunyama, which was situated at
the edge of a school athletic field. Yonabaru-ieegaa is in a small children's
park and bordered on two sides by high-rise apartment buildings. At one
time the entire area was forested.

A short drive from Yonabaru is Teda-ugaa, a most unusual site. Teda is
the name of the sun deity that appears in Okinawan myth and song. Alight-
ing from the car, we climbed a small hill and descended a steep slope to the
very edge of the sea. A concrete walkway made for an easy fifteen-minute
walk. A cousin mentioned that, in the past, he had walked along the exposed
reef to reach the pilgrimage site. After departing from Yonabaru Harbor,
the king and *kikoe-ōgimi* stopped here to ask for safe passage during their
trip to Kudaka Island. Water no longer flows from this sacred spring.

We made our way to Seefa-utaki, the most sacred site of the Okinawan
nation. Only women were allowed to enter during the days of the kingdom,
but now all are welcome, and the site is popular with both pilgrims and archaeologists. Seefa-utaki has six sites for prayers: Ujooguti, Ufuduui, Yu'inchi,
Sikyodayuru ga nuubii and amadayuru amika nuubii, Sanguui, and Urookaa.
Of these, Ujooguti, Sanguui, and Yu'inchi correspond to named sites in Shuri
Palace. Shuri Palace symbolizes the center of the secular world, and Seefa-
utaki is its spiritual counterpart. We offered rites at three sites, Yu'inchi,
Sikyodayuru ga nuubii and amadayuru amika nuubii, and a site just outside
the sacred precincts.

From a sun-drenched open field, we climbed a short set of stairs, passing two small stone lanterns to the left as we came to the top of a low ridge.
Our feet met with a narrow coral-cobbled pathway, and we were immediately drawn into a thick canopy of trees. The ascending pathway wound its

way past the remains of Ufuduui, the site where the initiation rites of the *kikoe-ōgimi* took place. The shrine was destroyed during the Battle of Okinawa and has not been rebuilt. The pathway continued deeper into the forested hills to Yu'inchi, the site of our first prayers. The ritual site is on a low raised stage set with large coral rocks. The altar faces a shallow hollow at the base of a brownish-yellow-colored cliff. The spacious circular clearing facing the shallow cave had the feel of an amphitheater. Yu'inchi bears the same name as an open courtyard in Shuri Palace. Viewing the elders on the ritual platform, I imagined the king, *kikoe-ōgimi,* and other religious functionaries in their white robes attending to the spiritual health of the nation.

After completing our rituals, we returned via a pathway that veered to the left. We entered a clearing, bordered on the right by a large sheltering coral overhang that seemed to have been pushed up from the earth. The dense tropical thicket on the left curved to the right to enclose the space. We encountered our second ritual site, Sikyodayuru-ga-nuubii and amadayuru-amika-nuubii. Rainwater dripped from two stalactites, collecting in large hollowed-out stones. The volume of water that is collected is an indicator of the coming year's agricultural yield. This water is also used for *ubiinadii.* Immediately to the left of the hollowed-out stones is a long low altar where we observed our second rite. Further to the left is an inverted-V passageway leading to the Sanguui worship site. This unusual geographic feature is formed by a perpendicular right wall that is buttressed by a second wall leaning against it. The darkened passageway dramatically frames the sunlit rock face at the far end. Walking through and turning left, the pea-green wisp of Kudaka Island floating in the deep blue ocean comes into view. This is the site of Seefa-utaki's *utuusi* to Kudaka Island.

Completing our rituals, we found our way back down the forested passageway into the midday sun. We reassembled for a final rite in a small hollow to the left of the pathway. This site was not one of the six sacred sites in Seefa-utaki, and I am not certain of its significance. But it did seem to be an ancient burial site. Shortly after, we broke up for lunch.

Although seemingly otherworldly, Seefa-utaki possesses a gentle ease that conveys a sense of reassurance. Its scale contributes to this impression. The trees are tall, and the rock cliffs are large but not overwhelming; the site has a number of sheltering caves and outcroppings and a thick forest that offered the earliest settlers safe haven from the rigors of sea travel and from frequent storms. The site also provided sustenance. Nearby are Ukinju and Hainju, the freshwater springs that are associated with the first rice fields. From the protected inlet, I imagined people harvesting fish and other foodstuff. On an earlier visit, my daughter, then fourteen years old, perhaps crystallized what might have been the feelings of the first inhabitants when she said, "This is a place where Totoro would live." Totoro are gentle myth-ical forest-dwelling creatures who are protectors of children. They can be seen only by children who love them.

After lunch at a local restaurant, we reassembled at Nakandakari-biijaa, an artesian spring, and a most pleasant site. Water flowed from four open-ings in the side of a small cliff into a large cistern made from finely cut coral. The sound of rushing water and the trees tempered the afternoon heat. To the front of the cistern was a large open area, which must have served as the village square, where women came to draw water and wash and men stopped to rest after a day in the fields. I have found no detailed informa-tion on the spring, but its proximity to Mintun-gusuku, the first permanent home of Amamikyu, suggests its association with the earliest settlers. At the small shrine, which stands above and to the left of the cistern, elders led us in prayers of thanksgiving.

Located above the rest of the village, and featuring a commanding view of the eastern Pacific, is a shrine cared for by the priestess of Tamagusuku. During the kingdom period, the Tamagusuku shaman, who belongs to one of the oldest families on Okinawa, performed thanksgiving and memorial rites with representatives from the court. The shrine is divided into two rooms with three altars. The altars held no images, only censors, offerings of greens and sake. I am not clear to whom these altars are dedicated, but it seems that the shrine held several ancient lineages. The elders offered incense to a select few censors. They also acknowledged *fii nu kang*, the hearth deity.[12] Unlike the Chinese, who understand the kitchen god to be a messenger or representative of the god on high, the Okinawans under-stand the kitchen god to be the most-distant ancestor.

Taking leave, we proceeded to Yabusatsu-utaki. This *utaki* is associated with Amamikyu arriving on the island, her first home, and the first rice fields. Leaving the green plateau, we descended through a narrow road to the foot of a steep cliff. The blue waters of the Pacific merged with the sky. We ar-rived at a narrow strip of sugarcane field sandwiched between the beach and the cliff. The planter had dedicated part of his field to a parking lot to accommodate the many pilgrims and to earn some extra cash. From the parking lot, we walked between the fields back toward the cliffs to Ukinju and Hainju, the artesian springs that are associated with the first rice field. Rising above the fully matured sugarcane plants, the path split. The path to the left led to Ukinju (see fig. 12). Hainju lay approximately twenty-five

Figure 12. Nakasone Jiro performing rites at Ukinju, 1996. Photograph courtesy Ronald Y. Nakasone.

feet to the right. I was struck by the humble nature of the springs. The waters that flowed were no more than a gentle trickle. It is hard to imagine their importance, but surely, for the weary immigrants who stumbled onto shore, fresh water must have been a blessing.

The observances at sacred well sites honoring the water spirit, clearly animistic, reveal the most fundamental religious sentiment of the Okinawan people. The Okinawans believe that the world is inhabited by myriads of supernatural and sacred spirits or *kami*. Prayers at these sites express gratitude to the water spirit for taking care of the ancestors and ask for health and prosperity for the family. Ukinju and Hainju, the first springs, are clearly the most important ritual water sites. The waters from Ukinju and Hainju flowed into two small fields of rice that had been planted a few weeks before. I was surprised to see them. They were too small to be of any commercial value. Someone had taken the time and effort to relive the myth. As I passed by, an elder remarked, "This is the beginning of Okinawa." He was a farmer. In a previous visit to another well site, another elder had expressed a similar sentiment: "Water sustained the life of the ancestors and supported their crops." At every well site, elders remarked on the reduced water flow. Teda-ugaa was dry.

After rites at Ukinju and Hainju, we made our way to Yaharajikasa, where, according to the myth, Amamikyu first set foot on Okinawa. The vast expanse of white sand between blue sea and green hills made for a most spectacular scene. The holy site, marked by a three-foot-tall stone pillar, stood in the sand, approximately twenty feet from the sea. The site is covered with water when the tide is in. We directed our prayers toward the low outline of Kudaka Island adrift in the distance. This site and the direction of the prayers recall Amamikyu's descent on Kudaka Island and her arrival on the mainland.

The myth and the landscape encouraged self-reflection and transformed my perceptions of the scene. What could have happened here? Gazing over the ocean expanse, I imagined tired men and women grounding their flimsy ships, stepping into the gentle surf, and dragging their waterlogged belongings behind them. Although their footprints had long since been erased, I stood in the tracks of my ancestors. Picturing this event in my mind's eye, I imagined them speaking to me directly. They related their relief at landfall, the heat of the burning midday sun as they drifted with the current, their longing for the home they had left behind. Imagining the past inspires thoughts of who one is, stimulating memories of distant ancestors. Perhaps someday my daughter will continue this pilgrimage.

We then proceeded a short distance to Hamagaa-utaki, nestled in a thicket just above the beach. On top of an approximately six-foot-high coral retaining wall, a small shrine marks Amamikyu's first home. From this temporary abode, she sought a more permanent home further inland and on higher ground, at Mintun-gusuku, where the graves of Amamikyu and Shinerikyu are located.

It took an hour to get from Hamagaa-utaki to Bin'nutaki, which is located about one mile east of Shuri Palace. Bin'nutaki is one of the seven sacred sites created by Amamikyu. This once-isolated site has an *utuusi* for Kudaka Island and Seefa-utaki. On ceremonial occasions, the king and other religious functionaries performed their rites. We dedicated prayers at two of the sites and at a shrine dedicated to four Okinawan kings, Shuten (1187–1237), Eiso (1260–1299), Satto (1350–1395), and Shō En (1470–1476), the founders of royal dynasties.

Our final stop was at Saki-biijaa. The site is located between the bottom of a rather high cliff and a densely built-up section of Naha City. We performed rites at two sites dedicated to Ryūsen no kami, Dragon Spring *kami*. This site is not included in the Agari-umaai, and I am unclear as to its importance for my family. At the conclusion of these final rituals, we enjoyed food and companionship before dispersing.

Reflections

The elders who led us on our pilgrimage are keenly aware that they bridge the past and the future. Carriers of the memory of a tradition estranged by modernization, they transmit ancestral memories through story, ritual, and prayer. Later that evening, over dinner and other stories, we were asked to continue their work. This was the last pilgrimage for Uncle Jirō. "Today, I had trouble walking the distance. I will be too old for the next pilgrimage." He is seventy-eight. The tone and content of the tradition are shaped by his life and those of the other elders. The next generation of elders struggling to find meaning in ancient rituals can look to the experiences of the Nedukuru brothers, Takashi and Mitsusaburo, in *Man'en gannen no futtobōru* or "Football of the first year of Man'en" by Ōe Kenzaburō, the 1994 Nobel Laureate.[13] The novel, renamed *The Silent Cry* in the English-language edition (Ōe 1974), is an attempt to bridge two historical periods, the first year of Man'en (1860) and Ōe's own time (1960). Ōe's metaphor of a football being kicked back and forth between the present and the past symbolizes the brothers' obsession with trying to come to grips with their past through their present. The two brothers return home in hopes of building a life for themselves. Looking toward the future, they search the past. The ball kicked in 1960 bounces into 1860, where it is kicked back to 1960.

Like the Nedukuru brothers, I, too, look to the past to understand my present self. The modern pilgrimage preserves memories of the past. Its sites, reminders of another time, inform me of my connections with what has happened here in the past. At its best, the past offers counsel and instruction, telling me who I am in terms of where my ancestors have been. Imagination transports me to the past and enables me to relive through the myth such ancestral memories as the joy of landfall and the struggle to survive in a new home. This history, recounted with each visit, is layered with every retelling, but this layering has not diminished the sense of gratitude toward the original ancestors and the importance of life-giving water. Participation in and observation of ritual and prayer reinforce history and myth. Memory relives the past, and imagination transforms it. Myth continues to grip the imagination and hold meaning for this pilgrim. Repeat visits will reward the ever-changing landscape of memory and imagination.

The legends and rituals that accompany the Agari-umaai pilgrimage reveal the intrusion of foreign religions. I note two. First, ancestral veneration, a key feature in the village *kamiugan* and Agari-umaai pilgrimage, shares many features with the ancestral cult in China. The ancient Chinese believed the relationship between parent and child to be fundamental. Filial piety required children to honor their parents while they were alive and to provide proper burial and observe regular memorial services after they had died. While alive, the parents reciprocated with care and love; after death, as ancestral spirits, they looked after the welfare of their descendants. Such beliefs must have found a receptive audience among the Okinawans, for whom offerings and prayers of gratitude to the ancestors were already an important part of ritual life.[14]

Second, I noted on two occasions the presence of shrines dedicated to a *fii nu kang,* or hearth deity. Scholars have noted the similarity between the *fii nu kang* and the Taoist hearth deity and maintain that it is of Chinese origin (Lebra 1966, 99–100). Sinologists speculate that the hearth deity appeared sometime before the sixth century B.C.E. Japanese scholars believe that the cult of the hearth deity is indigenous to Okinawa, as it is to many other early cultures (Kubo 1993, 63)—and that its Chinese veneer entered with immigrants from the continent (Nakamatsu 1990, 152–153). In China, the hearth deity is believed to be a lesser deity who reports the activities of the family to a higher deity, the lord in heaven. In contrast, the Okinawans believe that *fii nu kang* represent *ukami* or great *kami,* the first and earliest ancestors of the family lineage (Nakamatsu 1990, 152). The *fii nu kang* also serves as an *utuusi* to distant prayer sites. The incorporation in Okinawa of this and other religious practices demonstrates the resilience and the openness of a people who live on the periphery of more powerful cultural spheres.

My research and observations led me to other aspects of Okinawan religion and culture and to unresolved discrepancies. Other than that they followed the traditional pilgrimage route, I uncovered no logic or pattern in the sequence of sites we visited. Further, I also discovered inconsistencies in many of the details surrounding the myths. For example, the official myth states that Amamikyu descended on Fabuu-utaki on Kudaka Island, before making her way to the mainland. But seven other sites scattered throughout Okinawa also claim to be the spot where Amamikyu first alighted. Further, while the tombs in Mintun-gusuku claim to house the remains of Amamikyu and Shinerikyu, other devotees believe that Amamikyu rests in a crypt on Hamahiga, a tiny island just off the Katsuren Peninsula.

Further research is required if sense is to be made of these and other discrepancies. Some of them can be explained by the successive waves of immigrants settling at different sites and coming from different places. Families and regions evolved thematic variations of myths that add to the difficulty of arriving at definitive explanations. Such discrepancies, however, point to a spiritual tradition that is still vital and alive. In the absence of a "holy book" and a seminary where religious functionaries learn their faith and craft, the Okinawans, at least from what I observed, transmit their gratitude for the natural world and for their ancestors through participating in Agari-umaai and other ritual family observances. Through participation and observation, the pilgrims invest themselves in their Okinawan religion and identity.

In a journey that evoked memory and imagination, this pilgrim reached deeply into ancestral memories of creation, spirituality, death, and the afterlife. My memories, shaped at every turn by personal biographies and intellectual proclivities, sustain the myth and the pilgrimage. Retracing ancestral pathways brought to light layers of memories that commingle past and present. Places possess a marked capacity for triggering imaginative insight, inspiring thoughts about who one is, memories of ancestors, and musings on what one might become. The pilgrimage, a journey of places in the mind, must be repeated.

Notes

1. *Munchu* (patrikin; Jp. *monchu*) refers to sibling groups concerned almost exclusively with ancestral veneration.

2. In addition to Agari-umaai and Nakijin-nubui, each sibling group observes pilgrimages to its *muutuya* (house of origin; Jp. *motoya*), where the memorial tablet of the original patriarch is enshrined (*munchubaka*, "sibling-group crypt"; Jp. *monchu haka*), and other sites important to the first ancestor.

3. The Ryūkyūan kingdom began with the first Shō dynasty (1406–1469) and ended with the Japanese annexation in 1879. Historically, the kingdom can be divided into two phases, the early kingdom (1422–1609), which includes the first and second Shō dynasties, and the late kingdom (1609–1879), during which the second Shō dynasty was controlled by the Satsuma domain.

4. The four versions of the myth appear in the *Ryūkyū shintōki* (compiled in 1605 by Taichū), the *Omoro-sōshi*, the *Kikoe-ōgimi ogishiki*, and the *Chūzan seikan*. Although the *Omoro-sōshi* was completed in 1610, its songs and poems date to a much earlier period.

5. Shinerikyu is the male counterpart of Amamikyu. Scholars debate whether Shinerikyu is a second deity. Since Shinerikyu appears together with Amamikyu, Sakihara (1987) believes that the Shinerikyu is an echo expression for Amamikyu. Originally Amamikyu was gender neutral, but, under the influence of the Japanese myth of Amaterasu Omikami, Amamikyu and Shinerikyu were assigned gender.

6. The *utaki* is an indigenous feature of Okinawan religion. Every village, except those built since the Meiji period (1868–1912), has an *utaki*. The village *utaki*, located in

the adjacent hills and forest, is associated with the founding family of the village and its burial site. The most sacred precinct of the *utaki* is a small clearing in a wooded area and is marked by a flat stone, or more recently a cinder block, on which offerings are placed and over which prayer is offered. Beyond the "altar" may be an *ibi,* a stone that personifies the spirit of the *kami* of the ancestral founder of a village. Often, however, there may be just a natural formation. On appointed days, the ancestral *kami* journeys from *nirai-kanai,* their home, and descend to the *utaki.* It is here that the ancestors are met.

7. Sakihara (1987, 14–41) provides an extended discussion of the various forms of the myth. While Agari-umaai is specific to Okinawa, the myth of Amamikyu is strikingly similar to the Japanese creation myth related in the *Kojiki* and the Shintō religion. The Okinawans articulated their creation myth after the Satsuma invasion of 1609.

8. Mabuchi (1964) writes that, except for the Miyako Islands, belief in the sister patronage is widespread throughout the Ryūkyūs.

9. Niruya-unusi is also known as *Agari nu unusi.* "*Niruya*" refers to *nirai kanai,* the original home of Amamikyu. "*Unusi*" means "lord." Hence, Niruya-unusi is the "lord of the heavens."

10. "*Nirai*" means "country of origin (*nedukuru*) that lies beyond the sea." "*Kanai*" is an echo word. *Nirai-kanai* lies in the east and is associated with the home of ancestral spirits. The country of origin is the land of bliss and the place where the spirits of the deceased go. *Nirai-kanai* is also associated with the Buddhist Pure Land, which is located in the west. It is believed that, once a year, the spirits leave their homes to bring happiness to their progeny living in this world.

11. The *utuusi* is a prayer site, usually at the top of a hill or on the beach, from which one directs prayers toward a site that should be visited. In the home, the altar dedicated to *fii nu kang* (see n. 12 below) serves as an *utuusi.*

12. *Fii nu kang* is represented by three stones placed in an ash-filled censor. The placement of the stones resembles hearthstones on which a cooking pot can rest. Before the introduction of the *ifee* (Jp. *ihai*), or memorial tablet, in the seventeenth century, the *fii nu kang* represented the ancestors.

13. *Nedukuru* is a cognate of *nirai* (see n. 10 above).

14. The memorial tablet and memorial ritual observance are two other obvious adaptations that shaped much of the current Okinawan religious practice (see Nakasone 1996, 85–101).

Appendix

U.S. Facilities on Okinawa

Figures for land area and number of landowners are from the end of March 1999. The yearly lease-payment figures are from fiscal year 1998. *Source*: Okinawa prefectural government home page, http://www.pref.okinawa.jp/index/html.

Army Oil Storage Facility
> Land area: 1,255,000 square meters
> Number of landowners: 721
> Annual rental fee: ¥1.058 billion
> Number of Japanese employees: 95

> Army: storage

Awase Communication Site
> Land area: 552,000 square meters
> Number of landowners: 479
> Annual rental fee: ¥518 million
> Number of Japanese employees: 6

> Navy: communications

Camp Courtney
> Land area: 1,348,000 square meters
> Number of landowners: 585
> Annual rental fee: ¥1.082 billion
> Number of Japanese employees: 304

> Marine Corps: barracks

Camp Hansen
> Land area: 51,404,000 square meters

Number of landowners: 1,995
Annual rental fee: ¥6.112 billion
Number of Japanese employees: 398

Marine Corps: training

Camp Kuwae
Land area: 1,067,000 square meters
Number of landowners: 665
Annual rental fee: ¥1.293 billion
Number of Japanese employees: 323

Marine Corps: medical

Camp Mctureous
Land area: 379,000 square meters
Number of landowners: 245
Annual rental fee: ¥321 million
Number of Japanese employees: 19

Marine Corps: barracks

Camp Schwab
Land area: 20,627 square meters
Number of landowners: 492
Annual rental fee: ¥1.914 billion
Number of Japanese employees: 165

Marine Corps: training

Camp Shields
Land area: 701,000 square meters
Number of landowners: 251
Annual rental fee: ¥572 million
Number of Japanese employees: 87

Navy, Air Force: barracks

Camp Zukeran
Land area: 6,459,000 square meters
Number of landowners: 3,916
Annual rental fee: ¥7.370 billion
Number of Japanese employees: 1,980

Marine Corps: barracks

Deputy Division Engineer Office
Land area: 45,000 square meters
Number of landowners: 2
Annual rental fee: not available
Number of Japanese employees: 34

Army: office

Futenma Air Station
　　　　Land area: 4,806,000 square meters
　　　　Number of landowners: 2,563
　　　　Annual rental fee: ¥5.525 billion
　　　　Number of Japanese employees: 173

　　　　Marine Corps: airport

Gesashi Communication Site
　　　　Land area: 10,000 square meters
　　　　Number of landowners: 1
　　　　Annual rental fee: not available
　　　　Number of Japanese employees: 0

　　　　Navy: communication

Gimbaru Training Area
　　　　Land area: 601,000 square meters
　　　　Number of landowners: 130
　　　　Annual rental fee: ¥76 million
　　　　Number of Japanese employees: 0

　　　　Marine Corps: training

Henoko Ordnance Ammunition Depot
　　　　Land area: 1,214,000 square meters
　　　　Number of landowners: 50
　　　　Annual rental fee: ¥156 million
　　　　Number of Japanese employees: 27

　　　　Marine Corps: storage

Ie Jima Auxiliary Airfield
　　　　Land area: 8,015,000 square meters
　　　　Number of landowners: 1,148
　　　　Annual rental fee: ¥1.209 billion
　　　　Number of Japanese employees: 21

　　　　Marine Corps: airfield

Kadena Air Base
　　　　Land area: 19,950,000 square meters
　　　　Number of landowners: 7,444
　　　　Annual rental fee: ¥21.634 billion
　　　　Number of Japanese employees: 2,691

　　　　Air Force: airport

Kadena Ammunition Storage Area
　　　　Land area: 27,331,000
　　　　Number of landowners: 3,241

Annual rental: ¥9.717 billion
Number of Japanese employees: 215

Air Force, Marine Corps: storage

Kin Blue Beach Training Area
Land area: 386,000 square meters
Number of landowners: 227
Annual rental fee: ¥51 million
Number of Japanese employees: 0

Marine Corps: training

Kin Red Beach Training Area
Land area: 17,000 square meters
Number of landowners: 21
Annual rental fee: ¥12 million
Number of Japanese employees: 0

Marine Corps: training

Makiminato Service Area
Land area: 2,750,000 square meters
Number of landowners: 2,007
Annual rental fee: ¥3,839 billion
Number of Japanese employees: 1,141

Marine Corps: storage

Naha Port
Land area: 567,000 square meters
Number of landowners: 968
Annual rental fee: ¥1.698 billion
Number of Japanese employees: 110

Army: port

Northern Training Area
Land area: 78,332,000 square meters
Number of landowners: 70
Annual rental fee: ¥468 million
Number of Japanese employees: 0

Marine Corps: training facility

Okuma Rest Center
Land area: 546,000 square meters
Number of landowners: 248
Annual rental fee: ¥150 million
Number of Japanese employees: 84

Air Force: other

Senaha Communication Site
        Land area: 612,000 square meters
        Number of landowners: 381
        Annual rental fee: ¥320 million
        Number of Japanese employees: 50

        Air Force: communications

Sobe Communication Site
        Land area: 535,000 square meters
        Number of landowners: 448
        Annual rental fee: ¥319 million
        Number of Japanese employees: 32

        Navy: communications

Tengan Pier
        Land area: 32,000 square meters
        Number of landowners: 9
        Annual rental fee: ¥11 million
        Number of Japanese employees: 0

        Navy: port

Torii Communication Station
        Land area: 1,940,000 square meters
        Number of landowners: 923
        Annual rental fee: ¥1,191 billion
        Number of Japanese employees: 338

        Army: communications

Tsuken Jima Training Area
        Land area: 16,000 square meters
        Number of landowners: national land
        Annual rental fee: not available
        Number of Japanese employees: 0

        Marine Corps: training

Ukibaru Jima Training Area
        Land area: 254,000 square meters
        Number of landowners: not available
        Annual rental fee: not available
        Number of Japanese employees: not available

        Other: training

White Beach Area
        Land area: 1,568,000 square meters
        Number of landowners: 875

Annual rental fee: ¥861 million
Number of Japanese employees: 101

Navy, Army: port

Yaedake Communication Site
Land area: 37,000 square meters
Number of landowners: 2
Annual rental fee: not available
Number of Japanese employees: 6

Use and purpose: communications

Yomitan Auxiliary Airfield
Land area: 1,907,000 square meters
Number of landowners: 228
Annual rental fee: ¥139 million
Number of Japanese employees: 0

Marine Corps: training facility

Glossary

Agari-umaai	Eastern pilgrimage.
akimasyoo	Okinawan exclamation.
Amamikyu	Creator deity of the Okinawan people. Also Amamiku.
arayachi	Unglazed hard-biscuit stoneware. Also known as *nanbanyachi* and *Ryūkyū nanbanyachi.*
awamori	Okinawa's local liquor. Made from Thai rice and fermented with black malt yeast.
bankoku shinryō	"Bridge to all nations."
bankoku shinryō no tami	"People bridging all nations (the world)."
bashōfu	Fabric woven from the fibers from the *bashō,* a non-fruiting banana plant introduced from South Asia.
bingata	Polychrome stencil-dyed fabric
binsii	A ritual tool and supply kit; footed vases placed on the family altar.
Chūzan seifu	"Records of the ages of Chūzan." Continues the official history of the Ryūkyūan kingdom where the *Chūzan seikan* left off. In 1701, Saitaku (1644–1724) revised and edited the original *Chūzan seikan.* Saitaku's son Saion (1682–1761) made corrections and additions in 1724.
Chūzan seikan	"Mirror of the ages of Chūzan" by Haneji Chōshū (1617–1675; also known as Shō Jōken). The official history of the Ryūkyūan kingdom.
eisaa	Popular Okinawan folk dance that is traditionally

163

performed during the summer in conjunction with the annual Okinawan Buddhist Obon, a ceremony that honors the ancestral spirits. The villagers petition the ancestral spirits for prosperity and good health for each member of the household.

fii nu kang   Hearth deity. Unlike the Chinese, who understand the kitchen god to be a messenger or representative of the god on high, the Okinawans understand the kitchen god to be the most-distant ancestor.

Haole   European Americans in Hawaiian Creole English.

gyokusai   Crushed jewel.

imingaisha   Emigration companies.

issei   First generation.

jamisen   An expression created by the Japanese to refer to the Okinawan *sanshin*. "*Ja*" means "snake." The Okinawans never referred to their beloved *sanshin* as "*jamisen.*"

"other Japanese"   The Okinawans were referred to as "the other Japanese" in Mindanao, Philippines; "*otro Japones*" in Peru; "*Japan-pake*" (by mainland Japanese) in Hawaiʻi; and "*Japonese-kanaka*" in Micronesia.

Japonesia   A term coined by the novelist Shimao Toshio in 1961. It has since entered the Japanese cultural vernacular. *Japonesia* refers to a long and narrow cultural sphere in the northwest Pacific that stretches from Hokkaido in the north to Yonaguni Island in the south. The Ryūkyūan Archipelago, with Okinawa Island at its center, constitutes the southern sector of this great geographic arch.

kachaashi   An improvisational dance in which the audience is invited to participate. From the Okinawan "*kachaa-sun,*" meaning "to mix up."

kanaka   A pejorative applied to all Carolinians and Marshallese. The Japanese ranked the Yapese, who stubbornly resisted Japanese institutions, values, and administration, at the very bottom of their social scale. Thus, such expression referring to the Okinawans as "*naichijin* [Japanese] *no kanaka*" and "*Japonese-kanaka*" were pejoratives.

kamiugan   Prayers to *kami* by kin groups who visit sacred wells

	and springs, grave sites, and other reminders of their immediate ancestors. *Kami ogami* in Japanese.
kankara sanshin	*Sanshin* made from an empty tin can.
kasuri	Weaving with resist-dyed and patterned yarn.
kikoe-ōgimi	National high priestess under the Ryūkyūan kingdom. *Chifijin* in Okinawan.
Konkōken-shū	"Anthology of sacred words." With more than eleven hundred entries, it is the oldest Okinawan dictionary.
lao-lon	Thai liquor.
munchu	Sibling groups concerned almost exclusively with ancestral veneration. *Monchu* in Japanese.
Naichi	Japanese heartland. In Hawai'i, the expression referred to Japanese from mainland Japan.
naichijin	See *naichi*.
nanshin netsu	"Obsession for the southward advance." Refers to the enthusiasm that developed to colonize and exploit the Nan'yō or South Seas region.
nanshin ron	"Southward advance." An ideology that emerged in the Meiji period (1868–1912) from the exploitation of the Nan'yō Islands.
Nan'yō	South Seas. This is an extremely vague expression. At various times, it has included Micronesia, Melanesia, the South China Sea, and Southeast Asia from the Andaman Islands to Papua. *Uchi* (Inner) *Nan'yō* includes the Carolines, the Northern Marianas to the north, and the Marshall Islands to the east. Nan'yō is always in reference to Japan, geographically.
nirai-kanai	A place of abundance, the home of the *kami* and other ancestral spirits who bring happiness and treasures when they visit this world. *Nirai-kanai* also came to be associated with the Pure Land Buddhist's western paradise.
nisei	Second generation.
noro	Priestesses. *Nuru* in Okinawan.
obaachan	Grandmother.
ojiichan	Grandfather.
Okinawa *Kenjinkai*	Okinawa prefectural organization.

omoro	"Divine song," "songs sung in the sacred woods," "to think," "thoughts," and "reflections."
Omoro-sōshi	An anthology of ancient poems that date from the twelfth century.
otro Japones	"*Japones*" means Japanese in Spanish, and "*otro*" means "other." "*Otro Japones*" referred to the Okinawans, who were considered not to be "pure Japanese."
Ryūkyū shintōki	"Records of Shinto in Ryūkyū." Compiled in 1605 by Taichū.
sansei	Third generation.
sanshin	Three-stringed plucked lute. *Samisen* in Japanese. Often referred to as *jamisen*.
seiban	Aborigine. Referred to Japan's newly subjugated people, who were at the margins of the Japanese polity.
Seikatsu kaizen undō	Lifestyle Reform Movement.
Shinerikyu	Male counterpart of Amamikyu.
sonjinkai	Village association. Also *chōjinkai* (village block association). Based largely on the villages and regions from which members came. The early immigrants also established *shijinkai* (city-based associations) and even *azajinkai* (village hamlet associations).
sotetsu jikoku	"*Sotetsu*" refers to the sago palm, which is poisonous when improperly prepared, the food of last resort. In times of famine, Okinawans resorted to consuming it. "*Jikoku*" means "hell."
tama'n chaabui	Crown of the Ryūkyūan king. Formally called *hibenkan*. *Tama mi kabuiri* in Japanese.
Ubiinadii	A ritual of dabbing water from sacred springs on the forehead to ensure divine protection. *Obenade* in Japanese.
Uchinanchu	People from Okinawa.
umatchi	An annual observance that honors the family's founding ancestor.
utuusi	Sites for prayers from afar. The *utuusi* is a prayer site, usually at the top of a hill or on the beach, from which one directs prayers in the direction of a site that should be visited. In the home, the altar dedicated to *fii nu kang* serves as an *utuusi*. *Yōhaishō* in Japanese.

yonsei	Fourth generation.
yuimaaruu	Mutual help. Mutual help emerged from the farming communities at a very early period in the society's evolution. Mutual help was essential to maintain the community's agricultural production and livelihood.
Yamatunchu	People from mainland Japan.
yuta	Shaman; priestess.

References

Akamine Hidemitsu
1990   Nan'yō imin to wa nani datta no ka (What was South Seas immigration?).
        Shin Okinawa bungaku (New Okinawan literature), no. 84:72–89.

Alegria, Ciro, and Alfredo Saco
1943   Japanese spearhead in the Americas. *Free World* 2, no. 5 (February): 81–84.

Allen, David
1996   Futenma move pleases Okinawa's Ota. *Pacific Stars and Stripes,* 15 April, 1, 6.

Alvarez, David
1934   Why the Davao hemp industry is successful. *Philippine Journal of Commerce and Industry* 10, no. 11 (November): 6.

Amemiya, Kozy K.
1996   The Bolivian connection: U.S. bases and Okinawan emigration. Working paper no. 25. Cardiff, Calif.: Japan Policy Research Institute.

Anderson, Benedict
1991   *Imagined communities: Reflections on the origin and spread of nationalism.* 1983. Revised and extended ed. London: Verso.

Aniya Masaaki
1974   Kengai dekasegi to kennai ijū (Working outside the prefecture and migration within the prefecture). In *Okinawa Ken* (Okinawa Prefecture), ed. Okinawa Ken kyoiku inkai, 7:42–55. Tokyo: Sentoraru insatsujo.

Appadurai, Arjun
1996   *Modernity at large: Cultural dimensions of globalization.* Minneapolis: University of Minnesota Press.

Appiah, Kwame Anthony, and Henry Louis Gates Jr., eds.
1995   *Identities.* Chicago: University of Chicago Press.

Arakaki, Robert K.
1996   The politics of Okinawan identity: Forgetting, recovery, and empowerment. In *Reflections on the Okinawan experience,* ed. Ronald Y. Nakasone. Fremont, Calif.: Dharma Cloud.

Arbaiza, Genar
1925   Acute Japanese problems in South America. *Current History* 21, no. 5 (February): 735–739.

Aruga Tadashi
1994   The Cold War in Asia. *In Commemorative events for the twentieth anniversary of the reversion of Okinawa.* Tokyo: The Japan Foundation Center for Global Partnership

Asai Tatsuo
1944   Nihonjin (Japanese). In *Ponapetō seitaigaku kenkyū* (Ponape Island, ecological research), ed. and comp. Imanishi Kinji. Tokyo: Shōkō shoin.

Asato Noburu
1941   *Okinawa kaiyō hattsu shi* (History of Okinawan seafaring development). Tokyo: Sanseidō.

Ashcroft, Bill, Gareth Griffiths, and Helen Tiffin
1989   *The empire writes back.* London: Routledge.

Ayala, Alfredo Genes
1939   Davao—a growing city and a serious problem. *Commonwealth Advocate* 6, no. 12 (December): 13, 34–35.

Barkan, Elazar, and Marie-Denise Shelton, eds.
1998   *Borders, exiles, diasporas.* Stanford, Calif.: Stanford University Press.

Barnhart, Edward N.
1962a   Citizenship and political tests in Latin American republics in World War II. *Hispanic American Historical Review* 29 (August): 7–32.
1962b   Japanese internees from Peru. *Pacific Historical Review* 31, no. 2 (May): 169–178.

Barth, Fredrik
1969   *Ethnic groups and boundaries: The social organization of cultural difference.* Boston: Little, Brown.

Beals, Carleton
1938   Totalitarian inroads into Latin America. *Foreign Affairs* 17, no. 1 (October): 78–89.

Bello, Walden.
1996   The balance-of-power doomsday machine, resurgent U.S. unilateralism, regional realpolitik, and the U.S.-Japan Security Treaty. *Ampo: Japan Asia Quarterly Review* 27, no. 2:12–29.

Brook, Timothy
1998   *The confessions of pleasure, commerce, and culture in Ming China.* Berkeley and Los Angeles: University of California Press.

Buchignani, Norman
1980   The social and self-identities of Fijian Indians in Vancouver. *Urban Anthropology* 9, no. 1:75–97.

Castells, Manuel
1997   *The power of identity: Economy, society and culture.* Malden, Mass.: Blackwell.

Chalian, Gerard, and Jean-Pierre Rageau
1995   *The Penguin atlas of diasporas.* Translated by A. M. Berrett. Harmondsworth: Viking.

"Chiji jimu hikitsugi shorui"
1978   Chiji jimu hikitsugi shorui (Governor's office, supplementary documents). In *Okinawa ken shiryō kidai 1* (Modern Okinawa prefectural documents 1). Tokyo: Ganando.

China, Jōkan
1988   Okinawa no taiyō shinko to oken: "Tiidako" shisō no keisei katei ni tsuite (Sun worship in Okinawa: The development of the notion of "tiidako"). In *Okinawa no shukyō to minzoku* (Religion and people of Okinawa). Tokyo: Dai'ichi shōbo.

Christy, Alan S.
1997   The making of imperial subjects in Okinawa. In *Formation of colonial modernity in East Asia,* ed. Tani E. Barlow. Durham, N.C.: Duke University Press.

Clifford, James
1994   Diasporas. *Cultural Anthropology* 9 (August): 302–338.

Coates, David A.
1996   Yanagi Sōetsu and the Pure Land of Beauty. In *Reflections on the Okinawan Experience.* Fremont, Calif.: Dharma Cloud.

Cody, Cecil
1959   The Japanese way of life in prewar Davao. *Philippine Studies* 7, no. 2 (April): 172–186.

Cohen, Robin
1997   *Global diasporas: An introduction.* Seattle: University of Washington Press.

Cole, Fay Cooper
1913   *The wild tribes of Davao district, Mindanao.* Chicago, Field Museum of Natural History, no. 2.

Comissão de Recenseamento da Colonia Japonesa, ed.
1964   *The Japanese immigrant in Brazil.* Tokyo: Comissão de Recenseamento da Colonia Japonesa.

Cushman, Jennifer, and Gung Wu Wang, eds.
1988   *Changing identities of the Southeast Asian Chinese since World War II.* Hong Kong: Hong Kong University Press.

Daniels, Roger, Sandra C. Taylor, Harry H. L. Kitano, and Leonard J. Arrington
1986   *Japanese Americans: From relocation to redress.* Salt Lake City:
        University of Utah Press.

Dōgen
1970   Ūji. 1243. In *Dōgen,* Nihon shisō taikei, vol. 12. Tokyo: Iwanami shoten.

Duckworth, N. H.
1926   Leading plantations in the Davao Gulf region. *American Chamber
        of Commerce Journal* (January): 8–9.

Duus, Masayo Umezawa
1999   *The Japanese conspiracy: The Oahu sugar strike of 1920.* Berkeley and Los
        Angeles: University of California Press.

Emmerson, John K.
1978   *The Japanese thread: A life in the U.S. Foreign Service.* New York: Holt,
        Rinehart & Winston.

Esman, Milton O. J.
1986   Diasporas and international relations. In *Modern diasporas in international
        politics,* ed. Gabriel Sheffer. London: Croom Helm.
1994   *Ethnic politics.* Ithaca, N.Y.: Cornell University Press.

Estuar, V.
1937   Davao is a bustling city of the south. *Philippine Journal of Commerce and
        Industry* 13, no. 3 (March): 17.

Ethnic Studies Oral History Project, ed. (ESOHP)
1981   *Uchinanchu: A history of Okinawans in Hawaii.* Honolulu: Ethnic Studies
        Program, University of Hawai'i.

Farriss, Nancy M.
1995   Remembering the future, anticipating the past. In *Time, histories, and
        ethnologies,* ed. Diane Owens Huges and Thomas R. Trautmann, 107–138.
        Ann Arbor: University of Michigan Press.

Featherstone, Mike, Scott Lash, and Roland Robertson, eds.
1995   *Global modernities.* Thousand Oaks, Calif.: Sage.

Field, Norma
1993   *In the realm of a dying emperor.* New York: Vintage.

Figal, Gerald
1997   Historical sense and commemorative sensibility at Okinawa's corner-
        stone of peace. *Positions: East Asia Cultures Critique* 5, no. 3 (winter):
        745–778.

Frazer, James
1980   *The golden bough: A study in religion and magic.* 3d ed. 9 vols. 1913. Reprint.
        London: Macmillan.

Gabila, Antonio S.
1941   18,000 Japanese can't be wrong. *Graphic,* 10 July, vol. 15, 12–13.

Gardiner, C. Harvey
1975   *The Japanese and Peru, 1873–1973.* Albuquerque: University of New Mexico Press.
1981   *Pawns in a triangle of hate: The Peruvian Japanese and the United States.* Seattle: University of Washington Press.

Geertz, Clifford
1973   The integrative revolution: Primordial sentiments and civil politics in new states. In *The interpretation of cultures: Selected essays.* New York: Basic.

Gerbi, Antonello
1943   *Japanese in Peru.* N.p., January.

Gilroy, Paul
1993   *The black Atlantic: Modernity and double consciousness.* Cambridge, Mass.: Harvard University Press.

Glacken, Clarence J.
1955   *The Great Loochoo: A study of Okinawan village life.* Berkeley: University of California Press.

Gladney, Dru
1996   Relational alterity: Constructing Dungan (Hui), Uygur, Kazakh identities across China, Central Asia, and Turkey. *History and Anthropology* 9, no. 4:445–477.

Goitein, S. D.
1967–   *A Mediterranean society: The Jewish communities of the Arab world*
  1983 *as portrayed in the documents of the Cairo Geniza.* 6 vols. Berkeley and Los Angeles: University of California Press.

Goodman, Grant
1965   A flood of immigration: Patterns and problems of Japanese migration to the Philippines during the first four decades of the twentieth century. *Philippine Historical Review* 1, no. 1:170–193.

Hall, Stuart
1996   What is this "black" in black popular culture? In *Stuart Hall: Critical dialogues in cultural studies,* ed. David Morley and Kuan-hsing Chen. London: Routledge.

Hama Kunihiko
1998   "Jinshu" no kaitai to kokumin no kioku—Erikku Viriamuzu chūshin ni (Dismantling "race" and national memory—focus on Eric Williams). In *Fukusubunka no tame ni* (For the sake of multiple cultures), ed. Fukusubunka kenkyūkai. Kyoto: Jinbun shoin.

Hashimoto Mitsuru
1998   Yanagita Kunio's "Japan." In *Mirror of modernity,* ed. Steven Vlastos. Berkeley and Los Angeles: University of California Press.

Hattori Shunichi and Kakihara Seiya
1941   Nanpō hatten to Okinawa (South Seas development and Okinawa). In

Nanshin Nan'yō kenkyū (Southern advance and South Seas research)
35:1–35.

Haya de la Torre, Victor Raul
1940   Latin America. *Living Age,* October, 146–149.

Hayase Shinzō
1984a   Tribes on the Davao frontier, 1899–1941. *Philippine Studies* 33, no. 2:
        139–150.
1984b   Tribes, settlers, and administrators on a frontier: Economic development
        and social change in Davao, southeastern Mindanao, the Philippines, 1899–
        1941. Ph.D. diss., Murdoch University.
1985   American colonial policy and the Japanese abaca industry, 1898–1941.
        Philippine Studies 33, no. 4:505–517.

Higa Chōshin
1991   *Okinawa no shinko yōgo* (Okinawan religious expressions). Naha: Fudoki sha.

Higa Kōbun
1997   How has Okinawa changed? Greeting the twenty-fifth anniversary of Okinawa's
        return to Japan. *The East* 22, no. 6:6–13.

Higa Shunchō
1959   *Okinawa no rekishi* (History of Okinawa). Naha: Okinawan Times.
1971–   *Higa Shunchō zenshū* (Complete works of Higa Shunchō). 5 vols. Naha:
  1997 Okinawa Times.

Higaonna Kanjun
1941   *Awamori zōkō* (Miscellaneous reflections on *awamori*). Tokyo: Teikoku
        kyōikukai.

Higashide Sei'ichi
1943   *Adios to tears: The memoirs of a Japanese Peruvian internee in U.S. concen-
        tration camps.* Honolulu: E. & E. Kudo.

High Commissioner of the Ryukyu Islands
1957   Cultural Center Statistics, 1 April 1957–30 September 1957. *Civil Affairs
        Activities in the Ryukyu Islands* 5, no. 2:100.

Hobsbawm, E., and Terence Ranger, eds.
1983   *The invention of tradition.* Cambridge: Cambridge University Press. Trans-
        lated by Maekawa Keiji and Kajiwara Kageaki as *Tsukurareta dentō* (Tokyo:
        Kinokuniya shoten, 1992).

Hokama Shūzen
1986   *Okinawa no rekishi to bunka* (History and culture of Okinawa). Tokyo:
        Chuokōron sha.

Hokama Shūzen and Saigo Nobutsuna
1978   *Omoro sōshi* (Anthology of ancient poems). Tokyo: Iwanami shōten.

Hokama Shūzen and Shigemi Kuwahara
1991   *Okinawa no soshin Amamiku* (Amamiku, the ancestral deity of Okinawa).
        Tokyo: Chikuji shōken.

Holley, David
1995   U.S. likely to stay on Okinawa. *San Jose Mercury News,* 5 November, 10A.

Honan, William H.
1997   Hunt for royal treasure leads Okinawa to a house in Massachusetts. *New York Times,* 13 July, 12.
1999   Curators as partners in war crimes. *New York Times,* 27 July, E5.

Horowitz, Donald L.
1985   *Ethnic groups in conflict.* Berkeley and Los Angeles: University of California Press.

Hunt, Terence
2000   Clinton faces Okinawa tension. *San Jose Mercury News,* 21 July, 4A.

Ifa Fuyū
1907   "P" onkō (Studies on the *p* sound). In *Kō Ryūkyū* (Old Ryūkyū). Naha: Okinawa Kōronsha.
1911   *Kō Ryūkyū* (Old Ryūkyū). Naha: Okinawa Kōronsha.
1926   Onarigami (Sibling deities). *Minzoku* (Folkways) 2, no. 2:45–58.
1927   Onarigami (Sibling deities). *Minzoku* (Folkways) 2, no. 2:45–58.
1940   *Ryūkyū sōsho* (Collection of historical sources on the Ryūkyūs). 5 vols. Tokyo: Natori.
1942   *Okinawa kō* (Okinawan reflections). Tokyo: Sōgensha.
1945   *Nihon bunka no nanzen* (The southern terminus of Japanese culture). Tokyo: Rakurō

Inose Hijiri
1996   U.S. offers to reduce Okinawa bases by 30%. *Nikkei Weekly,* 26 February, 4.

Ishida Takeshi
1998   *"Dōka,"* seisaku to tsukurareta kannen to shite no nihon (jō) (Assimilation, policy, and Japan as a construction: Part 1). *Shisō* (Idea), no. 392:47–75.

Ishihara Masaie
1977   Okinawa taiken no shisōka to heiwa sōshutsu undō (Thoughts on the Okinawan experience and the establishment of the peace movement). In *Reisen-go no Nihon to Okinawa: Sono jiritsu, kyōsei, heiwa no tenbō* (Japan and Okinawa after the cold war, perspectives on self-support, cooperation, and peace), ed. Sakugawa Sei'ichi and Kamata Sadao. Tokyo: Tanigawa shobo.

Ishii Ryoichi
1937   *Population pressure and economic life in Japan.* Chicago: University of Chicago Press.

Ishikawa Tomonori
1976   A sociogeographic study of emigrants from Kin Village in Okinawa Prefecture. *Ryūkyū daigaku honbungakubu kiyo shigaku chirigaku hen* (Journal of the University of the Ryukyus Faculty of Law and Letters, history and geography edition) 19:55–92.
1980   Okinawa imin kankei shiryō tōkei, zuhyō, chizu (Data on Okinawan immigration: Statistics, tables, maps). *Shin Okinawa bungaku* (New Okinawan culture), no. 45 (10 June): 141–152.

Johnson, Chalmers
1996   *Go-banken-sama,* go home! *Bulletin of the Atomic Scientists* 52, no. 4 (July/August): 22–29.

Jumsai, Sumet
1997   *Naga: Cultural origins in Siam and the West Pacific.* Bangkok: Chalermnit/ DD.

Kagoshima daigaku suisan gakubu, ed.
1985   *Okinawa gyogyō shiryō shū* (A collection of historical materials on the Okinawan fishing industry). Kagoshima: Kagoshima daigaku suisan gakubu.

Kaigai Kenkyoshō, comp.
1937   *Gendai Okinawa kenjin meikan* (Modern directory of persons from Okinawa Prefecture). Tokyo: Kaigai Kenkyushō.

Kakazu Hiroshi
1992   Five economic trends in the Asia-Pacific region: Emerging issues and Japan's role. *Research Institute for Asian Development Bulletin* 1 (March): 101–138.

Kamakura Yoshitarō
1982   *Okinawa bunka no ihō* (The legacy of Okinawa culture). Tokyo: Iwanami.

Kamisato Kami
1968   *Ijū uchi de ikinuita, 50 nen* (Surviving fifty years in a place of migration). Los Angeles.

Kaneshiro, Edith Mitsuko
1999   Our home will be the five continents: Okinawan migration to Hawai'i, California, and the Philippines, 1899–1941. Ph.D. diss., University of California, Berkeley.

Kang Sang-joong
1988   Nihonteki orientarizumu no gendai (Present day Japanese orientalism). *Sekai* (World) 522 (1987): 133–139.
1989   Shōwa no shūen to gendai no *shinzō shiri-rekishi* (Last moments of the Showa period and the *mental image contours* of modern Japanese history). *Shisō,* no. 786 (1989): 26–55.

Kang Sang-jung and Mari Oka
1999   Posutokoroniaru to wa nani ka (What is postcolonialism?). *Shisō,* no. 897:75–93.

Kasamoto Takao and Umebayashi Hiromichi
1996   Toxic contamination of the U.S. military bases in Japan. Paper presented at the International Forum on U.S. Military Toxins and Bases Clean-Up, 24–26 November, Manila.

Kawashima, Mie
1997   Reversion bittersweet for Okinawa. *Japan Times Weekly International Edition,* 19–25 May, 7.

Kenjinkai, ed.
1985   *Peru-Okinawa kinenshi* (A commemorative history of Peru and Okinawa). Lima: Peru Okinawa Kenjinkai.

Kerr, George H.
1958   *Okinawa: The history of an island people.* Rutland, Vt.: C. E. Tuttle.

Kina Shōichi
1997   *Subete no buki wo gakki ni* (Transform all weapons into musical instruments). Tokyo: Booken sha.

Kirk, Gwyn, and Margo Okazaki-Rey
1996   Military security: Confronting the oxymoron. *Crossroads,* April/May, 4–7.

Kiyono Kenji
1942   Nanpō minzoku no soshitsu, nihonjin no nettai junka nōryoku (Ethnography of the South Seas and the acclimatization ability of the Japanese to the tropics). *Shakai seisaku jihō* (Social policy review), no. 260:95–130.

Kodani Jun
1984   The Japanese Peruvians of Lima and anti-Japanese agitation: 1900–1940. M.A. thesis, University of California, Berkeley.

Koizumi Fumio
1977   Ed. *Asian musics in an Asian perspective.* Tokyo: Heibonsha.
1978   *Nihon dentō ongaku no kenkyū 1* (Studies on Japanese traditional music 1). Tokyo: Ongaku no tomosha.
1979   *Minzoku ongaku kenkyū nōto* (Ethnomusicology research notes). Tokyo: Seidōsha.

Kojima Yōrei
1987   Agarimari—oken o sasaeru seichi no junpei (Agaimaai—pilgrimage to sacred sites that support royal authority). In *Nihon no kamiugami—jinja to seichi* (Gods of Japan—shrines and sacred sites), ed. Tanikawa Ken'ichi, vol. 13, *Nansei shōtō* (Southwest archipelago), 260–316. Tokyo: Hakusuisha.

Kristof, Nicholas D.
1995   Welcome mat is wearing thin for G.I.s in Asia. *New York Times,* 3 December, A14.
1996a   Doubts rising in Okinawa on giving up U.S. bases. *New York Times,* 2 June, A4.
1996b   Suit in Japan seeks to ban night flights at U.S. base. *New York Times,* 11 April, A10.
1997   Okinawa vote rejects new U.S. military base. *New York Times,* 22 December, A3.

Kubo Noritada
1993   *Okinawa no minkanshinkō, chugoku bunka kara mita* (Okinawan folk religion, as seen from Chinese culture). Naha: Hirugisha.

"Kurōzuappu 1"
1999   Kurōzuappu 1 (Close-up 1). *Nichiroku, 20 seiki* (Japan record, twentieth century), 23 March, 20–21.

Lebra, William P.
1966   *Okinawan religion, belief, ritual, and social structure.* Honolulu: University of Hawai'i Press.

Levathes, Louise
1994   *When China ruled the seas.* New York: Oxford University Press.

Levine, Ellen
1995   *A fence away from freedom: Japanese Americans and World War II.* New York: G. P. Putnam's Sons.

Linn, Brian M.
1997   *Guardians of empire: The U.S. Army in the Pacific, 1902–1940.* Chapel Hill: University of North Carolina Press.

"Liuqui guo-chuan"
ca. 643 Reprinted in *Suisho* (History of the Sui dynasty), chüan 81. Vol. 3 of *Twenty-five histories.* Shanghai: K'ai-ming shu-tien, 2532 [i.e., 1936].

Mabuchi Toichi
1964   Spiritual predominance of the sister. In *Ryūkyūan culture and society: A survey,* ed. Allan H. Smith. Honolulu: University of Hawai'i Press.

Makabe, Raul Araki
1979   Migracion japonesa al Peru: 80 anos, un largo camino (Japanese emigration to Peru: 80 years, a long road). In *Ensayos de integracion* (Exercises in integration). Lima: Asociacion Universitaria Nisei del Peru.

Martin, Akemi
1998   Interview conducted by Shirota Chika. 7 December.

Masalski, Kathleen Woods
1999   History as literature, literature as history: An interview with *Lost names'* author Richard E. Kim. *Education about Asia* 4, no. 2 (fall): 23–27.

Matsue Haruji
1932   *Nan'yō kaitaku jūnen shi* (A ten-year history of development in the South Seas). Tokyo: Nan'yō Kōhatsu.

Matsumoto Toshiaki
1996   Mikka-kan dake "kaihō sareta gate": Beigun "Kadean Kichi Fest" ni atsumatta kenmin no "kyōchū" (The gate "opens" to locals for only three days: The hearts of Okinawans at the "Kadena Base Fest"). *Friday,* 26 July, 14–16.

McDermott, John F., et al.
1980   *People and cultures of Hawaii, a psychocultural profile.* Honolulu: University of Hawai'i Press.

McKeown, Adam
1999   Conceptualizing Chinese diasporas, 1842 to 1979. *Journal of Asian Studies* 58, no. 2 (May): 306–337.

Metcalf, Barbara, ed.
1996   *Making Muslim space in North America and Europe.* Berkeley and Los Angeles: University of California Press.

Military Base Affairs Office, Okinawa Prefecture
1998   *Military bases in Okinawa, current situation and problems.* Naha: Military Base Affairs Office.

Military Violence and Women in Okinawa
1995   Pamphlet distributed at the NGO Forum on Women, Beijing, 7 September
        1995.

Minear, Richard H.
1999   Lost names, master narratives, and messy history. *Education about Asia* 4,
        no. 2 (fall): 30–31.

Mochizuki, Carmen Higa
1999   *Carmen Mochizuki et al. v. United States of America.* 43 U.S. Court for
        Federal Claims, p. 99.

Montville, Joseph V., ed.
1990   *Conflict and peacemaking in multiethnic societies.* Lexington, Mass.: Heath.

Morimoto, Amelia
1991   *Poblacion de origen Japones en el Peru* (The problem of the origins of the
        Japanese in Peru). Lima: Centro Cultural Peruano Japones.

Morton, Louis
1953   *The fall of the Philippines.* Washington, D.C.: Department of the Army.

Mukai Kiyoshi
1988   *Okinawa kindai keizai shi* (Economic history of modern Okinawa). Tokyo:
        Nihon keizai hyōronsha.

Murai Osamu
1992   *Nantō ideorogii no hassei* (Origins of ideology toward the Southern Islands).
        Tokyo: Fukumu shoten.

Murata Tatsuji
1941   Bunka eiga—shinario: Kaiyō minzoku, Okinawajima ki, 3-bu saku (Cultural
        Documentary—scenario: seafaring people: A record of Okinawa Island, in
        three parts). *Bunka Okinawa,* vol. 2, no. 5, 24–29.

Murayama Meitoku
1929   *Hiripin gaiyo to Okinawa kenjin* (An overview of the Philippines and people
        from Okinawa Prefecture). Davao.

Murayama Shichirō
1979   *Nihongo no tanjō* (Birth of the Japanese language). Tokyo: San'ichi shobō.
1988   *Nihongo no kigen to gogen* (Origins and rise of the Japanese language). Tokyo:
        San'ichi.

Naimubu ishokumin kei
1943   Okinawa ken imin jigyō kihon hoshin (Fundamental policy regarding immi-
        grant enterprises). In *Chiji jimu hikitsui shorui* (Governor's report, supple-
        mental documents). Naha: Okinawan Prefectural Government.

Nakamatsu Yashū
1990   *Kami to mura* (Gods and villages). Tokyo: Fukurousha.

Nakano Yoshio
1969   *Sengo shiryō Okinawa* (Postwar documents: Okinawa). Tokyo: Nihon
        hyoronsha.

Nakasone, Ronald Y., ed.
1996   *The Okinawan experience.* Fremont, Calif.: Dharma Cloud.

Namihira, Emiko
1997   The characteristics of Japanese concepts and attitudes with regard to human
        remains. In *Japanese and Western bioethics: Studies in moral diversity,* ed.
        Kasamasu Hoshino. Dordrecht: Kluwer Academic.

Nano, Teodoro V.
1935a   America, Japan, and the Philippines. *Commonwealth Advocate* 1, no. 1
        (January): 15–16.
1935b   To save or not to save—Davao. *Commonwealth Advocate* 1, no. 10 (October–
        November): 41–44.

Nan'yō kyōkai Nan'yō guntō shibu, ed.
1935   Mane shimbun (Bean [little] news). *Nan'yō guntō* (South Seas island group)
        1, no. 5:98.
1941   Nan'yō nyūzu (South Seas news). *Nan'yō guntō* (South Seas island group) 7,
        no. 7:56.

Nihon satō kyōkai, ed.
1930   *Satō nenkan* (Sugar annual). Tokyo: Nihon sato kyōkai.

Nihonjin Peru ijū 80 shūnen shukuten i'inkai, ed.
1979a   *Andesu e no kakehashi* (A bridge to the Andes). Lima: Nihonjin Peru ijū 80
        shūnen shukuten i'inkai.
1979b   *Peru to nikkei shakai* (Peru and the Japanese community). Lima: Nihonjin
        Peru ijū 80 shūnen shukuten i'inkai.

Nomura Kōya
1990   Uchinanchu no seikatsushi (A history of Okinawan life). Sophia University.
        Typescript.
1997a   Nihonjin e no kodawari (On resisting becoming Japanese). *Inpakushon*
        ("Impaction") 103:40–41.
1997b   Sabetsu, dōka, Okinawajin (Discrimination, assimilation, and the Okinawans).
        Sanyō gakuen tanki daigaku kiyō (Journal of Sanyō Junior College) 28:71–82.
1998   Okinawa ni okeru nashonarizumu to koroniarizumu ni kansuru yobiteki
        kōsatsu (Preliminary thoughts on nationalism and colonialism on Okinawa).
        Sanyō gakuen tanki daigaku kiyō (Journal of Sanyō Junior College)
        29:105–114.
1999   Sabetsu to shite no dōka—Okinawajin to iū ichi kara (Assimilation as
        discrimination—from the Okinawans' standpoint). *Kaihō shakai gaku
        kenkyū* (Liberation of humankind: A sociological review) 13:74–93.

Normano, J. F., and Antonello Gerbi
1943   *The Japanese in South America: An introductory survey, with special refer-
        ence to Peru.* New York: Institute of Pacific Relations.

"Nyuu-yangu-Okinawa"
1940   Nyuu-yanga-Okinawa (New young Okinawa). *Bunka Okinawa* 1, no. 1.

Ōe Kenzaburō
1974   *The Silent Cry.* Translated by John Bester. Tokyo: Kodansha International.
1995   *Japan, the ambiguous, and myself: The Nobel Prize speech and other lectures.*
        Tokyo: Kodansha International.

Office of the Resident Commissioner of the Philippines
1942   *Facts and figures about the Philippines.* Washington, D.C.: U.S. Government
        Printing Office.

Oguma Eiji
1998   *Nihonjin no kyōkai—Okinawa, Ainu, Taiwan, Chōsen, shokuminchi shihai
        kara fukki undō made* (The boundaries of the Japanese—Okinawa, Ainu,
        Taiwan, and Korea, from the colonial administration until the reversion
        movement). Tokyo: Shinyosha.

Okamoto Junya
1998   Ishikawa-shi (Ishikawa City). In *Eisaa 360-do, rekishi to gendai* (All about
        eisaa, history and present), ed. *Okinawa zentō eisaa matsuri jikkō i'inkai.*
        Naha: Naha shuppan sha.

Okamura, Jonathan Y.
1980a   Aloha Kanaka me ke aloha 'aina: Local culture and society in Hawai'i.
        Amerasia Journal 7, no. 2:119–137.
1980b   Why there are no Asian Americans in Hawai'i: The continuing significance
        of local identity. *Social Process in Hawai'i,* 35:161–178.
1998   The illusion of paradise: Privileging multiculturalism in Hawai'i. In *Making
        majorities: Constituting the nation in Japan, Korea, China, Malaysia, Fiji,
        Turkey, and the United States,* ed. Dru C. Gladney. Standord, Calif. Stanford
        University Press.

Okihiro, Gary Y.
1994   *Margins and mainstreams: Asians in American history and culture.* Seattle:
        University of Washington Press.

Okinawa Club of America, comp.
1988   *History of the Okinawans in North America.* Los Angeles: Asian American
        Studies Center, University of California, Los Angeles, and Okinawa Club of
        America.

Okinawa daihyakka jiten kankō jimukyoku, ed.
1983   *Okinawa daihyakka jiten* (Okinawa Encyclopedia). Naha: Okinawa Times.

Okinawa Ken
1974   *Okinawan Ken shi* (History of Okinawa Prefecture). Vol. 7, *Imin* (Emigra-
        tion). Tokyo: Iwanami.
1975   *Okinawan Ken shi* (History of Okinawa Prefecture). Vol. 10, *Okinawa sen
        kiroku* (Documents on the Battle of Okinawa). Tokyo: Iwanami.

Okinawa Ken chi'ikishi kyōgi kai, ed.
1989   *Nantō no haka* (Tombs of the Southern Islands). Naha: Okinawa shuppan.

Okinawa Ken kyōiku'inkai
1996   *Okinawa no rekishi* (History of Okinawa). Reprint, Naha: Ōzato insatsu.

Okinawa Ken seishi kakei daijiten hensan i'inkai, ed.
1991   *Okinawa Ken seishi kakei daijiten* (Dictionary of Okinawan surnames and
        family lineages). Tokyo: Kadokawa shoten.

Okinawa no shuzoku kenkyūkai, ed.
1986   *Munchu haishōmawari no tehiki* (A guide to clan pilgrimages). Naha: Geppan
        Okinawa sha.

Okinawa zentō eisaa matsuri jikkō i'inkai, ed.
1998   *Eisaa 360-do, rekishi to gendai* (All about eisaa, history and present). Naha:
        Naha shuppan sha.

Okinawan Prefectural Government
1992   *Keys to Okinawa culture.* Naha.
1995a   Military bases in Okinawa: The current situation and problems. Naha,
        November.
1995b   Reduction and realignment of U.S. military bases in Okinawa. Petition
        submitted to the United States Government. Naha, May.
1996a   Base return action program. Proposal. Naha, January.
1996b   The cosmopolitan city formation concept: Grand design for a new Okinawa
        aiming at the 21st century. Naha, November.

Okinawan Women Act against Military Violence
1996   *Okinawa women's America peace caravan (February 3–17, 1996).* Naha:
        Okinawan Women Act against Military Violence.

Omae, Kenichi
1993   The rise of the region state. *Foreign Affairs* 72, no. 2:78–87.

Ong, Aihwa
1997   Chinese modernities: Narratives of nation and of capitalism. In *Ungrounded
        empires: The cultural politics of modern Chinese transnationalism,* ed. Aihwa
        Ong and Donald M. Nonini. New York: Routledge, pp. 171–202

Ong, Aihwa, and Donald M. Nonini
1997a   Afterword: Toward a cultural politics of diaspora and transnationalism. In
        Ungrounded empires: The cultural politics of modern Chinese transnationalism,
        ed. Aihwa Ong and Donald M. Nonini. New York: Routledge, pp. 323–332.
1997b   *Ungrounded empires: The cultural politics of modern Chinese trans-
        nationalism.* New York: Routledge.

Ortiz, Fernando
1995   *Cuban counterpoint: Tobacco and sugar.* 1947. Reprint, Durham, N.C.: Duke
        University Press.

Ōta Masahide
1972   *Okinawa no kokoro* (Okinawan heart). Tokyo: Iwanami.
1987   *The occupation of Okinawa and postwar reforms in Japan proper, democrat-
        izing Japan: The Allied occupation,* ed. Robert E. Ward and Sakamoto Yoshi-
        kazu. Honolulu: University of Hawai'i Press.

1994   *Mieru Shōwa to mienai Shōwa* (Visible Shōwa and hidden Shōwa). Naha: Naha shuppan.

Paguio, Pedro Q.
1930   Who is to blame about Davao? *China Weekly Review,* 1 March, 15.

Pan, Lynn
1990   *Sons of the Yellow Emperor.* Boston: Little, Brown.

Peattie, Mark R.
1988   *Nan'yō: The rise and fall of the Japanese in Micronesia, 1885–1945.* Honolulu: University of Hawai'i Press.

Pollack, Andrew.
1996   Okinawans send message to Tokyo and U.S. to cut bases. *New York Times,* 9 September, A3.

Price, Willard
1936   Japan in the Philippines. *Commonwealth Advocate* 2, no. 7 (July): 14–17, 25.
1938   The far flung Japanese. *Asia: Journal of the American Asiatic Association* (February): 129–132.

The Publication Committee of the Art of Okinawa, ed.
1989   *Okinawa bijutsu zenshū* (The art of Okinawa), 6 vols. Osaka: Dai Nippon Printing.

Quiason, Serafin D.
1958   The Japanese colony in Davao, 1904–1941. *Philippine Social Science and Humanities Review,* 33:215–230.

Rabson, Steve
1989   Introduction. In *Okinawa: Two postwar novellas by Ōshiro Tatsuhiro and Higashi Mineo.* Berkeley, Calif.: Institute of East Asian Studies.

Radhakrishnan, Rajagopalan
1996   *Diasporic mediations: Between home and location.* Minneapolis: University of Minnesota Press.

Reischauer, Edwin O.
1977   *The Japanese.* Cambridge, Mass.: Harvard University Press.

Rucker, Warren Page
1970   U.S. Peruvian policy toward Peruvian Japanese persons during World War II. M.A. thesis, University of Virginia.

Ryūkyū daigaku Okinawa bunka kenkyū sho, ed.
1964   *Miyako shotō gakujutsu chosa kenkyū hōkoku: Chri, minzoku hen* (Miyako Island group scientific research survey report: Geography and folklore). Naha: Ryūkyū daigaku Okinawa bunka kenkyū sho.

Safran, William
1991   Diasporas in modern societies: Myths of homeland and return. *Diaspora* 1:83–99.

Said, Edward W.
1978   *Orientalism.* London: Routledge.
1994   *The pen and the sword: conversations with David Barsamian and Edward W. Said.* Monroe, Maine: Common Courage.

Saiki, Berry
1995a   After years of occupation, Okinawans still feel overrun. *Stockton Record Centennial,* 6 December, A11.
1995b   News reports from Okinawa stir old memories. *Stockton Record Centennial,* 22 November, A11.
1995c   Okinawans' fear, distrust of U.S., Japanese military easily understood. *Stockton Record Centennial,* 13 December, A13.

Saito, Natsu Taylor
1998   Justice held hostage: U.S. disregard for international law in the World War II internment of Japanese Peruvians! A case study. *Boston College Law Review* 40, no. 1 (December): 275–348.

Sakai Naoki, Kitshara Megumi, Kanou Mikiyo, and Ogura Toshimaru
1998   Mai'noriti to shite no nihonjin—nashonaruna aidentiti o do kokufuku suruka (Japanese as minority—on how to expunge national identity). *Inpakushon* ("Impaction") 111:63–93.

Sakihara, Mitsugu
1979   Jyobun ni kaete (Introduction). In *History of Ryukyuan accomplishments in Hawaii,* ed. Takenobu Higa. Honolulu: Hawaii Hochi.
1981   History of Okinawa. In *Uchinanchu: A history of Okinawans in Hawaii,* ed. Ethnic Studies Oral History Project and the United Okinawan Association of Hawaii. Honolulu: Ethnic Studies Program, University of Hawai'i.
1987   *A brief history of early Okinawa based on the Omoro Sōshi.* Tokyo: Honpo shōseki.

Saleeby, N. M.
1905   *Studies in Moro history, law, and religion.* Manila: Bureau of Public Printing.

Schultz, John, and Kimitada Miwa, eds.
1991   *Canada and Japan in the twentieth century.* Toronto: Oxford University Press.

Serei Kyoko
1995   *Watashi no ayunda hansei* (Reflections of my journey). Cordoba: Makoto Otsuka.

Sheffer, Gabriel, ed.
1986.   *Modern diasporas in international politics.* London: Croom Helm.

Shinjō Tokuyū
1977   *Agari-umaai no haishō kyuseki* (Prayer sites and ancient remains related to Agari-umaai). Naha: Mitsuhoshi.

Shiga Shigetaka
1887   *Nan'yo jijō* (Conditions in the South Seas). Tokyo: Maruzen.

Shimao Toshio
1961   *Japonesia no nekko* (Roots of Japonesia). Tokyo: Chikuma shobō.

Shiroma, Alberto
1997   *Eisaa.* On *Diamantes: Eisaa special, e.p.,* by Diamantes. Tokyo: Bad News
        Records.

Simons, Lewis M.
1995   Okinawa long has felt burdened by outsiders. *San Jose Mercury News,* 5
        November, 10A.

Smith, Robert Ross
1953   *Triumph in the Philippines.* Washington, D.C.: Department of the Army.

Sorensen, John
1991   Politics of social identity: Ethiopians in Canada. *Journal of Ethnic Studies* 19,
        no. 1:67–86.

Stavrianos, Leften S.
1968   The global distribution of man. In *World migration in modern times,* ed.
        Franklin D. Scott. Englewood Cliffs, N.J.: Prentice-Hall.

Struck, Doug
1999   Japan plans air base move, but U.S. balks at deadline. *San Jose Mercury
        News,* 23 November, 4A.

Study Tour
1981   Town and Village Association of Okinawa Prefecture and Okinawa City
        Mayors' Association, comps. The nisei/sansei Hawaii-Okinawa study tour.
        Unpublished reports and essays available through the Hawai'i Okinawa
        Center, Waipahu, Hawai'i, and the International Exchange Division of the
        Okinawa Prefectural Government Office, Naha, Okinawa.

Sugihara Toru
1990   *Oriento e no michi* (Road to the Orient). Tokyo: Shōkō shoin.

Sulit, Pablo F.
1929   Young and prosperous Davao. *Philippine Journal of Commerce and Industry*
        5, no. 7 (July): 3–4.

Taeuber, Irene B.
1958   *The population of Japan.* Princeton, N.J.: Princeton University Press.

Taira, Koji
1997   Troubled national identity: The Ryukyu/Okinawans. In *Japan's minorities:
        The illusion of homogeneity,* ed. Michael Weiner. New York: Routledge.

Takeda Akira
1990   *Sorei saihi to shirei kekkon, nikan hikaku minzokugaku no kokoromi* (Ances-
        tral spirit ritual and death spirit ritual, an attempt at a comparative folk
        religion between Japan and Korea). Tokyo: Jinbun shōin.

Tamamori, Terunobu, and John C. James
1995   *A minute guide to Okinawa: Society and economy.* Naha: The Bank of the
        Ryukyus International Foundation.
2000   Okinawa: Society and economy. Naha: The Bank of the Ryukyus Interna-
        tional Foundation.

Tarling, Nicholas
1992   *The Cambridge history of Southeast Asia, from c. 1500–1800.* Cambridge:
        Cambridge University Press.

Tasaki Hideaki
1996   Hi no uchi dokoro no nai riron (Theory with a negative). *Jōkyō* (Affairs)
        10:21–26.

Teruya Rinken, Naka Bokunen, and Murakami Akiyoshi
1995   *Okinawa no ima, gaido bukku* (A guidebook on present Okinawa). Tokyo:
        Iwanami.

Thomas, Helen
1995   *Dance, modernity, and culture: Explorations in the sociology of dance.*
        London: Routledge.

Tigner, James Lawrence
1954   *The Okinawans in Latin America: Investigations of Okinawan communities
        in Latin America, with exploration of settlement possibilities.* Scientific
        Investigations of the Ryukyu Islands report no. 7. Washington, D.C.: Pacific
        Science Board National Research Council.

Titiev, Misha
1951   The Japanese colony in Peru. *Far Eastern Quarterly* 10, no. 3 (May): 227–247.

Tomiyama Ichirō
1990   *Kindai nihon shakai to "Okinawajin"* (Modern Japanese society and the
        Okinawans). Tokyo: Nihon keizai hyōronsha.
1992   Sensō domin to senjō taiken (War laborers and the war experience). *Nihonshi
        kenkyū* (Studies on Japanese history), no. 355:111–139.
1993   Bōkyaku no kyōdōtai to senjō no kioku (Forgetfulness and the cooperative
        body: Battlefield recollections). *Yoseba* 6:53–70.
1995a   Colonialism and the sciences of the tropical zone. *Positions* 3, no. 2:367–391.
1995b   *Senjō no kioku* (Battlefield memories). Tokyo: Nihon keizai hyōron sha.
1996   Nashonarizumu, modanizumu, koronirizumu—Okinawa kara no shiten
        (Nationalism, modernism, and colonialism—the view from Okinawa]. In
        Nihon shakai to imin (Japanese society and immigration), ed. Yō Kumai.
        Tokyo: Akashi shoten.
1997   Ryūkyūjin to iu shutai—Ifa Fuyū ni okeru boryoku no yokan (The Okinawan
        subject—the premonition of violence in Ifa Fuyū). *Shisō* (Idea), no. 878:5–33.

Torres, Luis Rocca
1997   *Japonese bajo el sol de Lambayeque* (Japanese under the sun of Lambaye-
        que). Lima: Universidad Nacional "Pedro Ruiz Gallo," Facultad de Ciencias
        Historico Sociales y Educacion, Asociacion Peruano Japonesa del Peru, and
        Comision Comemorativa del Centenario de la Imigracion Japonesa al Peru.

Toyama, Henry, and Kiyoshi Ikeda
1981   The Okinawa-Naichi relationship. In *Uchinanchu: A history of Okinawans in
        Hawai'i,* ed. Ethnic Studies Oral History Project and the United Okinawan
        Association of Hawai'i. Honolulu: Ethnic Studies Program, University of
        Hawai'i.

Tsuneshige, Cesar, ed.
1998   *La gran aventura* (The great adventure). Lima: Asociacion Peruano Japonesa Comision Centenario de la Inmigracion Japonesa al Peru.

Uehara Tetsusaburō
1940   *Shokuminchi to shite mitaru* (A study of the [South Seas island groups as] colonies). Nan'yō guntō no kenkyū (Nan'yo Islands Group research), no. 59. Tokyo: Nan'yō bunka kyōkai.

Ukai Satoshi
1997   *Teikō e no shōtai* (Invitation to violence). Tokyo: Misuzu shobō.
1998   Posuto koroniarizumu—mitsu no toi (Postcolonialism—three questions). In *Fukusubunka no tame ni* (For the sake of multiple cultures), ed. Fukusubunka kenkyūkai. Kyoto: Jinbunshoin.

Ukai Satoshi, Sakai Naoki, Chong Yeong-hae, Tomiyama Ichirō, Murai Osamu, and Karatani Kojin
1996   Posuto koroniaru no shisō towa nanika (What is postcolonialist thought). *Hihyō kukan* (Critical space) 2, no. 11:6–36.

Umesao Tadao
1944   Kikō (Travelogue). In *Ponapetō seitaigaku kenkyū* (Ponape Island, ecological research), ed. Imanishi Kinji. Tokyo: Shōkō shoin.

Urashima Etsuko
1999   After Governor Ohta's defeat women's initiative for base-free Okinawa. *Ampo: Japan Asia Quarterly Review* 29, no. 1:19–23.

Urasoe Shi, ed.
1984   *Urasoe shi shi* (History of Urasoe City). Vol. 5, *Shiryōhen* (Manuscript volume), no. 4, pt. 5. Urasoe: Urasoe Shi kyōiku i'inkai.

U.S. Bureau of Insular Affairs
1913   *The Philippine Islands.* Washington, D.C.: U.S. Government Printing Office.

van Wolferen, Karel
1990   *The Enigma of Japanese power: People and politics in a stateless nation.* New York: Vintage.

Wagatsuma, Hiroshi
1975   Problems of cultural identity in modern Japan. In *Ethnic identity: Cultural continuities and change,* ed. George De Vos and Lola Romanucci-Ross. Palo Alto, Calif.: Mayfield.

Waku'ue Gen'o and Ōshiro Hideko
1997   *Okinawa no shōji* (Sacred sites of Okinawa). Nakagusuku: Mugisha.

Wang, Gung Wu
1988   *Changing identities of the Southeast Asian Chinese since World War II.* Hong Kong: Hong Kong University Press.
1991   *China and the Chinese overseas.* Singapore: Times Academic.

Watanabe Akio
1994   The significance of the Seminar on the Commemoration of the Reversion

of Okinawa. In *Okinawa reversion: Its long-term significance in U.S.-Japan relations—past and future.* Tokyo: Japan Foundation Center Global Partnership.

Weglyn, Michi
1976   *Years of infamy: The untold story of America's concentration camps.* New York: Morrow.

Weiner, Michael
1995   Discourses of race, nation, and empire in pre-1945 Japan. *Ethnic and Racial Studies* 18, no. 3 (July): 433–455.

Wilkinson, Jens, and Kiyokazu Koshida
1996   Overview: Time to scrap the Security Pact. *Ampo: Japan Asia Quarterly Review* 27, no. 1:14–23.

Wilson, Michiko Niikuni
1986   *The marginal world of Ōe Kenzaburō: A study in themes and techniques.* Armonk, N.Y.: East Gate.

Winichakul, Thongchai
1994   *Siam mapped: A history of the geo-body of a nation.* Honolulu: University of Hawai'i Press.

Wyatt, David K.
1984   *Thailand: A short history.* New Haven, Conn.: Yale University Press.

Yamazato Eikichi
1969   Japan is not our fatherland. *China Post,* June. This series of five articles was reprinted in an undated pamphlet that carries no publisher's name.

Yanagi Sōetsu
1972   *The unknown craftsman.* Tokyo: Kodansha International.

Yanagita Kunio
1925   *Kainan no shōki* (A short record of the South Seas). Tokyo: Daiokayama shoten.
1950   "Takaragai no koto" (The cowrie). *Bunka Okinawa* 2, no. 7. Reprinted in Yanagita Kunio, *Kaijō no michi* (Ocean road) (Tokyo: Iwanami, 1978).
1978   *Kaijō no michi* (Ocean road). 1961. Reprint. Tokyo: Iwanami bunko.

Yanaihara Tadao
1935   *Nan'yō guntō no kenkyū* (A study of the South Seas island group). Tokyo: Iwanami.
1942   Nanpō rōdō mondai seisaku no kichō (Basis for labor policy in the South Seas). *Shakai seisaku jihō* (Social policy review) 260:156–157.

Yokoyama Shigeru, ed.
1943   *Ryūkyū shintoki* (Records of Shinto in Ryūkyū). Tokyo: Ōkayama shoten.

Yoon Kun-cha
1989   Shokumin nihonjin no seishin kōzo (Spiritual makeup of Japanese colonists). *Shisō,* no. 778 (1989): 4–28.

Young, Crawford
1976   *The politics of cultural pluralism.* Madison: University of Wisconsin Press.

Yujo sillok
1981   *Yujo sillok* (Veritable records of the Yi dynasty). Translated by Kadena Sōtoku. In *Nihon shomin seikatsu shiryō shūsei,* vol. 27. Tokyo: San'ichi shobō.

Yu-Jose, Lydia
1996   World War II and the Japanese in the prewar Philippines. *Journal of Southeast Asian Studies* 27, no. 1:215–230.

Zielenziger, Michael
1996   Okinawans to have say on U.S. troop presence. *San Jose Mercury News,* 8 September, 1A, 16A.

Contributors

ARAKAKI MAKOTO is an assistant professor of cultural studies at Okinawa Christian Junior College. A graduate of the Asian American Studies Program of the University of California, Los Angeles, he is currently a Ph.D. candidate and research associate at Tsukuba University. He is interested in the Okinawan experience in Okinawa and overseas, especially in Hawai'i.

ROBERT K. ARAKAKI is a doctoral candidate in political science at the University of Hawai'i at Manoa. His dissertation focuses on the politics of religious pluralism in Southeast Asia. His essay "The Politics of Okinawan Identity: Forgetting, Recovery, and Empowerment" appeared in *Reflections on the Okinawan Experience* (1996).

HOKAMA SHŪZEN, emeritus professor of Hosei University, is the current director of the Okinawa gaku kenkyūsho. His publications include *Okinawa kōgo daijiten* [Encyclopedia of ancient Okinawan language] (1998), *Okinawa no rekishi to bunka* [History and culture of Okinawa] (1986), *Omorosōhi* (1972), and many other learned articles on Okinawan culture.

EDITH M. KANESHIRO received her Ph.D. in history at the University of California, Berkeley, in 1999. Her dissertation focused on the village of Kin, Okinawa, and the international labor migrations of Okinawans to Hawai'i, California, and the Philippines. At present, she is a postdoctoral fellow at Brandeis University.

RONALD Y. NAKASONE teaches Buddhist thought, ethics, and aesthetics at the Graduate Theological Union. His publications include *Ethics of Enlightenment* (1990), *The Okinawan Experience* (1996), and numerous articles on Buddhism and bioethics. His most recent article, "Religious Views on Biotechnology, Buddhism," appeared in the *Encyclopedia of Ethical, Legal, and Policy Issues in Biotechnology* (2000).

NOMURA KŌYA is an assistant professor of sociology at Hiroshima Shudo University. His most recent published articles include "Shokuminchi shugi to kyōhanka" (Colonialism and the making of its accomplices) and "Sabetsu to shite no dōka" (Assimilation as discrimination) in *Kaihōshakaigaku kenkyū* (Liberation of humankind: A sociological review). He has also published other articles on postcolonialism in Okinawa and Japan.

SHIROTA CHIKA is a doctoral student in cultural anthropology at Kyoto University and in sociology at the University of Hawai'i. Her published articles include "Dancing beyond the U.S. Military: Okinawan *Eisaa* as Identity and Diaspora" in *Theatre Insight* (1999) and "Odori tsunagaru hitobito: Hawaii ni okeru Okinawan eisaa no butai kara" [Dancers' network: Okinawan *Eisaa* in Hawai'i] in *Kinjō zukiai no fūkei: Tsunagari o saikō suru* [Rethinking neighborhood] (2000).

TOMIYAMA ICHIRŌ is a professor of Japanese studies at Osaka University. His publications include *Kindai nihon shakai to "Okinawajin"* (Modern Japanese society and the Okinawans] (1990) and *Senjo no kioku* [Battlefield memories] (1995).

WESLEY UEUNTEN is a Ph.D. candidate in the Ethnic Studies Department of the University of California, Berkeley. He has published several articles on Okinawan identity, including "The Maintenance of the Okinawan Ethnic Community in Hawaii" (1991), "Okinawan Music and Images of Okinawa" (1994), "Okinawans in Mainland Japan: Discrimination, Imeeji, and Identity" (1996), and "Yaju no ibukuro no nakade" [In the belly of the beast] (1999).

Artist

California-based sculptor RANDALL SHIROMA has exhibited widely throughout the Western United States. His most notable public art commissions are installed at the Hilton Towers at the City of San Jose, Safeway Corporate Headquarters at the City of Pleasanton, and State of California Crime Laboratory in Sacramento. He received the Eureka Fellowship from the Fleisshacken Foundation in 1994 and is represented by Gwenda Jay/Addington Gallery in Chicago. His most recent solo exhibit was at the Fresno Art Museum (2001).

Index

abaca, 74, 76, 78, 79; cultivation and stripping of, 77–79, 80; farm life, 76–80; marketing, 79

Agari-umaai, 6, 21, 142–155; and creation myth, 144–146; and identity, 143; and Kudaka Island, 149, 152; observed by the royal house, 142, 146; pilgrimage, 146–153; ritual, 142–143, 145, 147, 151; significance of, 153–155

    pilgrimage sites: Bin'nudaki, 146, 148, 152; Hainju and Ukinju, 149, 150–151; Hamagaa-utaki, 152; Nakandakari-biijaa, 146, 150; Saki-biijaa, 146, 147, 152; Seefa-utaki, 146, 147, 148–150, 152; Teda-ugaa, 146, 148, 152; Udunyama, 147; Yabusaatsu-utaki, 150; Yaharajikasa, 152; Yonabaru-iegaa, 146

Ajifu Kayu, 85

Ajifu Nae, 85

Ajifu Tatsu, 87

Aka, Raymond, xii

Aliaza Popular Revolucionaria Americana, 101

Alvarez, David, 77

Amabe people, 49, 144

Amamikyu, 142–144; as creator deity, 21, 49; and royal house, 145

Amami Oshima Islands, 142

Amaterasu Omikami, 21, 70n. 8

America. See United States (U.S.)

American Friends Service Committee, 133

American-Ryūkyūan Friendship *Bon Dance Festival*, 122

American Women's Welfare Association (AWWA), 125, 129n. 4

ancestors, 134, 135, 143, 150, 151–152. See also Agari-umaai

ancestral veneration, 6, 142–143, 146, 153–154

Anderson, Benedict, 28; *Imagined Communities*, 28

Appadurai, Arjun, 28; *Modernity at Large*, 28

Appiah, Anthony Kwame, 28; *Identities*, 28

Arakaki, Robert, 12, 33; "Politics of Okinawan Identity," 33

Arakaki Makoto, 20, 42–43

Armenia, 36

Asai Tatsuō, 63, 69n. 6

Asato Nobu, 66; *Okinawa kaiyō hattsu shi*, 66

assimilation, 18–21, 32, 33, 132; Americanization, 35; on becoming Japanese, 18, 19, 63–69, 130; and creolization, 34–35; and intellectual colonial control, 114–115; and Japanese nationalism, 66, 88, 113–114; replacing symbols, 102. See also diaspora; identity; identity *under* Japanese; identity *under* Okinawans

Atlas of Diasporas (Chalian and Rageau), 27

Bagobo people, 81, 82, 87
bankoku shinryō, 16, 131
bankoku shinryō no kane, 130, 141n. 1
bankoku shinryō no seishin, 131
bankoku shinryō no tami, 20, 131
Barkan, Elazar, 27, 28; *Borders, Exiles, Diasporas*, 27, 28
Barth, Fredrik, 33; *Ethnic Groups and Boundaries*, 33
Battle of Okinawa, 11–12, 109, 116
Benguet Road (Zig Zag Road), 72, 73, 74
Benjamin, Walter, 117; *Zur Kritik der Gewalt*, 117
Bin'nudaki, 146, 148, 152. *See under* Agari-umaai, pilgrimage sites
Black Atlantic, The (Gilroy), 27
Borders, Exiles, Diasporas (Barkan and Shelton), 27, 28
Buchignani, Norman, 33

Calderón, Francisco Garcia, 101
Canada and Japan in the Twentieth Century (Schultz and Miwa), 40
Carmen Higa Mochizuki et al. v. the United States of America, 90, 111
Castell, Manuel, 38; *Power of Identity*, 38
Chalian, Gerard, 27; *Atlas of Diasporas*, 27
Chamorro, 59, 60, 61, 62
Changing Identities of the Southeast Asian Chinese since World War II (Cushman and Gung), 27
chifijin. See *kikoe-ōgimi*
Chiji jimu hikitsugi shorui, 68
China and the Chinese Overseas (Wang), 27
Chinese Exclusion Acts, 75, 101
Chōdō Matsujirō, 58
Chō Kenkō (Nakachi Reishin), 51
Christy, Alan, 37
Chūzan seifu (Saion), 3, 24n. 1, 53n. 6
Chūzan seikan (Haneji Chōshū), 3, 24n. 1, 53nn. 4, 5, 144, 146; and myth of Amamikyu, 144–145
Civil Liberties Act (CLA), 92
Clifford, James, 27, 40, 141; "Diaspora," 27, 40
Clinton, Bill, (William Jefferson), 15
Cody, Cecil, 79
Cohen, Robin, 27, 28–29, 31, 33, 40; *Global Diasporas*, 27, 28, 29
Cole, Faye Cooper, 81
Colonial Okinawa, 18
colonialism, 112–119, 118n. 1; colonial soci-

ety, 61–63; and colonized, the, 112–113; complicity with, 112, 115–118; critique of, 113–114, 118; and imperialism, 113–114; intellectual, 115, 116; and nationalism, 113–118; the Okinawan experience with, 17, 19, 113–118; persisting, 112–113. *See also* discrimination; identity *under* Okinawans
Commonwealth Advocate, 86
Conflict and Peacemaking in Multiethnic Societies (Montville), 30
cowrie (*takaragai*), 48
creation myth, 45–46, 144–146, 153; Amamikyu, 144–145; brother-sister original ancestor, 46, 145
Crystal City internment camp, 103, 105
Cultural Anthropology, 27
Current History Magazine, 101
Cushman, Jennifer, 27; *Changing Identities of Southeast Asian Chinese since World War II*, 27

Davao Planters' Association, 74
Davis, William T., 3, 11, 22
Diaspora, 27
"Diaspora" (Clifford), 27, 40
diaspora: analysis, 28–29, 30–31; definition of, 29; and homeland, 35–37; and identity, 26, 36–38, 39 (*see also under* Okinawan); Japanese, 37, 39; journals on, 27–28; Okinawan, 21, 26–27, 36, 39, 40–41, 139; studies on, 27. *See also* diaspora experience; diasporic flows
Diaspora and Public Cultures, 27
diaspora experience, 32–39; definition of, 29; double diaspora, 37–39; hybridity and creolization, 32, 34–35; identity politics, 32–34; and *nihonjinron*, 33; Okinawan, 8, 34. *See also* diaspora; diasporic flows
diasporic flows, 26, 28–32, 34–39; definition of, 29; effect of nationalism, 32; English, 29–30; and global capitalism, 95, 103; and global history, 30; Okinawa Diaspora?, 109–110; types of, 32. *See also* diaspora; diaspora experience; identity
Diasporic Mediations (Radhakrishnan), 28
discrimination: American, 100–101; anti-Japanese sentiment, 99–103, 132; and assimilation, 79, 114–116; in Hawai'i,

101; in Peru, 99–102; toward Japanese and Okinawans, 132. *See also* labor, wages
Dōgen Zenji, 8
Dulles, John Foster, 22

education, 84–83; in Crystal City, 105; *fever*, 83–86; Japanese, 84–85, 102; migration, 85, 86; and nationalism, 83–86, 102, 128
Eisa (Shiroma), 128
eisaa, 120–129; as creative space, 121, 122, 127; in Hawai'i, 120, 126–128; and identity, 120–122, 127–128; as a political act, 121, 122–123, 127; postwar development, 121–125, 127; protest, venue for, 124–125; spiritual significance of, 121–122; and U.S. military bases, 122–126, 127
Eiso, 9, 152
Elisseeff, Serge, 22
emigration, 26, 29–30, 36. *See also* diaspora; diasporic flows
Esman, Milton, 31
Ethnic Groups and Boundaries (Barth), 33
Ethnic Groups in Conflict (Horowitz), 30
Exclusion Act (Immigration Act of 1924), 30, 96

Featherstone, Mike, 28; *Global Modernities*, 28
Festival for Asian-Pacific American Heritage, 120, 127
fii nu kang, 150, 154, 156n. 11, 12
Filipino: attacks on Okinawans, 87–88; fears of Japanese invasion, 85–86; *insurrectos*, 72, 76; perceptions of Japanese, 76; perceptions of Okinawans, 75, 79–80
Friday, 125
Fubuu-utaki. *See under* Agari-umaai
Futenma Air Station and Naha Port Reversions Affairs Office, 16

Gabila, Antonio, 85–86
Gardiner, Henry C., 40; *The Japanese and Peru, 1873–1973*, 40
Gates, Henry Louis, Jr., 28; *Identities*, 28
Gendai Okinawa kenjin meikan, 67
Geneva Convention Relative to the Protection of Civilian Persons in Time of War, 111n. 4

Gentlemen's Agreement, 75
Gerbi, Antonello, 40; *The Japanese in South America*, 40
German South Seas Phosphate Company, 59
Gilroy, Paul, 27; *The Black Atlantic*, 27
Gladney, Dru, 33
Global Diasporas (Cohen), 29, 40
Global Minorities (Featherstone, Lash, and Robertson), 28
Goitein, S. D., 27; *A Mediterranean Society*, 27
Goodman, Grant K., 89
Greater East Asia Co-prosperity Sphere, 37, 65, 70n. 6
gyokusai (crushed jewel), 58, 68

hagotan, 77
Hall, Stuart, 121
Hamagaa-utaki. *See under* Agaari-umaai
Hana (Kina), 128
Haneji Chōshū (Shō Jōken), 49, 53n. 4, 144, 146
Hashimoto Ryutarō, 16
Hawai'i Uchinanchu Business Group, 139
Hayase Shinzō, 72, 81
Higashi Mineo, 41
Higashionna Kanjun, 50
Higa Shunchō, 49, 53n. 6
Hirata Tentsū, 51
History of Okinawans in North America (Okinawa Club of North America), 8
Hobsbawm, Eric, 69
Hokama Shūzen, 23, 128n. 1
Horowitz, Donald, 30; *Ethnic Groups in Conflict*, 30
Hui O Laulima, 138
human rights, 92, 111n. 4

ibi, 147, 156n. 6
Identities (Appiah and Gates), 28
identity, 33; Castell's categories, 38; colluding, 38–39; and diaspora, 26, 33, 34, 36; and diasporic flows, 28–29, 36; essentialized, 19; fluidity of, 28, 33; hybrid and creole, 19, 29, 32, 34–35; and identification, 33; legitimating, 38; markers, 34; *Politics*, 32–34; and primordialism, 33; project, 20, 38, 39; resistance, 20, 38. *See also* diaspora; diasporic flows; identity *under* Japanese; identity *under* Okinawans

Ifa Fuyū, 46, 48, 49, 53n. 5, 116, 145;
    Okinawa-kō, 144
Igei Genichi, 87
Ijū uchi de ikinuita (Kamisato), 90, 99
Ikehara Hiroshi, 85
Imagined Communities (Anderson), 28
Imanishi Kinshi, 62, 63
immigration: Chinese, 86, 95; and racism,
    95–96; restrictions of, 30, 75, 96. *See
    also* diaspora; diasporic flows
        Japanese: to Hawai'i, 95; to Latin
            America, 95–96, 97, 101–102;
            to Philippines, 74, 75
        Okinawan: to Hawai'i, xi, 96, 131;
            Latin America, 95–96; Philip-
            pines, 71–76
Immigration Limitation Law (Australia),
    96
Inamine Kei'ichi, 16
Ishida Takeshi, 117
Ishihara Masaie, 124
Ishii Ryoichi, 76
Islam, 47, 81
Iwamuro Yoshiaki, 22

jamisen, 132, 141n. 2
Japanese: colonialism, 19, 112–119; colo-
    nial project, 37–38, 40; complicity
    with, 115–116; discrimination, 18, 38,
    63–70, 102–103, 132; education, 102;
    immigration, 86, 95–96; Imperialism,
    18, 19, 25n. 8, 69n. 8, 113; majority,
    112, 115, 116, 118; military, 11, 12,
    86, 87; and nationalism, 39, 113, 118;
    nation building, 37; orientialism, 63,
    64; perceptions of Okinawans, 18, 64,
    67; repatriates, 92; self-image, 39–40,
    63, 65–66; women, 84
        in Davao, Philippines, 76, 79–86;
            businesses, 76; expansion, 71;
            immigration, 75, 76, 86; military,
            87; schools, 84, 85; women, 84
        in Hawai'i, 101, 131–132
        identity, 114; "consciousness," 58,
            63; construction of, 18, 37, 39–
            40; vis-à-vis *gaijin*, 39–40; project,
            37, 39–40; *nihonjinron*, 33, 39–
            40; resistance to, 23, 25n. 6; 37;
            vis-à-vis *seiban*,18; uniqueness of ,
            18, 19, 33, 63
        in Nan'yō, 57–70; colonial society,
            61–63; imperialism, 58–61;

    investments, 59; perceptions
    of Okinawans, 64; treatment of
    Islanders, 58–59. *See also* labor;
    Okinawan
    in Peru, 35, 90–104; businesses, 97,
        98 table 3; camp life, 105–106;
        capture and internment of, 103–
        109; deportation and resettle-
        ment, 107
Japanese and Peru, The (Gardiner), 40
Japanese Constitution, 15
Japanese Diet, 15
Japanese Empire, 38, 71, 102
Japanese government, 112–113; discrimi-
    natory policies, 15, 38, 94, 116–117;
    leasing of lands, 15, 116–117; *sangyō-
    rikkoku*, policy of, 94; suppression of
    Okinawan language and culture, 18,
    36, 102, 114, 116
Japanese in South America, The (Normano
    and Gerbi), 40
Japanese Latin American (JLA): as
    hostage, 92; as illegal alien, 92, 93,
    106; immigration, 95; internment,
    107; petition for redress, 92–93.
    See also in Peru *under* Japanese
Japanese Peruvian Oral History Project,
    91, 111n. 1, 2
Japanese-United States Security Treaty,
    13
Japonese-kanaka. See stigmatization
    of *under* Okinawans
Japonesia, 42, 45–46
Japonesia no nekko (Shimao), 45
Journal of Transnational Studies, 27

kachaashi, 120, 125, 134
Kagoshima prefecture, 16, 94
kami, 21, 46, 147, 151, 154
Kamisato Kami, 90, 99; *Ijū uchi da
    ikinuita*, 90, 99
kamiugan, 142, 154
Kanaka, 59, 60, 61, 69n. 3
Kaneshiro, Edith, 19, 36, 42
Kang Sang-joong, 63
kankara sanshin, 105, 122
Kansai Okinawa Prefectural Association,
    38
Kenjinkai (Palau), 66
Kenjinkai (Ponape), 67
Kerr, George, 90, 102; *History of an
    Island People*, 90

kikoe-ōgimi, 6, 146, 147, 148; destruction
    of office, 21, 142; responsibilities of, 6,
    142, 145
Kina Shōkichi, 124, 128; *Hana*, 128;
    "Transform All Weapons into Musical
    Instruments," 125
Kishaba Shizuo, xii, 12, 22–23
Kiyono Kenji, 64–65
Kobashigawa Sakukichi, 83
Koizumi Fumio, 46
Kojiki, 39
Konkōken-shū, 3, 24n. 1
Kublai Khan, 9
*kugani ufu'n chanjasi (kogane ryūhan
    ōkanzashi)*, 3, 21, 24n. 1
Kurota Zenpachi, 83
Kyōei kai, 67

labor, 58, 72, 74; Chamorro, 59, 60, 61–
    62; Chinese, 30, 61, 74; *dekasegi*, 74,
    82; disputes, 60, 66; and global
    economy, 30, 95; Japanese, 60–61, 74;
    Kanaka, 59, 60, 61–62;
    karobos, 61; Korean, 61–62; Muslim,
    78; Okinawan, 58, 59,
    72, 74; recruitment of, 60, 74; slave, 28,
    30; Taiwanese, 61; Yapese, 61;
    yobiyose, 74. *See
    also* wages
Land Expropriation Law, 12
Lash, Scott, 28; *Global Minorities*, 28
Leadership Development Study Tour
    (1993), 136–138
Leadership Tour (1980), 134–136
League of Nations mandate, 57, 58, 62
Lemieux Agreement (Canada), 96
Lifestyle Reform Movement. *See* Seikatsu
    kaizen undō
lista negra, 103–104
Los Angeles Examiner, 101

Maehira Bōkei, 11, 12
magatama. See under tama kawara
makina goya, 78, 79
*Making Muslim Space in North America
    and Europe* (Metcalf), 31
Makiya Akira, 123
Man'en gannen no futtobōru (Ōe), 153
Margins and Mainstreams (Okihiro),
    110
Martin, Akemi, 125–126
Matsuda Michiyuki, 10, 119n. 3

Matsue Haruji, 57–58
Matsuoka Shizuo, 57
McKeown, Adam, 27
Mediterranean Society, A, (Goitein), 27
Meiji government. *See under* Japanese
    government
memory, 6–7, 16, 153; and imagination,
    7–9, 21, 143–144, 152–155; remem-
    bering Okinawa, 134–138, 144
Metcalf, Barbara, 31; *Making Muslim
    Space in North America and Europe*,
    31
Micronesians, 57, 61–62
migration, 44, 45, 48–50, 144. *See also
    under* diaspora; diasporic flows
Mindanao (Moro Province), 71, 73, 74
Mindanao Herald, 76, 77
Mintun-gusuku, 150, 152, 154
Mirukumunari (Ryūkyū-koku Matsuri
    Daiko), 125
Mitsubishi Bussan, 58
Mitsui Shōji, 58
Miwa, Kimitada, 40; *Canada and Japan in
    the Twentieth Century*, 40
Miyagi Saburo, 12
Mochizuki, Carmen Higa, 90, 110–111
Modern Diasporas in International Politics
    (Sheffer), 27
Modernity at Large (Appadurai), 28
Montville, Joseph V., 30; *Conflict and
    Peacemaking in Multiethnic Societies*,
    30
Muruyama Shichirō, 49
Murayama Tomo'ichi, 15–16
Muslims, 78, 81, 82

Naichi, 131–132
naichijin, 64. *See also Naichi*
nachijin no kanaka. See stigmatization
    of *under* identity, Okinawan
Nago City G-8 summit, 16, 24n. 3
Nakama Kamado, 87
Nakama Masanori, 80
Nakama Nabe, 85
Nakandakari-biijaa. *See under* Agari-umaai
Nakandakari Chiken, 51
Nakasone, Ronald Y., 42, 43
Nakasone Katsujirō, 105, 108
Nakijin-nubui, 142
Nano, Teodoro V., 86
nanshin netsu, 63
nanshin ron, 63

Nan'yō, 57–70, 69n. 3; boundaries of, 57, 69n. 1; as image of opportunity, 58, 63; and Japanese imperialism, 57–61, 63; League of Nations mandate, 57, 58, 62; military significance of, 57–58; and Okinawa, 57–58

Nan'yō Bōeki, 58, 59–60, 68

Nan'yō-chō (Nan'yō government), 57, 58; labor policy, 61; phosphate mining operations, 58, 60–61

Nan'yō Kōhatsu, 57, 58, 59–60, 67; attitude toward native workers, 59; businesses, 59; discriminatory wage policies, 60; employment categories, 59; hesitancy to employ Okinawans, 60; management, 60; sugar industry, 59

Nan'yō Takushoku, 58

Nikkei Weekly, 15

nirai-kanai, 21, 109, 144, 147, 148, 156n. 10

niruya-unusi, 147, 156n. 9

Nishimura Shokusan, 61

Nomura Kichisaburō, 58

Nomura Kōya, 19, 42, 102; "Uchinanchu no seikatsushi," 102

Nonini, Donald M., 31; Underground Empires, 31

Normano, J. F., 40; The Japanese in South America, 40

Norweb, Henry, 104

Ōe Kenzaburō, 4, 23, 153; Man'en gannen no futtobōru (The Silent Cry), 153

Ogawa, Joy, 136

Okihiro, Gary Y., 110; Margins and Main-streams, 110

Okinawa: in Asian and Pacific context, 9, 16, 23, 44, 46–48; economy, 16–17, 47; geopolitical importance of, 9; as Japanese colony, 37; as Japan's south-ern hub, 141; military importance of, 12; population, 17, 25n. 9, 94; pre-history, 44–45, 49; "reannexation" of, 130; reversion of, 13, 19, 116; taxes paid to Japan, 16, 94; and U.S. 22, 23, 114; U.S. occupation of, 12, 13, 19. See also Ryūkyū kingdom; United States military
    culture, 23, 45–53; Awamori, 50, 62, 137; ceramics, 51–52; complexity of, 50–52; dance, 120; dual

sovereignty, 4, 145; language, ix–x, 49, 53n. 5; lifestyle, reform of, 64–68 (see also Seikatsu kaizen undō); music, 46, 120; as periph-eral culture, 23; shamanism, 18, 100; society, 4–5, 144; sources of, 40–49; textiles, 10 fig. 4, 50–51

Okinawa kaiyō hattatsu shi (Asato), 66

Okinawa kō (Ifa), 144

Okinawan (Uchinanchu); aspirations, 6, 15–16, 20, 125; collusion with colo-nialism, 58, 68, 115–116; colonial experience, 113–119; double minority and double diaspora, 37, 41; immigra-tion, 17–18, 95, 96; migration, 17–18, 25n. 5, 36; mythic, origins of, 21, 144–146; pacifism, 7, 12; protests, 12, 110, 121–122, 123, 125; repatriates, 17, 19, 88, 108–109; self impressions of, 16, 65–68; separatism, 12, 18–19, 25n. 7, 149; sovereignty, 4, 8, 19; spirituality, 121–122, 142–144, 150–151, 153–155; women, 7. See also diaspora; diasporic experience; diasporic flows
    in Davao, Philippines, 71–89; com-munity life, 80–81, 82; context of, 71–72; descriptions of natives, 79, 81–83; education fever, 83–86; farm life, 76–79; immigration to, 75; as "the other Japanese," 79–80; relations with native popula-tion, 82–83; repatriates, 88; self impressions of, 81; war experience, 87–88; women, 78, 80, 82, 85
    in Hawai'i, 35, 110, 131–141, 135; as Japan-pake, 132; local identity and aloha spirit, 138; and Naichi (Japanese), 131–132; relationship to homeland, 131, 134–138; relief efforts, 133, 135
    identity, 7–8, 23–24, 34, 102, 105–106; affirmation of, 135; and Amamikyu, myth of, 143; ambiva-lence of, 37, 39, 113, 118, 132; on becoming Japanese, 18, 37, 38, 58, 62, 63–69, 113–115, 130; collec-tive, 131–134; colluding, 39; con-struction of, 37, 133; diasporic, 36–39, 128, 141; double minority, 37; imagining, 8, 18–21, 131; vis-à-vis Japanese, 19, 23, 26, 37–38, 39–40, 105–106; vis-à-vis

Japanese in Hawai'i, 131; non-Yamato, 23; vis-à-vis overseas cohorts, 131; pan-Okinawan, 37, 38, 128, 133–134; positive image of, 130–131; pride in, 25n. 6, 135; project, 39; resistence, 39, 118; self impressions of, 81; suppression of, 36, 67–68; toward, 9–18; transnational, 19, 43, 128; and *Uchinanchu* spirit, 138–139; vis-à-vis U.S. military presence, 122. *See also under* assimilation; memory
    in Nan'yō, 58–66; collusion with imperial vision, 58, 68; and colonial society, 61–63; enterprises, 68; immigration to Nan'yō Islands, 58; as *Japonese-kanaka*, 64; on becoming Japanese, 63–69; strategies to escape discrimination, 65, 66–68. *See also* identity
    stigmatization of, 32, 63–64, 102, 105–106, 113–116; *Japan-pake*, 37, 132; *Japonese-kanaka*, 19, 37, 65, 66, 68, 132, *naichijin no kanaka*, 64, 65; "the other Japanese," 19, 37; *otro Japones*, 19; *seiban*, 18
Okinawan Peruvians (Latin Americans), 90–111, 108; businesses, 97–98, 98 table 3; as illegal aliens, 106; immigrant life, 93, 96–104; immigration to, 95–96; internment, 103–106; as *otro Japones*, 102, 103; in Peruvian society, 98–99; pressure to escape discrimination, 105–106; repatriation to Okinawa, 108; resettlement, 106–109; women, 93
Okinawan Relief Clothing Drive Committee, 133
Okinawans in Latin America, The (Tigner), 17, 95
Okinawan studies, 38, 45, 48–49
Okinawan Women Act Against Military Violence, 7
Okinawa prefectural association. See *Kenjinkai*
Okinawa prefectural government, 13–15, 136; complaints against U.S. military bases, 13–14; petition for the reduction of U.S. military bases, 15–16; promotion of positive image, 130

Okinawa Television, 130
Okuma Shigenobu, 101
omoro, 6–7
Omoro-sōshi, 3, 6, 8, 11, 20–21, 50; Aniya version, 24n. 1; loss of, 4, 11–12; search for, 21–23; significance of, 6–7
Ong, Aihwa, 31; *Ungrounded Empires*, 31
Orientalism (Said), 28
Ortiz, Fernando, 95
Ōshiro Kōzō, 41, 72, 74, 75, 81
Ōshiro Tatsuhiro, 41
Ōta Development Company, 74, 78, 87
Ōta Kyōsaburo, 72–73
Ōta Masahide, 15, 16
otro Japones. See stigmatization of *under* Okinawan
Ōyama Chōjyō, 126

Pacific War, 11, 24n. 2, 89
Pan, Lynn, 27; *Sons of the Yellow Emperor*, 27
Peattie, Mark, 61
Peoples' Link around the United States Bases, 124
Peru, 97–10; anti-Japanese sentiment, 99–102, 103–104; collusion with U.S. 100–102; racism and immigration, 95–96; refuses Japanese and Okinawan reentry, 106; society, 100
Phelan, James, 101
Philippine-American War, 72, 73
Philippine Journal of Commerce and Industry, 76–77
Philippines, 71–89; American occupation of, 72–74; restrictions of Japanese immigration, 86
Politics of Cultural Pluralism, The, (Young), 30
"Politics of Okinawan Identity" (Arakaki, Robert), 33
popular culture, 121
Power of Identity (Castell), 38
Prado, Manuel, 104
Price, M., 122–123
Price, Willard, 72

Radhakrishnan, Rajagopalan, 28; *Diasporic Mediation*, 28
Rageau, Jean-Pierre, 27; *Atlas of Diasporas*, 27
Rekidai hoan, 48
remembering. *See* memory

Report on the Security Relationship between the United States and Japan, 15

Robertson, Roland, 28; *Global Minorities*, 28

royal crown (*kugani ufu'n chanjasi*, also *hibinkan*); description of, 3, 6 fig. 3; loss of, 11–12; search for, 21–23, 36; symbol of sovereignty, 3, 23

Ryūkyū, 3, 12. *Also see under* Okinawa

Ryukyu-American Cultural Center, 124, 129n. 3

Ryukyu American Historical Research Society, xii, 12, 23

Ryukyuan-American relations, 22, 23

Ryūkyū Archipelago, 9, 44, 45, 46, 48

Ryūkyū kingdom, 3–7; annexation of, 10–11, 119n. 3, 142; in *Asian Context*, 9–10, 46, 53, 130–131; and China, 3–4, 19; commercial activities of, 9, 15, 40, 47; dual subordination of, 23, 25n.10; government structure, 4, 145–146; image of, 131; and Japan, 9–11, 113–114; memories of, 130; and Satsuma, 10, 24n. 1, 25n. 10, 49; sovereignty, 4, 11

Ryūkyū-koku, 53n. 6

Ryūkyū-koku Matsuri Daiko, 125–128; in *Hawai'i*, 126–127, 128; Mirukumunari, 125

Ryūkyū-koku yuraki, 53n. 6

Ryukyu Shimpo, 73, 122, 123, 130, 141

Ryūkyū shintōki (Taichu), 144

Ryūsen no kami, 152

Safran, William, 27

Said, Edward, 28, 115, 118–119n. 2; *Orientalism*, 28

Sakai Naoki, 116

Saki-biijaa. *See under* Agari-umaai

Sakihara Mitsugu, 122, 155n. 5

sanshin, 37, 65, 67, 105, 121

Satsuma *han*, 10, 23, 24n. 1, 25n. 10; invasion of, 51. *See also* Okinawa; Ryūkyū kingdom

Satto, 152

Schultz, John, 40; *Canada and Japan in the Twentieth Century*, 40

Seefa-utaki, 146, 148–150, 152; relation with Shuri Palace, 148; ritual sites, 148

Seikatsu kaizen undō (Lifestyle improvement movement), 19, 38, 65–67

"Sekai no Uchinanchu," 130

Serei Kyoko, 107; *Watashi no ayunda hansei*, 107

Sheffer, Gabriel, 27; *Modern Diasporas in International Politics*, 27

Shelton, Marie-Denise, 27; *Borders, Exiles, and Diasporas*, 27, 28

Shiga Shigetaka, 57

Shima, George, 111

Shimao Toshio, 45; *Japonesia no nekko*, 45

Shinerikyu, 144, 145, 155n. 5

Shiroma, Alberto, 128; *Eisa*, 128

Shiroma Kikō, 123

Shirota Chika, 19–20, 42

Shō En, 152

Shō Hō, 51

Shō Jōken. *See* Haneji Chōshū

Shō Nei (king), 10

Shō Nei (queen), 20

Shō Shin, 12

Shō Tai, 10, 102

Shō Taikyu, 130

Shun Medoruma, 41

Shuri Palace, 10, 10 fig. 4, 11, 130; spiritual significance of, 148

Shuten, 152

Sino-Japanese War, 11, 95, 116

Sons of the Yellow Emperor (Pan), 27

Sorensen, John, 33

sotetsu jikoku (hell), 17, 59, 94, 109

Spanish-American War, 72

Sternfelt, Carl W., 3, 22

sugar industry, 60, 69n. 4, 94–95; collapse of, 59, 94; expansion in Micronesia, 59; Japanese pricemsupport of, 59; need for cheap labor, 95; strike in Hawai'i, 101; in Taiwan, 59

Sulit, Pablo F., 76

Taeuber, Irene, 83

Takazato Shizuyo, 7

Tamagusuku shaman, 146, 150

tama kawara (*magatama*), 3, 24n. 1

tama'n chaabui. *See* royal crown

Tamashiro, Pamela, 140

Teda, 145–146, 148

Teda-ugaa. *See under* Agari-umaai

Teruya Rinken, 127

Third Okinawa Promotion and Development Plan, 141

Thomas, Helen, 127

Tigner, James L., 17, 95, 97, 101; *The Okinawans in Latin America*, 95

time and being, 7–9
Tōjō Hideki, 66
Tomiyama Ichirō, 19, 42, 116
Torre, Raul Haya de la, 100–101
Tōyama Kyūzō, 41, 72
Tōyō Takushoku, 59
Toyotomi Hideyoshi, 9
"Transform all weapons into musical instruments" (Kina), 125

ubiinadii, 143, 149
Uchinanchu (Okinawan), 83, 130, 134, 135, 136; community, 141; and overseas cohorts, 131. See also identity under Okinawan
Uchinanchu, a History of Okinawans in Hawaii (Ethnic Studies Oral History Project), 8
Uchinanchu no seikatsushi" (Nomura), 102
Uchinanchu spirit, 123, 131, 136, 137, 138–139; and aloha spirit, 139; characteristics of, 138; as a counterdiscourse, 138; and Uchinanchu-at-heart, 139–141; and yuimaaruu, 141
Udunyama. See under Agari-umaai
Ueunten, Wesley, xii, 19, 42
Ukinju and Hainju. See under Agari-umaai
umatchi, 142
Umesao Tadao, 62, 63, 65, 69
Ungrounded Empires (Ong and Nonini), 31
United Okinawan Association (UOA), 133, 134, 136, 140, 141
United States Civil Administration of the Ryukyus (USCAR), 17, 122, 123
United States Department of Justice, 92, 105
United States government, 12, 22; administration of the Philippines, 72–73; expansion into Pacific region, 71–72; immigrant policies, 75–76, 95–96; internment of Japanese, 91–92; seizing JLAs as hostages, 92, 104
United States Immigration Restriction Act, 75
United States military, 14; in Okinawa, 108, 109–110, in Philippines, 72, 73, 87
United States military bases, 7, 13 table 1, 14 fig. 5, 22, 36, 125–126; appropriation of land, 12, 110; complaints of,

13–14; detriment to local development, 14–15, 116–117, 120; Futenma Marine Corp Air Station, 12, 14 fig. 5, 15, 16, 124; importance of, 12, 123; Japanese support of, 13, 15, 116–117; Kadena Air Force Base, 12, 123, 124, 125; location of bases, 14 fig. 5; occupation of, 12; petition for reduction of, 15–16; protests against, 7, 124–125; statistics, 13; violation of peace principle, 15; Yomitan Airfield, 12
United States War Department, 72
U.S. government. See United States government
utaki, 145, 155n. 6; list of, 145
utuusi, 149, 154
Uyehara, Kevin, 137

Versailles Treaty, 57

wages, 61 table 2, 79, 93, 97; discrimination, 60, 79; negotiating, 67
Wang, Gung Wu, 27, 31; Changing Identities of the Southeast Asian Chinese since World War II, 27; China and the Chinese Overseas, 27
Waniya, Wesley, 136, 137
Wanli, 3
Warner, Langdon, 22
War Relocation Authority (WRA), 92, 105, 107
Watashi no ayunda hansei (Serei), 107
Weglyn, Michi, 104
Worldwide Uchinanchu, 131
Worldwide Uchinanchu Business International (WUB), 20, 139
Worldwide Uchinanchu Business Investment, Inc., 20, 139
Worldwide Uchinanchu Business Network project, 139
Worldwide Uchinanchu Festival (1990 and 1995), 128, 139, 140 fig. 10
Worldwide Uchinanchu Goodwill Ambassador program, 139

Xuande, 3

Yabiku Shuko, 87
Yabusatsu-utaki. See under Agari-umaai
Yaharajikasa. See under Agari-umaai
Yaka bushi, 109
Yaka Camp, 109

Yamasato, Toshio, 91, 91 fig. 7
Yamatunchu, 83
Yamazato Eikichi, 25n. 6
Yanagita Kunio, 48–49; *Kaijō no michi*,
   48; *Kainan shōki*, 48; Takaragai no
   koto, 48
Yanaihara Tadao, 64, 65, 69
Yapese, 61, 69n. 3
Yijo sillok, 50–51
Yokusan undō, 65
Yonabaru-iegaa. *See under* Agari-umaai
Yonamine Shinji, 141

Yonashiro Shigeru, 78, 84
Yoon Kun-cha, 63
Yoshino Sakuzō, 115
Yoshizato Hiroshi, 22
Young, Crawford, 30; *The Politics of
   Cultural Pluralism,* 30
Young Okinawans of Hawai'i (YOH), 136
yuimaaruu, xi, 20, 138, 139–141

Zheng He, 9
Zig Zag Road. *See* Benguet Road
Zur Kritik der Gewalt (Benjamin), 117

www.ingramcontent.com/pod-product-compliance
Lightning Source LLC
Chambersburg PA
CBHW020703270326
41928CB00005B/242